*Jewish Religion
after
Theology*

EMUNOT: Jewish Philosophy and Kabbalah

Dov Schwartz (Bar-Ilan University),
Series Editor

Editorial board
Ada Rapoport-Albert (University College, London)
Gad Freudenthal (C.N.R.S, Paris)
Gideon Freudenthal (Tel Aviv University)
Moshe Idel (Hebrew University, Jerusalem)
Raphael Jospe (Bar-Ilan University)
Ephraim Kanarfogel (Yeshiva University)
Menachem Kellner (Haifa University)
Daniel Lasker (Ben-Gurion University, Beer Sheva)

JEWISH RELIGION
after
THEOLOGY

Avi Sagi

Translated by Batya Stein

Boston
2009

Copyright © 2009 Academic Studies Press
All rights reserved

ISBN 978-1-934843-56-7

Book design by Olga Grabovsky

Published by Academic Studies Press in 2009
28 Montfern Avenue
Brighton, MA 02135, USA
press@academicstudiespress.com
www.academicstudiespress.com

Contents

Preface vii

Chapter One
Are Toleration and Pluralism Possible in Jewish Religion? 1
    Notes 34

Chapter Two
Yeshayahu Leibovitz: The Man against his Thought 43
    Notes 64

Chapter Three
Leibowitz and Camus: Between Faith and the Absurd 67
    Notes 99

Chapter Four
Jewish Religion without Theology 107
    Notes 137

Chapter Five
The Critique of Theodicy: From Metaphysics to Praxis 141
    Notes 181

Chapter Six
The Holocaust: A Theological or a Religious-Existentialist Problem? 185
    Notes 203

Chapter Seven
Tikkun Olam: Between Utopian Idea and Socio-Historical Process 205
    Notes 230

Bibliography 235

Index 247

Preface

Is Jewish religion at all intelligible without theology? This question relates to both universal and particular aspects. A student of religions will ask: can we explain the religion phenomenon without theology? Is there any meaning to religion, at least in its monotheistic version, without God as its central, constitutive concept? From a particularistic perspective, can we understand the *lebenswelt* of Jewish religion if God is no longer its central element? These questions are not merely theoretical, but follow from the situation of the modern person living after the "death of God," after losing the primary innocence that is purportedly the foundation of the religious world. Modern individuals, who make their own lives the center of their being but nevertheless wish to remain loyal to a religious commitment, must face the problem of creating a religious life within this set of basic assumptions.

Since "the death of God," these questions have indeed become basic problems not only for the study of the religious phenomenon but also, and mainly, for believers. They find themselves at the eye of the storm, facing a cultural-religious legacy with a transcendent

God and a duty of obedience at its center confronting a modernist reflective experience where the protagonist is the individual.

This book offers an account of attempts to deal with this question in contemporary Jewish thought. It points to a post-theological trend that shifts the focus of the discussion from metaphysics to praxis and examines the possibilities of establishing a religious life centered on immanent-practical existence, with various chapters presenting different aspects of this shift.

First, I trace the manifestations of this shift in the work of contemporary Jewish thinkers who discussed it directly — Yeshayahu Leibowitz, Eliezer Goldman, Joseph B. Soloveitchik, and David Hartman. Each one offers a set of unique options for an immanent religious experience, centered on praxis and on a way of life rather than on a transcendent God. In this sense, this book continues and complements my *Tradition vs. Traditionalism: Contemporary Perspectives in Jewish Thought*.* Second, I reconsider basic issues of religious life through this perspective such as, for instance, the conditions for the development of a pluralistic world view within the context of a religious commitment in Chapter One, and the attitude to a flawed human reality in Chapter Seven. These chapters examine the borders of flexibility in Jewish religious life and lead to the conclusion that Halakhah, as a normative system perceived as conservative, allows for greater openness than the metaphysical theological perspective.

Although some of the chapters of the book have been published as separate articles and deal with specific issues, they are also part of a general argument presenting clearly and comprehensively the option of immanence in Jewish religious

---

*   *Tradition vs. Traditionalism: Contemporary Perspectives in Jewish Thought*, trans. Batya Stein (Amsterdam-New York: Rodopi, 2008). Both these books appeared in one volume in Hebrew entitled *A Challenge: Returning to Tradition* (Tel Aviv: Hakibbutz Hameuchad, 2003).

life. This book will obviously fail to exhaust the subject. Indeed, it is only the beginning or, more precisely, it is an invitation to re-examine an option that has been neglected due to an overstated concern with theology and metaphysics. My general starting point is the approach developed by Wittgenstein, who is the book's latent hero. According to this view, we must focus on a given culture's actual "forms of life" and prefer them to theoretical statements, of which metaphysics and theology are only one part.

This book could not have been written without the enriching dialogue that I have been conducting for decades with my colleagues and my students at the Shalom Hartman Institute in Jerusalem and at Bar-Ilan University. I am deeply appreciative of the opportunity for our sustained discourse. Thanks to Dov Schwartz, who occupies the Nathalie and Isidore Friedman Chair for the Teaching of Rav Soloveitchik's Thought, for his help in funding the translation. As ever, I am grateful to my dear friend Batya Stein for her accomplished rendition of the text from Hebrew. Batya has been my longstanding partner, and her subtle and critical reading of my work resonates in her translation.

I have been greatly privileged to enjoy close contacts with three of this book's protagonists: Yeshayahu Leibowitz, Eliezer Goldman, and David Hartman. My encounter with them afforded me a glimpse into a complex world of commitment as it attains realization, above all, in real life, and their readiness to share this has been a moment of grace for me. I remember with longing my conversations with Eliezer Goldman, whose philosophy is only now becoming more widely available. Eliezer, who taught at the Department of Philosophy of Bar-Ilan University and was a member of Kibbutz Sdeh-Eliyahu, drew the connection between Yeshayahu Leibowitz and Joseph Soloveitchik, who was his teacher. David Hartman, who began as my teacher and became my friend, taught me about commitment to values and beliefs accompanied by critical thought and a willing readiness to engage in their re-examination.

This book is devoted with love and appreciation, which did not blind my criticism, to the three thinkers I have known personally: Yeshayahu Leibowitz, Eliezer Goldman, and David Hartman, grateful for the privilege of our encounter and in deep appreciation of their contribution to my life.

Chapter One

ARE TOLERATION AND PLURALISM POSSIBLE IN JEWISH RELIGION?

J ewish religion holds certain beliefs about the world that it takes to be true, including theoretical assumptions and practical obligations. The theoretical assumptions include premises about the Torah's divine origin and the explicit duty of observance incumbent on every Jew. Practical halakhic obligations extend to most if not all spheres of life and, by dint of the theoretical assumptions, compel all members of the Jewish collective. Given these circumstances, can Jewish religion endorse notions of toleration and pluralism toward Jews who do not observe the Torah and the commandments without losing its fundamental meaning?

Two preliminary remarks are in place here. First, a clear distinction is required between my concerns in this book and displays of toleration, or even pluralism, in Halakhah. The saying "these and these are words of the living God" (BT Eruvin 13b), for instance, is often used as proof of Halakhah's support for tolerant or pluralistic attitudes. But this is not necessarily the case, since Jewish religion acknowledges multiplicity only *within* the system. Halakhah and Jewish religion do not rest on theoretical or empirical uniformity, and a diversified spectrum of thought and praxis indeed constitute Jewish religion as a culture of dispute.[1] Whatever is not part of the system, however, is not considered "words of the living God" but rather a deviation that the halakhic system will not necessarily tolerate and will certainly not approach in pluralistic terms.

The possibility of developing a tolerant and perhaps even pluralistic attitude toward non-Jews posed a fascinating challenge to Jewish tradition, but the difficulties raised by these questions are not comparable to the challenges posed by the attempt to apply these ideas to members of the Jewish collective. Gentiles are not compelled to observe the Torah and the commandments, whereas Jews are bound by these obligations by the very fact that they are Jews. In *Tolerance and the Jewish Tradition*, Alexander Altman reports the findings of a study on toleration and Jewish tradition and sums them up as ambivalent: "On the one hand, strictness in enforcing the religious discipline of the community, and on the other, a considerable measure of toleration towards the Gentiles."[2] When the other is wholly other, entirely beyond the borders of the Jewish community and Jewish culture, the potential threat to the core of identity is minimal. But when the other is inside a given society and culture, his or her very existence is a menace. No wonder, then, that Jewish tradition was tolerant of strangers.

Can Jewish believers adopt a tolerant or even a pluralistic stance toward non-observant members of the Jewish collective? Can Jewish tradition accept the other within itself, or must it reject these ideas? This is a vital issue, since it also determines the answer to the fundamental question: to what extent can Jewish believers open up to the outside world? Or, to what extent can they participate in a Western community that endorses notions of toleration and pluralism?

The following discussion will focus on the links between Jewish religion and ideas of toleration and pluralism, and less on the historical question of whether Jewish religion, as an actual historical-cultural phenomenon, displayed toleration toward deviants from halakhic norms or enabled pluralism. A preliminary conceptual analysis of toleration and pluralism is required here because in everyday language, and sometimes in philosophical terminology as well, these concepts appear as similar and sometimes as identical, although they actually represent different ideas.

Toleration and Pluralism

Toleration — Many scholars have pointed out that toleration is a paradoxical concept,[3] since it implies that we are willing to bear what we actually reject. Toleration, then, is built on a combination of two opposite trends. We oppose and reject the tolerated approach, but we also enable its existence. In Jay Newman's terms, this is a "split heart" stance.[4] This "paradoxical conclusion" of rejection and acceptance called toleration rests on several necessary and mutually related assumptions that explain one another.

First, the tolerated stance deviates from what is purportedly the right way. We will not say of a stance we consider worthy that we tolerate it, since we would not reject it in the first place.[5] The tolerant person, then, is neither a relativist nor a skeptic. Relativism and skepticism do not assume a truth-deviance relationship, since they do not support any outlook and thus cannot justify its rejection either.[6] Neither one reflects the paradox of tolerance or the split heart.[7]

Evidence of the essential role of the truth-deviation relationship within the toleration idea is the historical context that fostered the growth of toleration. The idea of toleration was born in a culture that assumed an objective truth and a monopolistic perception of values, and was neither skeptical nor relativistic. The conceptual meaning of the term "toleration" also reflects this assumption, since toleration is not agreement but rather readiness to bear or suffer what is wrong, despite disagreement.[8] John Locke, whose *Letters Concerning Toleration* are among the most significant expressions of the toleration idea, illustrates the link between adherence to a stance and readiness to bear what is perceived as mistaken.[9]

Similarly, speaking of tolerating something we do not care about is pointless. Toleration is predicated on the negative value assigned to the tolerated stance, but not on indifference or obliviousness to it.[10] The right to be called tolerant applies only when the tolerated attitude conveys deviation from something that tolerant individuals consider worthy. Otherwise, they would not need to exercise discretion to refrain from acting against the tolerated attitude, which is meaningless to them and hence unworthy of their concern.

Second, tolerant individuals can adduce good reasons to substantiate their objection to the tolerated position. Their opposition is not the product of a capricious whim. If tolerant individuals lack justified reasons for opposing the tolerated view, in what sense are they tolerant? Their opposition must have a rational basis.[11] In everyday language, the concept of toleration is used in a broader sense to include not only opposition based on rational grounds but also on feelings. We say that X is tolerant of her children's dress code or of their favorite music. We expand the use of the concept of toleration to include everything that is unbearable, regardless of the rational grounds that justify this opposition.[12] This use of the term reflects what could be called "descriptive toleration," which is a psychological portrayal of the kindness typical of the person called tolerant. From this description, however, we can hardly draw conclusions about the value of toleration and decide whether it deserves praise or contempt. Descriptive toleration often reflects what Newman calls "moral weakness."[13] A father unable to deal with his children allows them to do whatever they want. Toleration would hardly be a moral quality or a praiseworthy ethical stance if objection to the tolerated stance were simply a matter of personal taste without any rational grounds.

Third, the tolerant person has good reasons not only to oppose the tolerated stance but also to act against it. This assumption does not follow directly from the previous one, since the right to act against the tolerated view cannot be derived from the existence of rational grounds for opposing it. To justify this right, tolerant individuals require additional assumptions. For instance, a tolerant person could claim a right to act against deviants in order to help them find truth, or to prevent them from harming other members of the community, and so forth. Without believing in the existence of this right, abstention and self-restraint do not denote toleration, because refraining from action could simply follow from the absence of a right to take steps against the tolerated position in the first place.[14]

Fourth, tolerant individuals have counterarguments to substantiate their self-restraint. Without entering into a detailed analysis of the range of reasons that have been suggested in history for the idea of toleration, reasons for toleration can in principle be classified under two main rubrics: utilitarian and value-based. One instance of a value-based consideration could be respect for the other person's autonomy as a free entity. As for utilitarian considerations, their range is extremely broad and spans, *inter alia*, claims about lack of power to coerce the truth, unsatisfactory results from this coercion, or acknowledgement of the tolerated view's *instrumental* value, which helps to justify the tolerant person's self-perception as such. Thus, for instance, one argument for tolerating Jews adopted in Christian tradition from Augustine to Thomas Aquinas was that Jews should not be forced to convert since their inferior status attests to the truth of Christianity.[15] The value-based consideration assigns great importance to the dignity of the individual as a person able to choose, who cannot be deprived from this essential characteristic even in the name of truth.

All these grounds for toleration share one common denominator: they rule out the possibility of the tolerated position having any intrinsic value. Tolerant individuals claim that they have the truth but, for various reasons, endorse self-restraint. At times, they do not acknowledge even instrumental value in the tolerated position but refrain from acting against it for utilitarian reasons; at times, they view the tolerated stance as a means to their own ends.

Even when respecting the other and allowing him freedom of thought and action, one need not acknowledge any intrinsic value in his position. One may respect the person's freedom and agree to practice self-restraint without necessarily respecting the tolerated position per se.

Utilitarian and value-based reasons for supporting toleration differ in the level of commitment they command. Utilitarians, for instance, might renounce their commitment to toleration if they believed it useful to oppose the tolerated position.[16] Toleration advocates who rely on the idea of human dignity would find it hard or probably impossible to relinquish their commitment to toleration since no other consideration could possibly override this idea. If we ascribe moral value to toleration and we praise tolerant individuals, we probably intend the kind of toleration that rests on the idea of human freedom. People who are tolerant for utilitarian reasons would not warrant moral acclaim for displays of self-restraint given that, in other circumstances, they might not refrain from intolerant attitudes.

This analysis enables us to separate a prima facie tolerant stance from one of genuine toleration, a distinction that will prove crucial. Individuals often refrain from opposing the other's stance due to paternalistic considerations. Paternalists ascribe features to the tolerated position that enable them to view it as different from what it actually is. For instance, paternalists may claim that, although the tolerated position is founded on a mistake, the people who support it are not responsible for it — they are coerced and are not epistemically liable. At times, paternalists offer an alternative interpretation of the tolerated stance and claim it actually represents *their* own truth, or at least does not contradict it, even if its supporters are unaware of it. Viewing supporters of the tolerated position in this light enables paternalists to justify their abstention from action. The common denominator of all these paternalistic claims is that they dismiss the "paradox of tolerance" because they do not view the opposite stance as genuine. Paternalists will use analysis to refrain from *punishing* their opponents, but will not be truly ready to bear the tolerated stance as presented by its supporters. Refraining from punishment is not evidence of a tolerant position because this abstention could be motivated, as noted, by the collapse of the "paradox of tolerance."

Once toleration is characterized through these parameters, the question is: what is its object? What exactly is the tolerant person willing to bear? Ostensibly, toleration could relate to three different objects: views, deeds, and people. Since the tolerant person does not ascribe intrinsic value to either the views or the deeds of the tolerated person, however, it might be more correct to claim that people are the true object of toleration. The tolerant person is ready to tolerate specific people, despite their ideas or deeds.

The discussion has so far focused on the necessary conditions for making the concept of toleration meaningful. This analysis, however, does not deal with the degree of toleration: How tolerant am I? What is it that I can or may do and I do not? Types of toleration can be classified according to the type of reaction that tolerant people could implement if they were not tolerant, or according to the type of self-restraint they actually practice. The latter leads to a distinction between various levels of weak or strong toleration.[17] Weak toleration implies that tolerant people do not impose their views on the tolerated person and refrain, for instance, from applying physical force or direct coercion. It could also be broader and include absence of indirect coercion, implying that the tolerant person does not resort to rejection mechanisms that might lead others to change their views. This type of toleration is obviously stronger than lack of physical coercion, since it requires greater restraint. In both these displays of toleration, the tolerant person does not deny the other's freedom of action.

But supporters of this type of toleration have other means of conveying their negation of the other's position while still expressing lesser willingness to tolerate the other. Non-use of these means, which requires great restraint, reflects strong types of toleration. At the first level, tolerant individuals go beyond lack of coercion to argue they are waiving their right to prohibit the social and political expression of the tolerated stance. This type of toleration is evident mainly at the declarative level, in the abstention of proclaiming this prohibition. The three expressions of toleration I have examined so far share a behavioral dimension. The strongest level of toleration, requiring the greatest form of self-restraint, is toleration as a disposition or an attitude of the mind. In this type of toleration, not only does the tolerant individual refrain from banning public displays of the tolerated stance but also avoids deriding it, condemning it, or developing negative attitudes toward it. Developing this disposition is easier when toleration is value-based rather than utilitarian, relying on considerations of human dignity and liberty and viewing human beings as free agents whose mistakes should not be scorned.

Another classification distinguishes between various types of toleration according to the public means enabling the tolerant position to exist. In this context, the distinction is between negative and positive toleration. Negative toleration does not interfere with the deeds of others, and neither forbids views nor forces its own. This is not an appropriate reflection of the idea of toleration, since non-interference could simply reflect weakness. Powerless to negate the tolerated stance or coerce others to accept their own, tolerant individuals are deterred from action. In practical terms, this consideration is only temporary and could change with changing circumstances. By contrast, positive toleration represents a view stating that non-interference is insufficient, and imposes obligations on the tolerant person to ensure continued protection of the tolerated position by means of legislation or through other ways.[18]

Pluralism — Since toleration assumes that the tolerated stance is wrong and unjustified, it must contend with the paradox of pluralism and answer the question: why not act against it or, at least, develop a negative disposition toward it? Note that, historically, the idea of toleration played an important role in such cultures as Christianity, which assumed total certainty about its own truth and denied any value to tolerated positions. At first, the idea of toleration reflected the position of the majority vis-à-vis the minority and, from the seventeenth century onward, it also came to include deviant individuals.[19]

The idea of pluralism is radically different, both in its historical and sociological contexts, in that it is part of a cultural liberal framework that affirms free thought and free action without ensuring the majority view a preferable status. One of the main historical differences is that a tolerant culture is basically a monopolistic religious culture, whereas a pluralistic culture prevails in a liberal-secular environment where religions may even compete with one another. "The pluralistic situation" is one of unbridled competition, without any preferences or advantages.[20] As Berger describes it: "The pluralistic situation is, above all, a market situation," in which religion is sold as any of the other goods available in the market.[21] The transition from a tolerant to a pluralistic culture is not sharp and all-inclusive. A pluralistic culture may also include islands of toleration or even of intolerance, indicating it does not accept the market situation in some areas. A prominent instance is the change in the attitude to homosexuality in pluralistic cultures, shifting from intolerance to toleration and from toleration to indifference. This type of relationship is never found in a market situation. A conceptual analysis of pluralism will further understanding of this historical-sociological reality.

Conceptually, pluralism does not reflect a paradox of opposition and acceptance. Pluralists do not "tolerate" different views because they are, as it were, ready to tolerate the people expressing them. Rather, a pluralist considers the other's view valuable and, therefore, respects the person who represents it. Pluralists have views and values to which they attach certainty, and pluralism is not synonymous with an absolute skepticism incapable of substantiating anything. When no stance can be substantiated, "anything goes" and shifting positions is a matter of whim rather than discretion. This state of affairs does not reflect pluralism but lack of care. No stance is preferable to another and, therefore, all positions are irrelevant.[22]

In this sense, a distinction is required between descriptive pluralism, which merely states that people hold different positions, and normative pluralism, which is part of a wider, usually liberal, value system. Descriptive pluralism neither justifies nor rejects anything. It describes the factual datum of a multicultural society, which enables this multiplicity out of indifference. By contrast, normative pluralism is not a substitute for rational value allegiance to specific attitudes but reflects a certain commitment that is also rationally substantiated and hence affirms or rejects specific positions. Normative pluralists believe in their own attitudes and preferences and think them well substantiated. They do not agree with the views of others because, logically, their views differ.[23]

Pluralists still differ from tolerant people, however, in that they are not committed to refrain from acting against others since pluralists do not assume any grounds justifying such action in the first place. A pluralist does not view the other's stance as deviant, shameful, or evil, and demanding a reaction. Value preferences do not lead a pluralist to negate the other's views. Unlike tolerant people, pluralists assign to other views the same value they assign to their own, as evident in their respect for the views and the deeds of the other[24] rather than only for the other's basic human freedom. In other words, value-based toleration may lead a tolerant person to respect someone upholding the tolerated stance, but never its contents. Pluralists, however, respect also the contents of the contrary views. They engage in a genuine discourse with opposite views, not only because they consent to tolerate people and allow their freedom but because they are truly interested in the other's stand and consider it valuable.

Given that pluralists do have value preferences, however, why do they ascribe intrinsic value to other positions? This is the litmus test for distinguishing between two main versions of pluralism, to which I will refer as "weak" and "strong" pluralism. Weak pluralism does not entirely renounce the assumption of one truth and the need to find it, but rests on a skeptical position and argues that this truth can only emerge through constant confrontation with contrary views. John Stuart Mill advances this view, as does Karl Popper, who relies on Voltaire. Their shared basic assumption is that human beings are fallible creatures.[25] Hence, the only way of avoiding mistakes is to contend with contrary views. An open market of attitudes and actions is the best course for human beings, whose cognition is so fragile, to reach truth. Both Mill and Popper reject skepticism and relativism. Mill states: "As mankind improve, the number of doctrines which are no longer disputed or doubted will be constantly on the increase."[26] Mill views the development of humanity as a ceaseless process of rejecting mistaken attitudes and as a "gradual narrowing of the bounds of diversity of opinion."[27] Pluralism, then, is temporary by definition. In an infinite time perspective, it will disappear once truth is revealed. Popper's formulation is not as radical, but he too painstakingly emphasizes the distinction between "fallibilism" and relativism. Human fallibility assumes:

> There is such a thing as truth...Fallibilism certainly implies that truth and goodness are often hard to come by, and that we should always be prepared to find that we have made a mistake. On the other hand, fallibilism implies that we can get nearer to the truth or to a good society.[28]

Skepticism, then, is a temporary situation rooted in human reality rather than a metaphysical stance compelling relativism.

This analysis enables us to sharpen the distinction between the weak pluralist and the tolerant person. Tolerant individuals are likely to approach mistaken views as a means for reaching the truth but assume, according to the common definition, that truth has already been found and that they have it, whereas other views are only of instrumental, pedagogical, or epistemic value. By contrast, pluralists do not assume the absolute preference of their views over those of the other, since their own views could turn out to be mistaken. Tolerant individuals do not accept the idea of fallibility and, therefore, cannot relate to other views as they relate to their own, whereas pluralists, even when they do have a preferred view, do not claim it is absolutely preferable. In Hare's words, "the best that he has so far discovered."[29] In Popper's terms, the preferability of the pluralist's position means it has so far not been refuted. The other's position, however, is important for pluralists precisely because they are conscious of human fallibility.

Contrary to weak pluralism, strong pluralism does not assume the existence of one truth, not even ideally. Whereas weak pluralism views the confrontation between opposite views as a means to approximate truth, strong pluralism does not ascribe any instrumental value to contrary positions and considers every stance in the open market of ideas intrinsically valuable, beyond the temporary.

If Voltaire provided the foundation for weak pluralism, Rousseau adopted the strong version of pluralism. The multiplicity of ideas expresses human difference and the value of individuality.[30] Prominent modern champions of this version are Mill, in Chapter Three of *On Liberty*, Robert Nozick, and Joseph Raz. Whereas in Chapter Two of *On Liberty* Mill emphasizes the instrumental value of contrary views, in Chapter Three he sharply reverses his position. The basis for pluralism is now an acknowledgement of the value of individuality as embodied in human differences: "It is not by wearing down into uniformity all that is individual in themselves...that human beings become a noble and beautiful object of contemplation."[31] Human differences thus create variety and a diversity of lifestyles. Nozick too relies on this justification of pluralism, arguing that we do not know any specific lifestyle equally good for everyone, and a utopian society is one that enables all human beings to realize themselves as long as they respect the rights of others.[32] The recognition of human variety is a descriptive but also a prescriptive statement, which assumes the value of individuality and claims it can only be preserved in a pluralistic worldview.[33]

Joseph Raz proposes another version of strong pluralism. In his view, pluralism is a necessary condition of human autonomy. Autonomous individuals shape their lives and control their own destiny as far as possible, as evident in their choices. But freedom of choice, claims Raz, is not sufficient for autonomy and individuals must be able to choose between contrary options. Autonomy is an empty notion in the absence of options, but the choice must not be only between good and evil and must also involve choice between various possibilities of the good.[34]

Contrary to toleration, then, the common denominator of all versions of pluralism is their adoption of some form of relativism. Weak pluralism is committed mainly to epistemic and hypothetical pluralism, meaning that the truths assumed by the pluralist may emerge as false. Strong pluralism is committed to a particular form of value relativism, meaning there is no one absolute right for an individual, or even for all human beings. But this relativism is limited, since it acknowledges the existence of various forms of the good but also discerns the existence of various forms of evil. Some things are illegitimate and entirely lacking in value.[35] This conclusion is entirely compatible with the formal characterization of pluralism as a stance within a normative system that distinguishes between forbidden and allowed, worthy and despicable.[36] The difference between the two versions of pluralism is that, at least in principle, weak pluralism ascribes equal value to legitimate views as an expression of epistemic limitations, whereas strong pluralism ascribes intrinsic value to various versions of the good.

Jewish Religion and Toleration

Since toleration developed in a system that assumed value certainty, tolerant individuals had to justify their abstention from action in ways appropriate to their certainties. Indeed, this is how toleration developed. What might be the arguments favoring religious toleration? As noted, Augustine and Thomas Aquinas justified their toleration of the Jews as a conclusion ensuing from Christian certainty. An interesting and highly influential version of the idea of toleration rests on a voluntariness argument, which also draws on religion.

The first one to propose this argument was Sebastian Castellion (1515–1563), who argued that conversion is voluntary by definition and, therefore, cannot be coerced. Jesus never forced anyone to join Christianity, which is essentially endorsed voluntarily.[37] Castellion was a liberal Protestant thinker who began his career as a friend of Calvin. An elaborate and refined version of this argument was lucidly formulated by Locke in his *Letters Concerning Toleration*. Locke's argument, as Castellion's before him, rests on the Protestant approach,[38] suggesting a clear division between church and state.

The state was founded only for one purpose: "The commonwealth seems to me to be a society of men constituted only for the procuring, preserving, and advancing of their own civil interests. Civil interests I call life, liberty, health, and indolence of body."[39] A church, however, is different: "A church, then, I take to be a voluntary society of men, joining themselves together of their own accord in order to the public worshipping of God in such manner as they judge acceptable to Him, and effectual to the salvation of their souls."[40]

Given this distinction between church and state, Locke argues that both must endorse religious toleration. As for the state, Locke raises three arguments: First,

The care of souls is not committed to the civil magistrate...It is not committed unto him, I say, by God, because it appears not that God has ever given any such authority to one man over another as to compel anyone to his religion. Nor can any such power be vested in the magistrate by the consent of the people, because no man can so far abandon the care of his own salvation as blindly to leave to the choice of any other, whether prince or subject, to prescribe to him what faith or worship he shall embrace. (17)

Second, a state can coerce "but true and saving religion consists in the inward persuasion of the mind, without which nothing can be acceptable to God" (19). In other words, an act performed under coercion has no religious meaning.

Third:

For there being but one truth, one way to heaven, what hope is there that more men would be led into it if they had no rule but the religion of the court and were put under the necessity to quit the light of their own reason, to oppose the dictates of their own consciences, and blindly to resign themselves up to the will of their governors. (21)

Locke points out that, given that the princes of the world have many views on religion, the way to heaven is extremely narrow (21). Should we wish to widen it, on the assumption that it is improper for God to bestow his grace on so few, the basis for attaining redemption for all human beings must be their reason and their conscience rather than a political doctrine.

After divesting political rulers of the power to enforce their authority on matters of faith, Locke shows that the church does not have such power either. As a voluntary association by definition, the church cannot, in his view, rely on coercion.

Locke does not doubt the truth of Anglican Christianity, nor is his view based on skepticism or relativism. Both Locke and Castellion before him thought that toleration rested on religion and on religious truths: Locke traced a clear link between salvation and voluntarism.

The voluntariness argument substantiates only a weak version of toleration — it simply forbids coercion, and this is indeed all that Locke concluded from it. Furthermore, since the source of Locke's argument is his religious approach, all he is endorsing is negative toleration: one should not interfere to deprive deviants from their freedom, but it does not thereby follow that, within the political framework, one should seek to ensure additional rights for them beyond this minimum requirement.[41]

Can Jewish tradition adopt a tolerant attitude toward non-observant Jews? If so, can it adopt only the weak version that refrains from coercion or can it endorse stronger versions of toleration? Furthermore, can it embrace only negative toleration or can it also support positive toleration?

Historically, several sources can be pointed out supporting Locke's argument of voluntariness in one way or another. Moses Mendelssohn, who endorses a version of Locke's argument,[42] draws a distinction between the inter-subjective and the religious realms:

> The relations between man and man require action as such... An action beneficial to the public does not cease to be beneficial, even if it is brought about by coercion, whereas a religious action is religious only to the degree to which it is performed voluntarily and with proper intent.[43]

Incipient signs of a measure of support for the claim of voluntariness appear also in halakhic literature.[44] Thus, for instance, Solomon Kluger writes about coerced observance:

> Concerning matters that the Torah does not command us to impose, we have proof that the Torah wanted observance to be voluntary and never coerced. Hence, if the court did coerce someone, he is not considered to have complied with the commandment, since he did so under duress rather than willingly.[45]

But Kluger does not claim that the Torah forbids coercion altogether or that, in principle, a commandment fulfilled under duress has no value. Instead, he claims that no coercion should be applied on matters that the Torah does not coerce because the very fact that the Torah did not require coercion shows that the value of this particular commandment depends on the individual's will. No general conclusions about coercion follow from this.

The validity of the argument of voluntariness depends on the meaning ascribed to the religious act. Intolerant positions claim that the religious act is intrinsically valuable, regardless of the performer's will, so there is logic to its coercion. By contrast, tolerant positions argue that the value of the commandment is contingent on the performer's intention, so that an act performed under duress has no religious significance.[46]

The argument seems to fit a religion such as Protestantism, which makes voluntarism a cornerstone of its self-perception. It is less relevant, though still possible to some extent, in Judaism, where religious obligations have traditionally been compelled upon all members of the collective.

An alternative basis for weak toleration in Jewish religion assumes its reliance on considerations of result. Coercion is pointless if it does not lead to observance of the commandment or if it violates the conditions required for the performance of the religious act. Meir Simha Hacohen of Dwinsk appears to support this view. Maimonides rules that a man who is legally compelled to divorce his wife is coerced to do so until he says, "I consent." Maimonides does know that a coerced divorce is invalid, and thus presumes:

> Inasmuch as he desires to be of the Israelites, to abide by all the commandments and to keep away from transgressions — it is only his inclination that has overwhelmed him — once he is lashed until his inclination is weakened and he says "I consent," it is the same as if he had given the *get* voluntarily.[47]

This source seemingly argues that coercion is allowed only when we know for sure that this person wants to belong to the Jewish collective and resists only because he is overwhelmed by his inclination. Meir Simha Hacohen of Dwinsk indeed claims: "If the court knew for sure that he definitely does not want to [grant a divorce], and it is obvious to them as it is to Heaven that coercing him will be useless and he is willing to die for it, they would forbid laying a hand on him."[48]

Prima facie, refraining from coercion in this case means applying a consideration of result.[49] Yet, the scope for drawing inferences from this source is extremely limited, since we have no proof that considerations of result can be used to justify a wider thesis of weak toleration. Meir Simha Hacohen is drawing a legal inference related to the specific conditions for divorce. A coerced divorce is halakhically invalid, and divorce requires free consent. In this specific realm, then, personal intention is crucial. But does this consideration apply to all other commandments as well?

Elsewhere, however, Meir Simha Hacohen relies more broadly on a result consideration when he excludes the possibility of beating "to death" someone who is unwilling to observe a commandment: "What will we gain? The commandment will not be observed in any event."[50]

Although this source is more precise, it only justifies refraining from direct coercion. Are other forms of coercion, besides beating, also excluded? Is excommunication also forbidden? Reliance on result considerations does not dismiss the option of indirect coercion. For instance, removal and excommunication could be perceived as conveying the collective's attitude toward the deviant. These means may appear necessary so as to deter others, to prevent the damaging effects of deviance on other members of the collective, or to express scorn and revulsion. Abstaining from action in a given situation due to result considerations justifies limited toleration, which could change with the circumstances or due to other result considerations.

Historically, the Jewish collective did not refrain from using a range of means (not necessarily direct coercion) to combat deviance, repeatedly resorting to exclusion and excommunication. Jews sometimes abstained from these measures, not so much out of a desire to refrain from interference in the others' lives but rather due to their fear of the consequence — the irrevocable expulsion of the Jewish deviant from the Jewish people. Sometimes, however, they did impose such sanctions when the consequences were clear. Thus, for instance, Radbaz argues that dispensing with punishment for fear of its effects on the deviant should be dismissed in favor of attention to the potential damage to the community: "Should we fear this [that the person could abandon the Jewish collective], the Torah may have to be repealed since all will know that, due to this fear, we overlook the wrongs of the wicked."[51]

Signs of weak toleration are nevertheless present in Jewish tradition and a tolerant approach is conceptually compatible with full commitment to the tradition. This is not true of the strong version of toleration, which refrains from openly forbidding the deviant act. The voluntariness aspect is irrelevant here, and we must look for a kind of result consideration. The general talmudic principle "better that they should sin in ignorance than deliberately" (BT Betsah 30a and others), designed to avoid damage to the individual, could serve to justify the strong version — the deviant stance should not be forbidden so as not to turn the deviant into a deliberate transgressor. But whether conclusions drawn from this halakhic principle could be relevant to all prohibitions and in all situations is questionable. Many halakhic sages pointed to the limitations that qualify the implementation of this principle. Some emphasized that this principle applies only when individuals transgress unwittingly. When they wantonly transgress a prohibition, however, "you will rebuke them, curse them, reprimand them, and dismiss them...and even if they do not listen, you will have saved your soul."[52] Other sages pointed out that this principle does not apply to explicit Torah injunctions.[53]

But even according to sages who assumed that this principle applies to wanton transgressions of Torah injunctions as well, this view denotes indifference to evil rather than its toleration. In the formulation of Moses of Coucy: "A man should not say something that will go unheeded, as is written, 'Do not reprove a scorner, lest he hate thee' [Proverbs 9:8]."[54] According to this approach, what appears as strong toleration is a classic case of turning the deviant into an evil wrongdoer for whom society is no longer responsible. The halakhic principle relevant to this approach is "stuff the wicked until he dies." The wrongdoer's freedom to act as he pleases and the failure to rebuke him for his transgression denote his removal from the Jewish collective rather than a readiness to tolerate him.[55]

Beyond these caveats, this principle obviously applies only when all members of the collective are committed to the Torah but transgress a specific commandment, be it wantonly or mistakenly.

When large sections of the collective do not acknowledge the validity of Halakhah, however, its applicability becomes questionable. In these circumstances, this principle could also entail a heavy religious price: abstaining from declaring certain matters forbidden could have serious implications for members of the religious collective, who will conclude that these matters are permitted and will become transgressors.[56] Hence, although this principle could conceptually be used to justify strong toleration, turning it into a general rule applicable in all circumstances without a more basic transformation of Jewish religion seems unreasonable.

Could Jewish religion adopt the idea of toleration as a mental disposition? I noted above that toleration as a mental disposition is generally based on the value of human freedom. People who err should not be scorned, because their freedom could also lead them to make mistakes. Can someone who is religiously tolerant endorse this view? Can someone for whom religious truth is cardinal prefer the value of human autonomy instead? Religious individuals also believe in the importance of choice, since this is one of the basic assumptions of their religious activity, but the value of choice *per se* can hardly justify the endorsement of toleration as a disposition.

Believers find it easier to adopt a paternalistic attitude toward deviants, thus precluding feelings of disdain and scorn for them. Much of what passes for "toleration" in the writings of Abraham Yitzhak Kook[57] is merely a form of paternalism that does not address the deviant stance as genuine. This paternalism emerges in two forms: ascribing cognitive irresponsibility to deviants, and attempting to understand their "disease." The first is manifest, for instance, in the following statement about the *zeitgeist* "seducing our young with its many wiles to follow its shameless ways.... They are definitely acting under duress, and we should not, Heaven forbid, judge coercion as we would free will."[58]

Although this approach makes it easier not to despise or scorn others, it also precludes genuine respect for them since it neither recognizes them as cognitively responsible individuals nor does it acknowledge the deviation as a true position. Paternalism, then, although not affected by the paradox of toleration, is by nature limited. Deviants cannot forever be viewed as coerced, unless it is assumed they are cognitively handicapped.

The second form of "toleration" leads Kook to an attempt to understand "the disease of the generation."[59] According to this analysis, the source of deviance is not the denial of religious truth but the search for a deeper truth and disaffection with religiosity as it is.[60] The analysis of the deviants' motives may enable us to avoid despising them and may perhaps lead us to respect them, but it rests on the negation of the deviant's self-interpretation of their world and their longings. This negation also reflects the collapse of the paradox of tolerance, since it does not relate to the other's view as genuine.

This type of paternalistic rhetoric may express a tolerant religious approach, which cannot be formulated openly because it hinges on the tension between its halakhic foundation and its readiness for toleration. For toleration as a mental disposition, however, this rhetoric exacts a high price — it does not show respect for the others' freedom and their ability to formulate alternative views. This analysis of R. Kook's view sheds new light on the problems hindering believers from developing a tolerant disposition toward deviance.

All potentially acceptable versions of toleration will, at best, be confined to abstention. Since traditional Jewish religion holds itself absolutely true and valid for every member of the Jewish collective, its believers will hardly engage in a struggle to protect the rights of deviants to realize their ideals. This task can only engage those who view freedom as a cardinal value.

Tolerant persons are not required to renounce any of their beliefs and, conceptually, traditional Jewish religion can therefore be tolerant. Can it also endorse a pluralistic outlook without becoming self-subversive? Can the believer respect the other as a person as well as the other's views, beliefs, and deeds as having equal and also intrinsic value? Given the believers' perception of Jewish truth as divine, can they respect contrary views without breaching their own religiosity?[61] Are pluralism and religious authenticity compatible? Endorsing a pluralistic view requires a deep conceptual transformation, a religious revolution enabling the believer not to view the other's stance as deviant. Is such a revolution possible? And if possible, is it worthwhile? Given that the cradle of pluralism is the secularization process,[62] the question then is: can Jewish religion internalize the ideas of secularization and still remain meaningful to its believers?

Jewish Religion and Pluralism

These questions need to be examined vis-à-vis the two types of pluralism I proposed, weak and strong. As noted, supporters of weak pluralism assume there is truth and that the stance they uphold is one that has been substantiated in the best way or, at least, has so far not been refuted. These assumptions might be compatible with a religious approach, since religious pluralists willingly acknowledge the limitations of human cognition. In this sense, weak pluralism does not relinquish its clear preference for its own view, and its relativism is mainly cognitive and hypothetical rather than normative. Jewish believers, then, can be pluralists without renouncing their beliefs, but endorsing this view exacts a high price since Jewish beliefs could, at least hypothetically, prove false. The religious pluralist cannot continue supporting the belief that, even at a later time, "this Torah will not be changed," as Maimonides states in his Thirteen Principles of Faith. Furthermore, even if this price were reasonable, weak pluralism is incompatible with halakhic language and halakhic deeds. Since this problem is also relevant to strong pluralism, I discuss it below.

Strong pluralism, even though upholding normative relativism, is not necessarily committed to epistemic relativism. The pluralist, therefore, is not necessarily committed to the derogation of the value system that pluralism supports. Conceptually, one may acknowledge the existence of parallel value systems without in principle assuming that they cancel each other out. In this sense, strong pluralists are not committed to the temporariness of their beliefs and their values.

Yet, to enable this kind of pluralism, a fundamental conceptual revolution about the meaning of religious statements is required. Believers supporting strong pluralism must renounce a traditional assumption inconsistent with strong pluralism, namely, that religion is true. Renouncing this option seems impossible in a religious context, since believers cannot agree with the assumption that religion is false. The renunciation, however, could be interpreted to mean that religion is only praxis, and categories of truth and false are irrelevant in its regard. Truth claims about the world, about God, and about crucial events such as the Sinai theophany, are religiously irrelevant. In other words, religion is a value system that neither relies upon nor reflects metaphysical assumptions or factual data that could be translated into truth claims.[63] In John Searle's terms, religion is a constitutive system,[64] shaping a world of procedures and meanings that do not assume their sense from a specific state of affairs but from the system itself. The religious system formulates norms defined as commandments, and even formulates beliefs applying to these norms, the central one being the perception of these norms as God's word at Sinai. In religious terms, the historical fact of the Sinai theophany is not what validates the normative system. If this historical fact is a relevant constitutive rule, it will assume meaning only from the system itself and is, in Searles's terms, an "institutional fact."[65] In this light, the religious fact of the Sinai theophany can be viewed as a kind of judgment and evaluation of halakhic norms. The believer is then commanded to accept that these norms, all or some, are God's word at Sinai, deserving honor and respect as defined by the system itself. According to this outlook, Jewish religion is not founded on statements about the world; rather, like other constitutive systems, it shapes a world of meaning and internal coherence that is not conditioned by outside facts.

As part of this revolution, individuals deciding to embrace Jewish religion seek to actualize a world of norms and meanings articulated by the system, which they consider especially valuable. People's motivations when adopting this system are no different from those driving many to embrace a specific lifestyle: the wish to live within a certain system whose cluster of values they consider worthy of realization, to create a better world for themselves, and so forth.

The religious revolution required to enable strong pluralism relies on the following claims:

(1) Jewish religion is a value system that does not make truth claims about the world or about God but constitutes a value system.
(2) The system's meaning is internal, implying it is not contingent on outside facts. Instead, it emerges as a conclusion from an analysis of the cluster of norms and values through which Jewish religion is constituted.
(3) A person's commitment to religion results from an autonomous decision to realize these particular religious values.

This conceptual revolution enables the existence of value systems that also have inner value, since none of them formulates truth claims that might prove false. This analysis restricts the meaning of religious statements, thus making room for other value systems that do not make competing truth claims.

Conceptual-theoretical revolutions in religious tradition in general and in Jewish tradition in particular are not new. One of the most basic ways in which traditional societies cope with new challenges is the conceptual transformation of their world of values. This transformation enables the translation of the old world of values into a new conceptual language, without precluding commitment to these values.[66] Jewish intellectual history abounds with such examples, and Maimonides seems to have prompted the deepest theoretical revolution in traditional culture by creating a new language for the biblical-talmudic world so as to adapt it to the philosophical challenge.

Our revolution does differ from that proposed by Maimonides, since Jewish religion has now become an individual concern. Jewish religion is diverted from the collective-historical context to the individual one; it is a matter of choice or preference, as Berger noted: "Private religiosity, however 'real' it may be to the individuals who adopt it, cannot any longer fulfill the classical task of religion, that of constructing a common world within which all of social life receives ultimate meaning binding on everybody."[67]

But even if a conceptual religious revolution were possible and worthwhile, it is not easily compatible with halakhic language and action, which seem to be more rigid. A Jew who does not observe the Torah and the commandments is described in halakhic language as a transgressor, as ignorant of the law, as acting under duress, and so forth. The transgression of certain commandments is considered synonymous with the violation of the entire Torah, and breaking the Sabbath in public is particularly important in this context.

The special status of the Sabbath, as Rashi noted, is related to its theological meaning: "The Sabbath transgressor denies His acts, and falsely attests that the Holy One, blessed be He, did not rest on the Sabbath."[68] If this is the status of the Sabbath, the conceptual revolution faces a hard challenge because this status points to the presence of a deep metaphysical sediment in the halakhic realm. No less important, however, is the halakhic implication that follows. A mainstream halakhic tradition, stretching from *Halakhot Gedolot*[69] through the literature of the early authorities[70] and up to modern halakhic literature[71] speaks of Sabbath breakers in public as complete idolaters no longer included in the Jewish collective.[72] Various sages, however, developed a more tolerant attitude toward Sabbath breakers for other reasons. Some relied on considerations of result, claiming that an approach that views public Sabbath breakers as Gentiles would lead them to abandon the Jewish people. Others relied on a sociological consideration, arguing that the precondition for breaking the Sabbath in public is the existence of a society that observes the Sabbath. However:

> In our times, they are not called public Sabbath breakers because this is what most people do. When most Jews are not guilty, the few who dare to transgress are denying the Torah, committing an abomination, and excluding themselves from the Jewish people. Unfortunately, however, when most Jews are transgressors, the individual believes this is not such a serious offense and one need not hide.[73]

The transgressor's intention is thus a necessary condition for determining the seriousness of the offence. In light of secularization, the Sabbath breaker has no consciousness of being a sinner and, therefore, is not in the category of a public Sabbath breaker.

These considerations might, at best, substantiate weak toleration, but they cannot justify pluralism. Pluralism contradicts Halakhah's basic assumption, which holds that all Jews are compelled to observe the Torah and the commandments by virtue of the Sinai covenant, making pluralism an extremely difficult position to sustain in religious terms. First, pluralism is committed to a deep religious-conceptual revolution. Second, this revolution is not sufficient either, since Halakhah might be compatible with toleration but not with pluralism. In other words, the maximum possible is a pluralistic consciousness and halakhic toleration.

Is pluralism then entirely incompatible with Jewish religion? Halakhah is indeed hard to integrate with a pluralistic stance, but a religious revolution is not a negligible feat even if it cannot be directly translated into practice. It creates a new consciousness that could be significant in and of itself and, indirectly, could also contribute to practical trends. Even if unable to foster a pluralistic Halakhah, it might promote tolerant trends that will somehow progress toward pluralism. The religious pluralist may be doomed to live in permanent tension, fluctuating between a religious and pluralist pole on the one hand and, on the other, a halakhic pole that, at best, will be tolerant. This tension is a good illustration of the pluralist's participation in two communities — a Western community that endorses pluralism and a halakhic Jewish community unreservedly committed to its own directives. Membership in these two communities at times leads to a deep value conflict. Yet, as I have shown elsewhere,[74] affirming a conflict between two different value systems is, in logical terms, a measure of the deep commitment felt toward both. The conflict, then, is the quintessential affirmation of membership in both communities.

Finally, do religious believers have any reason for embracing religious pluralism despite the heavy religious price it exacts? The answer to this question is highly complex. Good religious reasons can be adduced for doing nothing at all, due to the religious concessions expected from tradition, to the ultimately conflictual effects of any action, and to its future implications for life in general and for religious truths in particular. A believer choosing to remain within a traditional framework could hardly accept arguments that might lead to its erosion and would have no reason to adopt a pluralistic outlook. The question is only relevant to a believer leaning toward pluralism — can rational justifications be found for this inclination? The reasons justifying the pluralistic believer's preferences will not make traditional believers change their minds, but are extremely valuable to the pluralist. These reasons are a conscious reconstruction of the pluralistic believer's world, an explication of the first datum in the pluralist's consciousness. In other words, these reasons provide pluralistic believers a theoretical foundation for the religious world they have long inhabited.

A serious attempt to contend with the questions raised by pluralism is to be favored on three counts. First, pluralism poses a serious challenge to traditional believers who see themselves as members of Western liberal societies by compelling them to examine the extent to which they can negate the intrinsic value of the other's world without hindering this membership. Second, concerning many public and value-based questions, believers who have opened up to the world endorse a pluralistic outlook. If they translate this outlook into actual behavior, they have to meet the theoretical challenge of formulating a pluralistic religious world view. Third, one interesting reaction of modern believers striving to preserve their religious beliefs and values is a perception of the religious world as a unique type of religious experience. Several scholars have indicated that religiosity in the modern world is no longer based on a rational-metaphysical cognition but on a personal subjective experience. This experience is an autonomous realm that cannot be exhausted or understood through any other context, and is thus the starting point of the religious domain.[75] The crucial role of subjectivity in human existence paves the way for a renewed justification of religion through the acknowledgement of subjective religious experience, which believers view as an autonomous realm out of which they relate to and interpret the world.[76] Adopting this approach compels what Hick called the "intellectual Golden Rule":[77] believers must allow others what they take for themselves, meaning they must recognize the justified value of the experience of others who are not like them.[78]

In sum, this chapter was an attempt to offer an initial outline for a discussion of the possibility of toleration and pluralism within a religious outlook. My conclusion is that, conceptually, toleration is an easier stance for the believer to accept and might be compatible with a traditional world view. Endorsing pluralism requires a religious revolution and exacts a heavy religious price, and yet, it is pluralism rather than toleration that challenges believers living in our modern-liberal world.

Notes

1. For an analysis of halakhic pluralism and its borders see my book, *The Open Canon: On the Meaning of Halakhic Discourse*, trans. Batya Stein (London: Continuum, 2007).
2. Alexander Altman, *Tolerance and the Jewish Tradition* (London: The Robert Waley Cohen Memorial Lecture — Council of Christians and Jews, 1957), 8. A classic expression of the halakhic tendency to coerce all members of the Jewish collective is evident in the work of Raphael Cohen, rabbi of Altona-Hamburg, a prominent eighteenth-century halakhic scholar: "The foundation of the Torah and the commandments is to coerce and punish transgressors...and whoever has seen the lights of Torah in his lifetime knows that the...foundation of the Torah and the commandment is built upon coercion" (Raphael Cohen, *Da'at Kedoshim* [Altona: Judah Brothers, 1797), 48a.
3. See D. D. Raphael, "The Intolerable," in *Justifying Toleration: Conceptual and Historical Perspectives*, ed. Susan Mendus (Cambridge: Cambridge University Press, 1988), 140; Preston King, *Toleration* (London: George Allen and Unwin, 1976), 29ff.
4. Jay Newman, "The Idea of Religious Tolerance," *American Philosophical Quarterly* 15 (1978), 187.
5. Compare Jeremy Waldron, "Locke: Toleration and the Rationality of Persecution," in *John Locke: A Letter Concerning Toleration in Focus*

(New York: Routledge, 1991), 100. Waldron indicates (121, n. 8) that Joseph Raz does not agree with this. As will be shown, even though Raz uses the term "toleration" he is referring to pluralism, which explains why he does not endorse this assumption.

6   King, *Toleration*, 25–26.
7   Newman, "The Idea of Religious Tolerance," 189.
8   The claim that the idea of toleration was born in a climate rejecting the concept of objective value is thus groundless. See, for instance, Roberto Mangabeira Unger, *Knowledge and Politics* (New York: Free Press, 1984), 76.
9   See Waldron, "Locke: Toleration," 105–106.
10 Some hold that caring is the opposite of toleration, as opposed to others who hold that the opposite of toleration is intolerance rather than indifference, since caring is a pre-condition of toleration but is not identical with it. See Peter Nicholson, "Toleration as a Moral Ideal," in *Aspects of Toleration*, ed. John Horton and Susan Mendus (London: Methuen, 1985), 162.
11 This formulation endorses Nicholson's view. See ibid., 160.
12 See Mary Warnock, "The Limits of Toleration," in *On Toleration*, ed. Susan Mendus and David Edwards (Oxford: Clarendon Press, 1987), 125–126.
13 Newman, " The Idea of Religious Tolerance," 194.
14 Nicholson further claims in "Toleration as a Moral Ideal" that tolerant people must have the power to act against the tolerated position. Assuming otherwise means they are forced to admit it exists without genuinely allowing it, since the tolerated stance does not depend on them at all. In the absence of such power, one can only speak of toleration in the limited sense of claiming that, if they had power, they would nevertheless refrain from exercising it (161). This assumption fits the definition of toleration as a behavioral stance, restraining the power to act, but does not apply to toleration as a mental stance or a disposition toward the tolerated attitude, where the power to act is irrelevant. The tolerant person will be one who does not reject, derive, curse, or assume a similar attitude toward the tolerated position, without considering the question of power. For a discussion of these types of toleration, see below.

[15] For an analysis of Augustine and Thomas Aquinas and their implications for a tolerant attitude toward Jews, see Alex Bein, *The Jewish Question: Biography of a World Problem*, trans. Harry Zohn (New York: Herzl Press, 1990), chs. 2 and 3.

[16] For a detailed critique of consequential considerations see Albert Weale, "Toleration, Individual Differences, and Respect for Persons," in *Aspects of Toleration*, ed. John Horton and Susan Mendus (London: Methuen, 1985), 19–23.

[17] Warnock, who also differentiates between various types of toleration, chose the first option I suggested, so that what I call weak toleration is for her strong toleration (Warnock, "The Limits of Toleration," 126–127). I prefer the second option since the value of toleration is determined precisely by the level of self-restraint it reflects.

[18] On this distinction, see Lord Scarman, "Toleration and the Law," in *On Toleration*, ed. Susan Mendus and David Edwards (Oxford: Clarendon Press, 1987), 49.

[19] Locke's *Letters Concerning Toleration* are good examples of this turnabout. Locke does not necessarily refer to a tolerated minority group but to deviant individuals.

[20] Peter Berger, *The Sacred Canopy* (New York: Anchor Books, 1990), 135. See also John Rawls, *A Theory of Justice* (Cambridge: Harvard University Press, 1971), 28–29; Charles E. Larmore, *Patterns of Moral Complexity* (Cambridge: Cambridge University Press, 1987), 22–23; Michael Sandel, *Liberalism and the Limits of Justice* (Cambridge: Cambridge University Press, 1982), 1.

John Kekes is deeply critical of the link between liberalism and pluralism. His main claim is that, whereas the pluralist cannot be committed to a specific system of values that overrides all others, liberalism in its various versions does evince this type of commitment. See John Kekes, *The Morality of Pluralism* (Princeton, NJ: Princeton University Press, 1993), 199–217. Kekes' critique is unpersuasive because his claims about pluralism are far too strong. To assume that pluralists hold that in all situations and concerning all issues there are no overriding values is implausible. Indeed, Kekes himself acknowledges the existence of unjustified options or ways of implementation (ibid., 14), in which case a liberal world view could be seen as the minimum condition for removing them. But even if Kekes is right, the historical fact is that pluralism did indeed originate in a secular-liberal culture, and Kekes' analysis does not satisfactorily account for this.

21   Berger, *The Sacred Canopy*, 138.
22   Compare Søren Kierkegaard, *Either/Or*, vol. 1, trans. Howard V. Hong and Edna Hong (Princeton, NJ: Princeton University Press, 1987), 38–40. For an incisive critique of American culture as indifferent, see Allan Bloom, The *Closing of the American Mind* (New York: Simon and Schuster, 1987), Part Two.
23   See Richard M. Hare, *Freedom and Reason* (Oxford: Clarendon Press, 1982), 178.
24   Ibid.
25   John Stuart Mill, *On Liberty* (Hammonsdworth, England: Penguin, 1984), 77; Karl Popper, "Toleration and Intellectual Responsibility," in *On Toleration*, ed. Susan Mendus and David Edwards (Oxford: Clarendon Press, 1987), 18.
26   Mill, *On Liberty*, 106.
27   Ibid.
28   Popper, "Toleration and Intellectual Responsibility," 25.
29   Hare, *Freedom and Reason*, 180.
30   Nicholas Dent, "Rousseau and Respect for Others," in *Justifying Toleration: Conceptual and Historical Perspectives*, ed. Susan Mendus (Cambridge: Cambridge University Press, 1988).
31   Mill, *On Liberty*, 127.
32   Robert Nozick, *Anarchy, State, and Utopia* (Oxford: Basil Blackwell, 1974), 310.
33   This is the solution to the naturalistic fallacy in this version of pluralism, pointed out in Milton Fisk, *Ethics and Society: A Marxist Interpretation of Value* (New York: New York University Press, 1980), 87.
34   See Joseph Raz, "Autonomy, Toleration, and the Harm Principle," in *Justifying Toleration: Conceptual and Historical Perspectives*, ed. Susan Mendus (Cambridge: Cambridge University Press, 1988) 156–157. Compare also Stanley I. Benn, "Freedom, Autonomy, and the Concept of a Person," *Proceedings of the Aristotelian Society* 76 (1975–1976): 123–128.

There is a clear link between the value of individuality that Mill and Nozick emphasize, and the value of human autonomy that Raz emphasizes. Autonomy in the sense of shaping and organizing life based on a personal decision is a classic expression of individuality, though the versions proposed by Mill and Nozick are slightly different from that offered by Raz. Raz sees the various options as competing alternatives that are a condition of autonomy, whereas Mill and Nozick are not committed to that view. They do not see these options as mutually competing necessarily but as reflecting, above all, the various possibilities of different people.

35 As noted, according to Raz, the condition of autonomy is a choice between good options, and not only between good and bad options. For additional distinctions between pluralism and relativism, see Kekes, *The Morality of Pluralism*, 8, 14, 31–32, 46–47.

36 Nevertheless, the relativism assumed by Nozick is broader than that assumed by Raz because Nozick's relativism relies on the variety and multiplicity of human experience.

37 For an analysis of his position, see King, *Toleration*, 78–80.

38 See Waldron, "Locke: Toleration and the Rationality of Persecution," 117.

39 John Locke, *A Letter Concerning Toleration*, ed. Mario Montuori (Hague: Martinus Nijhoff, 1963), 15.

40 Ibid., 23.

41 See also Waldron, "Locke: Toleration and the Rationality of Persecution," 111–115.

42 On the relationship between Mendelssohn and Locke, see Julius Guttmann, *Religion and Science* (in Hebrew) (Jerusalem: Magnes Press, 1955), 212–213; for an analysis of Mendelssohn's toleration see Jacob Katz, *Exclusiveness and Tolerance: Studies in Jewish-Gentile Relations in Medieval and Modern Times* (Oxford: Oxford University Press, 1961), ch. 14.

43 Moses Mendelssohn, *Jerusalem: On Religious Power and Judaism*, trans. Allan Arkush (Hanover: University Press of New England-Brandeis University Press, 1983), 72.

44 Michael Zvi Nehorai, "Can a Religious Deed Be Coerced?" (in Hebrew), in *Between Authority and Autonomy in Jewish Tradition*, ed.

Avi Sagi and Zeev Safrai (Tel Aviv: Hakibbutz Hameuchad, 1997), 364-381. Nehorai argues that Halakhah sees no basis or justification for coercing a religious act. Although his view is unquestionably one-sided, evidence definitely points to sources that support, or at least come close to, a tolerant stance.

[45] Solomon Kluger, *Hokhmat Shlomo* on *Shulkhan Arukh*, *Hoshen Mishpat*, 107a. This commentary appears in all the standard editions of Joseph Caro's code, the *Shulkhan Arukh*.

[46] See Nehorai, "Can a Religious Deed Be Coerced?." See also Jacob Levinger, *From Routine to Renewal: Pointers in Contemporary Jewish Thought* (in Hebrew) (Jerusalem: De'ot, 1973), ch. 9. Levinger holds that this tension is evident in the contrast between the positions of Judah Halevi and Bahya ibn Pakuda. Judah Halevi attaches metaphysical value to the actual performance of the commandments regardless of subjective intentions, whereas Bahya holds that the religious act is meaningless unless performed intentionally.

[47] *The Code of Maimonides*, *The Book of Women*, trans. Isaac Klein (New Haven: Yale University Press, 1972), Laws of Divorce 2: 20.

[48] Meir Simha Hacohen of Dwinsk, *Or Sameah*, *ad locum*. Note the changes in the interpretation of Maimonides. Raphael Cohen views Maimonides' statement as a basis for the possibility of coercion and, in clear contrast to Mendelssohn's view, although familiar with it, he concludes from Maimonides: "When a Jew observes a commandment, even if under duress, he will be seen as having done so willingly, because coercing him is only meant to weaken his evil inclination" (*Da'at Kedoshim*, 42a). On Cohen and his attitude to Mendelssohn see Jacob Katz, *Halakhah in Straits: Obstacles in Orthodoxy at its Inception* (in Hebrew) (Jerusalem: Magnes Press, 1992), 21-42.

[49] As Levinger and Nehorai indeed attempted to conclude.

[50] *Or Sameah* on Maimonides, Laws of Kings 4: 3.

[51] David b. Zimra (known as Radbaz), *Responsa* (Bnei Berak, 1975), 1: 187.

[52] Shlomo b. Yitzhak (known as Rashi), *Responsa* (Bnei-Berak: 1980), #20.

[53] Asheri, *Responsa* (Jerusalem: Or Hamizrah, 1994), 28: 13; Isachar Ber Illenburg, *Sefer Beer Sheva* (Jerusalem, 1982), #22, and others.

54 Moses of Coucy. *Sefer Mitzvot Gadol* (Bnei Berak, 1988), end of commandment 11.
55 For an analysis of the principle "stuff the wicked until he dies" see Yosef Ahituv, "'Stuff the Wicked Until He Dies': Refraining from Saving a Sinner" (in Hebrew), *Tehumin* 9 (1985): 156–170; Herzl Henkin, "Better For Them To Be Mistaken Than Wanton" (in Hebrew), *Tehumin* 2 (1981), 272–280.
56 *Shitah Mekubetset* (BT Betsah 30a) cites the view of Yom-Tov ben Avraham Ishbili (known as Ritba), ascribed to "French sages, among them the Maharam of Rottenburg." According to this view, "this idea ['better for them to be mistaken'] was meant only for their time [the talmudic period], but in our generation, which is more lenient, we ought to place a fence on the Torah, even if it is rabbinical, and we should fine them until they no longer transgress, whether mistakenly or wantonly." This is also the view of Yitzhak Abulafia, who claims: "And if they [the French tradition quoted above] said so about their own ancient times, what should we say in our bad days, so far removed from the early generations, of blessed memory...Surely if we say 'Let them be and so forth,' the Torah will disappear altogether...even more so since have no power to chastise them, fine them, and force them to mend their ways. Even so, we must rebuke them and abide by what our law requires" (*Penei Yitzhak*, Part 5 [Izmir, 1898], 4a-b)." Zvi Zohar, *Tradition and Change* (in Hebrew) (Jerusalem: Ben Zvi Institute, 1993) notes that Abulafia "tends to rely on a single Ashkenazi source against a majority of the sages" (224, n. 88). Even if true, however, the key question is not the source that the halakhist relies upon but the halakhic policy that should be applied in a reality of increasing secularism.
57 For an analysis of R. Kook's tolerant thought see Benjamin Ish-Shalom, "Tolerance and its Theoretical Basis in the Teaching of Rabbi Kook" (in Hebrew), *Daat* 20 (1988): 151–168; Zvi Yaron, *The Philosophy of Rabbi Kook*, trans. Avner Tomaschoff (Jerusalem: WZO, 1991).
58 Abraham Yitzhak Kook, *Iggerot ha-Rayha* (in Hebrew) (Jerusalem: Mosad Harav Kook, 1962), 171.
59 See "Ha-Dor" [The Generation] in Abraham Yitzhak Kook, *Eder HaYakar v'Ikvei Ha'Tson* (Jerusalem: Mosad Harav Kook, 1972), 109.

Notes

60 See Benjamin Efrati, *The Defense in Rav Kook's Philosophy* (in Hebrew) (Jerusalem: Mosad Harav Kook, 1959), 20–27; Benjamin Ish-Shalom, *Rav Avraham Yitzhak Ha-Cohen Kook: Between Rationalism and Mysticism* (Albany: SUNY Press, 1993), 133–134.

61 Compare Mordechai Piron, "The Principles of Religion v. the Perceptions of Toleration" (in Hebrew), *Mahanayim* 5 (May 1993), 51.

62 Berger, *The Sacred Canopy*, ch. 6.

63 Ahituv refers to this trend as "concept minimization and reduction." In his view, "the 'non-fundamentalist' Jew will try as far as possible to minimize religious-halakhic and theoretical concepts, so as to be able to accept them without a need for ontological-metaphysical assumptions." See Yosef Ahituv, *On the Edge of Change: A Study of Contemporary Jewish Meanings* (in Hebrew) (Jerusalem: Ministry of Education, 1995), 59. As noted in previous chapters, instances of this trend in Jewish philosophy can be found in the thought of Yeshayahu Leibowitz and Eliezer Goldman.

64 John Searle, *Speech Acts* (Cambridge: Cambridge University Press, 1980), 33–42.

65 On the distinction between "institutional fact" and "brute fact," see ibid., 50–53. The obvious link between Searle and Leibowitz is pointed out in Asa Kasher, "Paradox, Question Mark" (in Hebrew), *Iyyun* 26 (1976): 236–241.

66 On three reactions of traditional societies to new challenges, including transformation, see Samuel N. Eisenstadt, *Tradition, Change, and Modernity* (Malabar, Fla.: Robert Krieger, 1983), ch. 14.

67 Berger, *The Sacred Canopy*, 133–134.

68 Rashi, BT Hulin 5a, *s.v. ilema mumar*.

69 *Sefer Halakhot Gedolot*, ed. Azriel Hildesheimer (Berlin, 1888), 516.

70 See, for instance, Abraham b. Yitzhak of Narbonne, *Sefer ha-Eshkol*, ed. Shalom and Hanokh Albeck (Jerusalem, 1984), Part 2, 105; R. Yitzhak bar Sheshet Barfat (known as Ribash), *Responsa* (Jerusalem: Machon Yerushalayim, 1993), #4, *Beth Yosef, Yoreh Deah*, 119 and others.

71 See, for instance, R. Moshe Sofer (known as Hatam Sofer), *Responsa* (Jerusalem, 1970–1972), Part 3, Deletions, # 195; Rabbi Moshe Schick (known as Maharam Schick), *Responsa* (Jerusalem, 1984), *Hoshen*

Mishpat, # 61; Hayyim Elazar Shapira, *Responsa Minhat Eliezer* (New York, 1958), Part 1, # 74.

[72] Ribash, *Responsa*, #4, *Beth Yosef*, *Yoreh Deah*, 119; Maharam Schick, *Responsa, Hoshen Mishpat*, # 61.

[73] David Zvi Hoffman, *Responsa Melamed Leho'il* (Frankfurt: Hermon, 1926–32), 1: #29.

[74] See my article, "The Suspension of the Ethical and the Religious Meaning of Ethics in Kierkegaard's Thought," *International Journal for Philosophy and Religion*, 32 (1992): 83–103.

[75] Peter Berger refers to this approach as inductive. See Peter L. Berger, *The Heretical Imperative: Contemporary Possibilities of Religious Affirmation* (New York: Anchor Press, 1979), ch. 5. See also John Hick, *Problems of Religious Pluralism* (New York: St. Martin's Press, 1985), 16–27.

[76] Compare, John Hick *An Interpretation of Religion: Human Responses to the Transcendent* (New Haven: Yale University Press, 1989), ch. 13.

[77] Ibid., 235.

[78] Note that Hick devoted a great deal of attention to the question of inter-religious pluralism. In an earlier work, *God Has Many Names* (Philadelphia: Westminster Press, 1982), Hick founded inter-religious pluralism on the decisive role of the person's past in the creation of the religious experience (ch. 6), but did not deal with the implications of this idea for developing a pluralistic stance toward the secular world. Resorting to the subjective basis of the religious experience was a response to the secular world, which had made subjectivity and autonomy its central ideas. But why limit the application of this strategy to the justification of inter-religious pluralism? Its logic requires acknowledging secular experience too as intrinsically valuable, lest we lose the possibility of founding the religious experience on the individual's subjective past.

Chapter Two

YESHAYAHU LEIBOVITZ: THE MAN AGAINST HIS THOUGHT

THE previous chapter dealt with the possibility of pluralism within Jewish tradition. Yeshayahu Leibowitz developed a pluralistic position, yet one that epitomizes a perspective of cognitive dissonance described by Peter Berger as typical of many representatives of Jewish Orthodoxy.[1] According to Berger, the lives of Orthodox Jews are marked by dissonance between modern values, which they endorse, and the traditional conservative consciousness through which they describe and explain their world. Leibowitz's philosophy indeed lays foundations for pluralism, although he explicitly negates this option.

The Value Infrastructure

The fundamental problem that Leibowitz confronts in his thought is how to justify religious commitment without basing it on factual or metaphysical truths. This problem is far removed from the mainstream philosophical tradition of Judaism in general and Orthodoxy in particular, which assumes as obvious a series of truth claims about the world, about God, and about human reality.

The most prominent instance of a factual truth in Jewish tradition may be the belief in the Sinai revelation as the foundation of Jewish religion. Leibowitz raises a new problem here, which emerges from a modern cultural context that is typically characterized by secularization, and from the adoption of a stringent empirical criterion that leaves little room for metaphysical truths. In such a world, classic religious truths, be they factual or metaphysical, can no longer justify religious faith. Awareness of this state of affairs therefore raises a question concerning the renewed justification of religiosity, the key issue occupying Leibowitz. This is his contribution to the remapping of these theoretical problems.

Leibowitz's pioneering work offers an entirely new solution to this problem. The "Copernican revolution" he proposes is a view of Judaism as a value-normative system rather than as a system of truth claims about the world, about God, and about human reality. This deflection of Judaism to the value-normative realm is a radical innovation in Jewish tradition that, historically, had seen Judaism not only as a system of norms but also as a system of beliefs about the world and about God. Incipient signs in this direction had already been evident in the thought of Spinoza and Mendelssohn, but neither developed this issue as consistently and profoundly as Leibowitz.

In seemingly commonplace and simplistic language, Leibowitz proposes an entirely new philosophy. One is almost tempted to say that the simplistic language is a kind of smokescreen intended to conceal the depth of his revolution. This technique of esoteric writing had also been widespread in medieval thought that, *inter alia,* relied on a special and complex use of language. Only the cultural elite knew the secret of language, the key to the translation from natural to philosophical language. Only the elite, which had long been familiar with concealed philosophical contents, knew that natural language using everyday terms about God must be translated in entirely different ways. Leibowitz, however, does not resort to this concealment technique. He uses natural language in its standard meaning, and this simplification is itself the quintessential tool of concealment.

This difference between the two forms of writing reflects their different purpose. In the Middle Ages, concealment was guided by religious and social considerations: the true contents of religion had to be hidden from the unprepared masses. In Leibowitz's thought, concealment is part of an entirely different trend: it reflects an attempt to subsume the revolution into the continuum of the tradition. Leibowitz, who strives to describe historical-empirical Judaism and tries to preserve the continuity of tradition in changing times, uses day-to-day rhetoric to integrate a philosophical revolution. He is not proposing any changes, as it were, but merely acting as the tradition's "mouthpiece." Leibowitz did not, in my view, adopt this move out of a conscious attempt to blur the revolutionary nature of his philosophy and, more probably, used this technique in the somewhat naïve belief that he was indeed not suggesting any radical innovations. His thought, however, blazes a new trail in Jewish philosophy, and the following passage from Isaiah Berlin's "Two Concepts of Freedom" will serve to illustrate its revolutionary nature:

> It may be that the ideal of freedom to choose ends without claiming eternal validity for them, and the pluralism of values connected with this, is only the late fruit of our declining capitalist civilization: an ideal which remote ages and primitive societies have not recognized, and one which posterity will regard with curiosity, even sympathy, but little comprehension. This may be so; but no sceptical conclusions seem to me to follow. Principles are no less sacred because their duration cannot be guaranteed. Indeed, the very desire for guarantees that our values are eternal and secure in some objective heaven is perhaps only a craving for the certainties of childhood or the absolute values of our primitive past. "To realize the relative

validity of our convictions," said an admirable writer of our time, "and yet stand for them unflinchingly, is what distinguishes a civilized man from a barbarian." To demand more than this is perhaps a deep and incurable metaphysical need, but to allow it to determine one's practice is a symptom of an equally deep, and more dangerous, moral and political immaturity.[2]

My analysis of Leibowitz's philosophy will be conducted in light of this statement. Leibowitz's thought is indeed free from metaphysical longings and from the search for objective value guarantees. Neither the historical event of the Sinai theophany nor any worldly facts constitute a basis for the validity of religious (or moral) values, only human decision does. The centrality of human decision in Leibowitz's thought clearly conveys this liberation from the metaphysical values baggage. A believer in a value system whose accuracy is based on correspondence with a particular state of affairs in the physical or metaphysical world does not ascribe such decisive meaning to the act of choice. For a rational person, aware of facts as they are, a decision to choose the correct answer is the clear and even necessary product of this rationality. Such a person will not acknowledge any conflict or contradiction between values, claiming that the conflict is merely apparent and reflects a failure in the exercise of discretion. When a decision is based on specific circumstances, there is only one choice appropriate to the given situation. In other words, this person adopts a monistic theory of values.

Toward Pluralism

This emphasis on the act of decision, whatever the normative meaning ascribed to it, acknowledges that an accurate description of external reality is not a sufficient condition for the justification of a normative decision. Historically, one of the prominent differences between monistic and pluralistic theories of values is precisely the question of the status of values: the monist anchors values in external circumstances or in cognition, and theories that anchor values in natural law or in human rationality are prominent examples of such approaches. By contrast, pluralists recognize that different values reflect different perspectives and assessments — one good is never valid for all or exclusively justified. For various people, or even for one individual, various goods (which are not determined by external forces) reflect human diversity,[3] and hence the importance of decisions.

Applying this approach to Judaism is obviously an innovation, but this is precisely the move that Leibowitz proposes: turning Judaism from a religion based on truth claims into a normative religion whose only justification is a value decision — faith as a choice.[4] To justify this shift, Leibowitz proposes two mutually complementary arguments.

The first, which even if not explicitly formulated is at the basis of his theory of values, is that we do not have a common measuring unit for values (the incommensurability of values).[5] This argument, which is rather pervasive in value theory, seems to reflect two possible claims: first, values in the normative realm cannot be reduced to one common denominator that justifies and ranks all of them — happiness, freedom, or any other. Different values express different perspectives that cannot build upon one another. Second, different value theories express different goods. We have no universal value language, and the meaning of different value languages and theories is time and culture-bound. The claim common to both versions of this argument is that we do not have a supreme value enabling us to compare two incommensurable value systems and choose between them.

What is the relationship between value conflicts and the incommensurability of values? Obviously, whoever fails to acknowledge value incommensurability will not acknowledge the existence of value conflicts either, since values that appear to be mutually contradictory in a particular situation are not genuinely opposed — only one of them is worthy and the other is rejected. Only if we assume that the validity and meaning of values is not mutually conditioned and that values cannot build upon one another, can we support a view of value conflict as genuine.[6] Logically, however, upholding a perception of values as incommensurable does not require the assumption that value conflicts are genuine. We could claim that, even if we lack a *shared* criterion for comparing different values, another criterion for deciding between them could be offered. The opposite, however, is indeed true: if we consider value conflicts genuine, we must assume that values are incommensurable — if some criterion can be used to compare them, the conflict is not genuine because the overriding value can easily be determined.

The incommensurability argument is a pillar in the value stance formulated by Leibowitz, who supports a radical theory of value conflict. According to this theory, the conflict is not only genuine but is also the standard pattern in value action. The various value conflicts that Leibowitz suggests between religion and morality or even between different value systems — such as Eleanor Roosevelt's glass of milk as opposed to general Tojo's honorable death in the war for the emperor, an example of which Leibowitz is particularly fond[7] — all rely on the notion that values are incommensurable.

Leibowitz uses this argument to illustrate the importance of a value decision contradicting rational action on the one hand, and the relativity of values on the other. But neither conclusion is necessary. The first conclusion will be rejected below on the grounds that Leibowitz's use of the term "rational" is uncritical. The second conclusion is also unnecessary, and an analysis of different versions of value relativism would show it is not conditioned by the incommensurability argument. Such an analysis exceeds the scope of this work, however, and I will confine myself to one central claim: although relativism is close to a theory that recognizes value incommensurability in that both reject monism, these two approaches differ clearly on one count. The incommensurability argument points out that monism is an invalid value theory and that we do not have a general criterion for choosing the overriding value, but does not negate the claim that values must be justified. By contrast, one of relativism's most prominent versions assumes that values are adopted solely on a subjective basis, when the term "subjective" refers to random elements that do not constitute a justification.[8] Leibowitz supported the subjectivization of values as part of his discarding of the rational element from the value discourse. Although neither one of these conclusions is necessary, as noted, this is the argument that established for Leibowitz the importance of the decision dimension.

The second argument suggested by Leibowitz draws on the Kantian legacy and rests on the idea that the "ought" should not be derived from the "is." Norms should not be derived from the actual state of affairs in the world, and Leibowitz expanded the concept of "state of affairs in the world" not only beyond physical facts but also beyond metaphysical facts. The Sinai revelation, therefore, cannot serve as the basis for an obligation to obey God:

> Even if notarized evidence were found showing that the *Shekhinah* descended on Mount Sinai and gave the Torah to the Jewish people, I could still say: So what! Every single one could still react by saying he does not wish to observe the Torah. Can notarized evidence be a sufficient argument for accepting the yoke of the Torah and the commandments?... After all, this is what the sages said... that a person can recognize the truth and still rebel against it, and this goes back to the "is" and "ought" problem.[9]

Leibowitz endorsed both these arguments, as noted, and they complement the value transformation he proposes: values have no factual or metaphysical basis and they reflect different assessments and perceptions; conflicts of values are real and hence the crucial importance of an act of decision.

The thesis about the genuineness of value conflicts in Leibowitz's thought could ostensibly be dismissed on the grounds that if, as he claims, every conflict involves a decision, the decision could itself be proof that one value overrides another and the conflict is therefore not genuine. Believers, for instance, reject morality by invoking the religious world of values, and their decision is unequivocal. What is left, then, of the claim about genuine conflict?

Many philosophers do indeed claim that only a conflict that is in principle insoluble is genuine. Thus, for instance, McConnell argues:

> If the situation is *genuinely* dilemmatic, then one is presented with two conflicting ought-claims and no further moral consideration is relevant to resolving the conflict. By contrast, a situation is merely apparently dilemmatic if two ought-claims conflict, but there are overriding moral reasons for acting on one rather than the other. [10]

Sartre also supported this concept of conflict, and his famous example is that of a student who cannot decide between remaining with his sick mother and joining the forces fighting in the Second World War.[11]

This view of value conflict, however, may be too radical. The seemingly crucial difference between supporters and opponents of the genuine conflict theory is the opponents' claim that a principle of "overridingness" is at work in any conflict situation, based on a universal and rational scale of values. We will always find a value that is more justified, and hence overrides and dispenses with other values or with the obligations that follow from them. By contrast, supporters of a genuine conflict theory, like Leibowitz, acknowledge that in every value conflict, human beings decide. Their decision, however, is not the result of a rational-universal solution based on one scale of values ranking the order and preference of obligations. Above all, the decision is the expression of a practical need: every conflict situation ultimately requires some action, and the choice will reflect an individual or cultural-traditional value preference.

What is the difference between advocates of "a correct answer" theory and supporters of a genuine conflict theory? "Correct answer" supporters assume that the value to be realized utterly rejects the discarded value, which is perceived as mistaken. Supporters of genuine conflict assume that the overriding value cannot negate the worth of the rejected one, which could be significant to other individuals or societies, and the decision is based on a tradition or a culture that cannot undermine the value or on another tradition or culture claiming the rejected value is preferable.[12]

This analysis enables us to point to the option emerging from Leibowitz's thought, an option that Leibowitz rejects: developing a Jewish philosophy committed to the Torah and the commandments without negating the value of alternative world views. In other words, my thesis is that Leibowitz offered a model of Jewish thought that is both Orthodox and pluralistic.

The argument about the incommensurability of values, which we discussed above, is one of the main justifications used in pluralistic value theories. Values cannot be compared since they represent different goods, and this is the basic predicament of all value systems.[13]

Supporters of value incommensurability, however, are not compelled to adopt a pluralistic world view because they can argue that the choice between incommensurable values will be made elsewhere. Acknowledging that values are incommensurable, however, does usher in a pluralistic world view. Since values are incommensurable, other value systems cannot be dismissed as worthless, enabling at least what we could call weak pluralism.

Weak pluralism assumes, as noted, that different value systems are of *equal value*, and cannot be ordered hierarchically. Weak pluralism, therefore, confines itself to a description of the logical relationship between the various systems and pronounces them equivalent. Strong pluralism makes a more compelling claim: not only are value systems equally worthy, but they also have *internal* or *intrinsic value*. In this light, the incommensurability of values could be said to lead to strong pluralism, given that its starting assumption is that values cannot be compared. From this assumption, we can move a step further and claim that the epistemic problem arises because value systems rest on an intrinsic value that cannot be based on something else and value systems are therefore incommensurable. This analysis is a plausible conclusion from Leibowitz's assumptions.

Pluralistic theories, unlike monistic ones, also infuse further meaning into the very act of decision making, resembling the move endorsed by Leibowitz. Isaiah Berlin, the classic representative of the pluralistic stance, points to the typical relationship between value incommensurability, the meaning of choice, and pluralism:

> If I am right in this, and the human condition is such that men cannot always avoid choices, they cannot avoid them not merely…[because] there are many possible courses of actions and forms of life worth living, and therefore to choose between them is part of being rational or capable of moral judgment; they cannot avoid choice for one central reason (which is, in the ordinary sense, conceptual, not empirical), namely, that ends

collide; that one cannot have everything... The need to choose, to sacrifice some ultimate values to others, turns out to be a permanent characteristic of the human predicament.[14]

Leibowitz the man did not keep step with the options offered by his theory. His typical reaction to the pluralistic implication of his view is one of struggle between values: confronting a reality of value incommensurability, he calls for a struggle to impose his values. This approach is not easily compatible with relativism. What would be the justification of a struggle seeking to impose a value system if the value of all systems is merely relative? Relativism is supposed to weaken the struggle and perhaps even lead to indifference, as Allan Bloom successfully argued in *The Closing of the American Mind*. A struggle to impose values assumes that one value is better and fairer than the other. Again, we learn that Leibowitz is not a relativist but he is not a pluralist either since, except for exceptional cases touching on the foundations of existence, a pluralist recognizes the value of different and diverse positions. Only monists would muster their forces and turn the struggle into the standard response to other value systems, yet Leibowitz drew this conclusion from the pluralistic stance, and a striking implementation of this approach is his attitude toward non-Orthodox interpretations of Judaism.

Pluralists, as noted, are not committed to an unrestricted version of relativism incapable of denying any values or norms. Pluralists too can reject values lacking any worth or meaning and deserving condemnation. Concerning certain values, pluralists also acknowledge that people who violate them are "moral idiots. We sometimes confine them in lunatic asylums. They are as much outside the frontiers of humanity as creatures who lack some of the minimum physical characteristics that constitute human beings."[15]

Berlin, like Kekes after him,[16] draws a distinction between "primary values" and "secondary values." Primary values relate to vital needs of human existence, and they are common to "all conceptions of a good life."[17] By contrast, secondary values diversify and change. Obviously, then, pluralists are not committed to the claim that all value systems, including those harmful to primary values, are valid.

But Leibowitz went further, moving from an assumption of value incommensurability to the total rejection of all the alternative values rejected in his own specific world view. According to the logic at the foundation of Leibowitz's value system, this is simply a mistake. It does not follow from the pluralistic predicament or from the individual's specific value decision because, according to Leibowitz's assumptions, a value decision neither has nor could have universalistic pretensions. This is an individual decision in the sense that it reflects no more than the action of the deciding subject and his or her value system.[18]

Moreover, Leibowitz holds that this decision cannot be justified in any way, and here too he is mistaken. As Kekes shows, this mistake is based on the unnecessary assumption that a justification, by its very nature, is universal. In a pluralistic approach relying on the recognition of many possible goods, the justification neither is nor can be universal, lest it undermine the very existence of pluralistic assumptions. Like Leibowitz, other scholars also conclude that a decision in a pluralistic context will be arbitrary. Kekes points out that many of our value justifications, albeit personal, are good enough without being universal.[19] Yet, the radical view claiming arbitrariness actually assumes pluralistic latitude even more strongly: since you have no justification for your own decisions, how can you possibly reject the world of the other?

Leibowitz could suggest two approaches for dealing with this contradiction. The first is to adopt an arbitrary value "theory" within which everything is permitted, including an unjustified struggle against the other. Leibowitz, however, not only fails to endorse this conclusion but also rejects it in the fundamental moral pathos characterizing his thought.

Another and more sophisticated option is the attempt to draw a distinction between the incommensurability of values and the development of a pluralistic world view. Typical pluralism acknowledges not only the factual existence of another value system but argues, at least minimally, that it is equally worthy. The difference between the pluralist and the tolerant person, as noted, is that tolerant individuals claim they have the truth but, in certain circumstances, are ready to bear the other's mistake. By contrast, pluralists present a different picture: their minimalist claim is that the other's world is not only bearable but is at least equally worthy. If so, the claim will be that the incommensurability of values does not lead to the acknowledgement of the other's world as equally worthy. We can, therefore, support the argument of incommensurability and also negate the world of the other.

This answer, however, is conceptually mistaken. If incommensurable values are in a hierarchical relationship and one value system is preferable to the other, meaning only one is worthy and the other only tolerated, we are not confronting genuine incommensurability. The relationship between something that is worthy and something that is worthless and mistaken is the relationship between truth and falsehood, or good and evil. In these circumstances, the criterion for testing values is their closeness to truth. Clearly, if my values are closer to the truth or the good, they should be preferred to others. Logically, value incommensurability means we have no shared criterion for comparison, and this is not the case when conflicting values are in a hierarchical relationship. In other words, a genuine value conflict requiring a decision must assume that the values involved in the conflict cannot be ranked. For instance, the conflict between religion and morality is for Leibowitz a genuine conflict that requires believers to decide, because religion and morality have unconditioned internal value and individuals must choose between them.[20]

The conclusion, then, is that Leibowitz's approach enables and even compels a pluralistic outlook. Leibowitz refused to accept this view even when confronted with it. The man who succeeded in implementing the idea that a value-religious commitment in Judaism does not rely on truth claims about the world was reluctant to apply this idea to the disputes within the Jewish world. Indirectly, then, he returned to the claim that Judaism in its Orthodox interpretation is based on truth claims!

The richness and innovativeness of Leibowitz's philosophy in its justification of a Jewish pluralism, which is opposed to his own assessment of this move, reemerge in the analysis of an issue that is crucial in Leibowitz's thought: his shifting of the question about the reason for a religious world from a causal to a meaning context.

This shift is extremely significant and reflects the closeness between Leibowitz and the Wittgenstein tradition. One of Peter Winch's fundamental claims in *The Idea of Social Science* is that we understand social behavior through a meaning rather than a causal category. The causal category does not relate to social behavior as the ultimate datum, to be understood from within, seeking instead justifications in truth claims about the world. By contrast, according to the category of meaning, a specific social behavior is the ultimate datum, so that the concepts of a particular society, say "primitive society," can only be interpreted "in the context of the way of life of those peoples."[21] In other words, the context that constitutes meaning is the socio-cultural context rather than any metaphysics or cosmological world picture, which constitutes the rational basis of social norms and concepts.[22]

Winch is highly critical of trends in anthropology that seek to examine the meaning of a given culture by analyzing the congruence between its conceptual world and reality. Winch claims that a society's conceptual terms cannot be understood by comparing them to external reality. The conceptual system of a given culture converges with its practice, and the concepts can therefore be understood only within the context of the culture. From the outside, we cannot even determine what is real and what is not: "what is real and what is unreal shows itself in the sense that language has."[23]

Winch's approach is an application of Wittgensteinian ideas, and shared by such thinkers as Norman Malcolm and D. Z. Phillips. In their view, "meaning" is not an essential attribute but a way of configuring concepts and practices. Thus, for instance, the meaning of a chess game is not some attribute outside the game but the entirety of the game's laws and goals. Understanding the game means understanding its laws and their goals. Similarly, the understanding of a culture grows from the understanding of an entire form of life within which and from which we will also draw the conceptual system fitting its description. This is a context that allows for comparisons between cultures, since they are not seen as competing over the correct causal description of the relationship between the world and its culture. This theory, traced here in broad outlines, enables the re-legitimization of myths because, according to this view, myths do not compete with science for a correct description of the world but provide instead an account about a form of life and of meaning within a given culture.

These thinkers applied their approach to the study of religion as well. Phillips claimed that "one of the scandals of the philosophy of religion" is that the study of religion begins from external speculative philosophical assumptions offering claims about the world, an argumentation course Phillips calls foundationalism.[24] These scholars emphasized that the research object of religion is a particular religious community, organizing its ways of life in a complex of patterns and concepts. The study of religion is a description and decoding of a living historical phenomenon rather than of theoretical concepts.

One obvious conclusion from this approach is that, in principle, negating another cultural world becomes impossible within the restricting circumstances described above. The digression from causality to meaning or the digression from rational justification to the values embodied in the concrete way of life of a given culture pre-empts the possibility of a monistic world view and paves the way for a pluralistic culture.

In his description of the halakhic world, Leibowitz resorts to the meaning category. His analysis of halakhic obligations relies precisely on the attempt to describe the meaning of this world through its internal concepts rather than founding it on any metaphysical world picture. In his view, the concept that unites the totality of the normative-halakhic system is the worship of God. This meaning, rather than superimposed from outside, is the one Leibowitz sees emerging from an analysis of the halakhic system.[25]

Leibowitz's philosophy thus plays out as a variation of Wittgensteinian conceptions, although Leibowitz was not influenced by Wittgenstein's later work, which endorsed these ideas, or by Wittgensteinian tradition. A programmatic article including the incipient formulations of theses that were to become the backbone of this approach appeared long before the publication of Wittgenstein's later writings or those of his followers.[26] His views on this question entail a radical innovation in the study of religious phenomena, according to any criterion. In his view, Judaism as an "institutional" phenomenon means that the religious world cannot be understood through its correspondence with reality. The world of religion is an internal pattern for organizing life, whose meaning is internal. It is impossible and even forbidden to compare this pattern and its meaning to others and their meaning, just as a chess game cannot be compared to a basketball game — the meaning of these two games is internal and derives from their constitutive laws.

The Man against his Thought

The extent to which Leibowitz the man remained far removed from the pluralistic options raised by his thought is now clear, and this gap has several dimensions. First, the shift from the causal to the meaning context reaffirms the pluralistic stance at the foundation of Leibowitz's philosophy. If the meaning of this activity is internal, there is no room for comparison and for proposing a shared criterion to examine the worth of other value systems. Weak pluralism ascribes equal value to the entire range of possible options and strong pluralism also ascribes inner and intrinsic value to the other's position. Leibowitz's stance enables strong pluralism as well. According to his view, concepts such as "inner value" or "intrinsic value" can be understood in the meaning context described above. The claim that a position has inner value means that its meaning is found within it, within the world of the practices and the understandings it gives rise to, and cannot be based on external elements. For Leibowitz to negate this approach, which is the obvious foundation of his value stance, is a rather puzzling step.

Second, Leibowitz accepts the idea that meaning is not an attribute but rather an expression of the form assumed by cultural practice, and he invests philosophical efforts in attempting to understand the form assumed by Jewish religion. In his view, the meaning of this form of life is absolute obedience to God's command. When the form is simple, understanding its meaning is also simple. Understanding a chess game does not pose hard problems, since the form of the game is clear and concisely formulated within the laws of the game itself. We do confront hard problems when decoding the meaning of complex forms of organization such as Judaism. Does this form have one purpose or many? Does God's command play a central role in the understanding of this activity? These basic questions, pointing to the crucial interpretive role of the philosophical observer in an active value system, can hardly be ignored. Interpretive pluralism is thus a rather natural conclusion of renouncing speculative criteria.

Third, if the datum is Judaism as a historical-empirical phenomenon, Leibowitz should have acknowledged that historical cultures are not static. They undergo gradual changes at both practical and conceptual levels, and their meaning does not remain fixed and stable. If the measure is practice, different practices could have different meanings that might be more or less related. In Wittgenstein's terms, these practices could belong to the same family because of their prominent resemblances. They are different and still close. Thus, a secular Judaism preserving a practice that is close to traditional Judaism offers a form that is both similar to, and different from, traditional practice. This is probably the most obvious legitimation of a pluralistic world view, not only in its interpretation of Jewish religion but also in its suggestion of alternative meanings to a dynamic historical phenomenon. Judaism, then, is not only a religion but also a culture and these forms, even if different, bear a family resemblance.

Leibowitz's work is thus richer than what Leibowitz the man acknowledged and affirmed. It enables value pluralism, and even Jewish pluralism. All Jewish interpretive systems offers different assessments and judgments, even concerning the meaning of Judaism itself.

Possibly, the source of this incongruence between the man and his thought is a genuine tension between Leibowitz's innovative philosophical world and his membership in an Orthodox culture that rejects this option outright. The fact that Leibowitz stands against his own theory is an expression of the cultural tension between new and old, embodied in his life and his thought in the duality he formulated. The contradiction between his work and his consciousness reflects, perhaps radically, something about the duality characterizing the life of the modern Jewish believer, who lives in various value communities and is not always able to coordinate between them. But Leibowitz went even further in the very presentation of a broad theory that enables believers to live as believers, without the affirmation of their religious world requiring them to negate the positions of the other.

The rejection of the pluralistic view often relies on the assumption that you do not truly believe in your values and are not fully committed to them unless you reject the other's world. But this need not be the case. Our commitment to our values is not measured by the extent of our rejection of the other's world but by the willingness to endorse these values consistently in our life and by our unwavering commitment to them. Loyalty to our values is related to our disposition toward them and not necessarily to their cognitive superiority. This lesson emerges clearly from Leibowitz's work, even if he failed to admit so explicitly.

Notes

1. Peter L. Berger, *The Heretical Imperative: Contemporary Possibilities of Religious Affirmation* (New York: Anchor Books, 1979), 29-30.
2. Isaiah Berlin, *Four Essays on Liberty* (Oxford: Oxford University Press, 1969), 172.
3. This issue is extensively discussed in Isaiah Berlin, *The Crooked Timber of Humanity: Chapters in the History of Ideas,* ed. Henry Hardy (London: J. Murray, 1990), 207-237.
4. See Yeshayahu Leibowitz, *Judaism, Human Values, and the Jewish State,* trans. Eliezer Goldman et. al. (Cambridge, MA: Harvard University Press, 1992) (henceforth *Judaism*), 37-38; Yeshayahu Leibowitz, *Conversations about Moshe Hayyim Luzzato's "The Path of the Upright"* (in Hebrew) (Jerusalem: n. p., 1995), 225-234.
5. For a precise and profound analysis of this argument, see Daniel Statman, *Moral Dilemmas* (Amsterdam: Rodopi, 1995), ch. 3.
6. John Kekes, *The Morality of Pluralism* (Princeton, NJ: Princeton University Press, 1993), 53-59.
7. See Yeshayahu Leibowitz, *Between Science and Philosophy* (in Hebrew) (Jerusalem: Academon, 1987), 270, 279; Leibowitz, *Conversations about Moshe Hayyim Luzzato,* 223-224, 390.
8. See Kekes, *The Morality of Pluralism,* 13-14.
9. Leibowitz, *Conversations about Moshe Hayyim Luzzato,* 225. Obviously, these two arguments are not necessarily related, and one can

support the second argument without endorsing the first. Kant is a classic example. He adopted and sustained the second argument while negating the first. In his view, values can be compared and ranked, and value conflicts are only apparent. Every value dilemma has one correct solution: "If it is our duty to act according to one of these rules, then, to act according to the opposite one is not our duty and is even contrary to duty." Immanuel Kant, *The Doctrine Of Virtue: Part II of The Metaphysics of Morals*, trans. Mary J. Gregor (New York: Harper and Row, 1964), 23. Kant does not accept value incommensurability, and claims we can always compare values and decide which one overrides another.

[10] Terrance C. McConnell, "Moral Dilemmas and Consistency in Ethics," *Canadian Journal of Philosophy* 8 (1978), 271.

[11] Jean Paul Sartre, *Existentialism and Humanism*, trans. Philip Mairet (New York: Haskell House, 1977), 23.

[12] I agree with Kekes on this point. See his analysis in *The Morality of Pluralism*, ch. 5.

[13] Ibid., 21–22 and ch. 4; Berlin, *The Crooked Timber of Humanity*, 70–90.

[14] Berlin, *Four Essays on Liberty*, Introduction, li.

[15] Berlin, *The Crooked Timber of Humanity*, 204.

[16] Kekes, *The Morality of Pluralism*, ch. 3.

[17] Ibid., 38.

[18] Leibowitz's mistake probably results from his choice of particularly extreme examples of value incommensurability. He compared General Tojo with Eleanor Roosevelt, or Eichmann's values with those of others, turned them into paradigmatic examples, and drew conclusions that were too general. Pluralists like Berlin or Kekes, however, understood the difference between values that, as pluralists, we will accept, and values that we will altogether reject. Hence, values fundamentally harmful to human existence deserve condemnation and utter rejection, but values presenting various human goods do not, since they are intrinsically worthy. According to Kekes' formal distinction between "primary" and "secondary" values," primary values are related to our very existence, aimed at the actual preservation of life and the aversion of injury. These values, contrary to Leibowitz's view, are shared by all human beings since they are related to their common human nature. Secondary

values are culture, time, and place-bound. Some apply the primary values to a given culture and some are the product of this culture. Pluralists argue that people who pay no heed to primary human values remove themselves from human existence. We should therefore fight against them. Not so, however, concerning secondary values. Leibowitz is also wrong concerning primary values themselves. The Nazis did agree that killing human beings is forbidden, as demonstrated by the fact that in order to kill Jews or members of other nations they were forced to proclaim that they were not human beings. This is an unacceptable idea, but it need not lead to the conclusion that the inevitable outcome of every value conflict is war.

[19] Kekes, *The Morality of Pluralism*, 95.
[20] For an additional analysis of this issue, see Avi Sagi and Daniel Statman, *Religion and Morality*, trans. Batya Stein (Amsterdam and Atlanta, GA: Rodopi, 1995), 119-125; Avi Sagi, "The Suspension of the Ethical and the Religious Meaning of Ethics in Kierkegaard's Thought," *International Journal for the Philosophy of Religion* 32 (1992): 83-103.
[21] Peter Winch, "Understanding a Primitive Society," in *Rationality*, ed. Bryan R. Wilson (Oxford: Basil Blackwell, 1985), 95.
[22] See also D. Z. Phillips, *The Concept of Prayer* (London: Routledge and Kegan Paul, 1968), 24-27.
[23] Winch, "Understanding a Primitive Society," 82.
[24] D. Z. Phillips, *Faith After Foundationalism* (London: Routledge, 1988), 3.
[25] The other thinker who developed this insight in profound and original directions is Eliezer Goldman. See, in particular, his article "The Commandments as the Basic Datum of Religion" (in Hebrew), in *Expositions and Inquiries: Jewish Thought in Past and Present*, ed. Avi Sagi and Daniel Statman (Jerusalem: Magnes Press, 1996), 306-315. Goldman told me that he lectured the contents of this article at a conference and Leibowitz was supposed to speak after him. When Goldman concluded, Leibowitz said he had nothing to add!
[26] See Leibowitz, "Religious Praxis: The Meaning of Halakhah," in *Judaism*, 3-29. This article is a translation of *"Mitzvot Ma'asiyyot,"* a transcription of a lecture he delivered in 1953.

Chapter Three

LEIBOWITZ AND CAMUS: BETWEEN FAITH AND THE ABSURD

THIS chapter draws a comparison between Yeshayahu Leibowitz and Albert Camus, who both made the renunciation of metaphysics the cornerstone of their thought. Any attempt to draw comparisons between these two thinkers, ostensibly representing two entirely alien worlds, appears "absurd." Leibowitz's philosophy is religious, not only because religion is at the center of his philosophical concern but also because his thought is that of a believer, who relates to God's command and to the obligation to obey it as the supreme value that pushes all others aside. By contrast, Camus does not place God at the center of his philosophy,[1] but human reality. More than that, Camus rejects the religious option and considers it "philosophical suicide": even if God exists, he is an irrelevant entity, vexing and obstructing human attempts to contend with reality.[2] If Leibowitz's religious philosophy is theocentric,[3] Camus' philosophy is anthropocentric. This chasm notwithstanding, several shared features do lay the ground for a fruitful comparison between them:

CHAPTER THREE

(1) Concrete reality as the only reality

Both recognize concrete empirical reality as the only one relevant to the individual. According to Camus, what characterizes the absurd individual is precisely the refusal to find a solution to the absurd in a turn to the transcendent. The absurd individual lives in a world without any hope for transcendent redemption, and adopts existent circumstances as the ultimate human reality. Hence, adopting a religious or a rational stance that confer absolute meanings is, in Camus' terms, "escape."[4] Camus acknowledges that human beings yearn for the transcendent, and recognizes the presence of a "nostalgia for unity" and an "appetite for the absolute."[5] But to recognize these yearnings is not equivalent to affirming their concrete manifestations as they have emerged throughout the history of philosophy. Human beings are doomed to live with this yearning, although they acknowledge it cannot be realized. They must accept this world,[6] with its tension, as the ultimate human reality. In Camus' words, they must recognize that "outside it [the world] there is no salvation."[7]

Some hold that Camus' stance is irrational.[8] But the fact that Camus rejects a rationalist metaphysical explanation that assumes one general principle from which to infer the structure of reality[9] does not mean that Camus rejects rational thought altogether. Rather, he bases his refusal to endorse a rationalist world picture on critical thought per se:

> I do not want to found anything on the incomprehensible. I want to know whether I can live with what I know and with that alone. I am told again that here the intelligence must sacrifice its pride and the reason bow down. But if I recognize the limits of the reason, I do not therefore negate it, recognizing its relative powers. I merely want to remain in this middle path where the intelligence can remain clear.[10]

This programmatic passage outlines in detail the rationality of Camus' stance. In his view, classic rationalism is "incomprehensible," that is, cognition is incapable of grasping the principle or principles of reality or, in sum, cognition cannot know reality. But the awareness of cognition's limitations is itself a product of critical thought. In this sense, the very acknowledgement of the absurd is a consequence of critical thought,[11] aware of the fact that the passion for clarity and unity cannot be realized with the tools of human cognition and we therefore experience the absurd.

In line with the pattern of removing unsubstantiated transcendence from the human world, Camus determines the borders of cognition: "It is useless to negate the reason absolutely. It has its order in which it is efficacious. It is properly that of human experience."[12] Camus' ontological approach, then, which negates the relevance of the transcendental world, overlaps the borders of cognition. In other words, the only known and meaningful reality is the reality grasped with the tools of human cognition.

Similarly, Leibowitz argues that Jewish religion offers a "realistic" perception of human reality: "It perceives man as he is in reality and confronts him with this reality — with the actual conditions of his existence rather than the 'vision' of another existence."[13] The "anti-illusory," "anti-visionary" character of the halakhic world prevents the "flight," according to Leibowitz — Camus' "escape" — to a different and sublime reality.[14] Recognizing the concrete world as the believer's absolute reality entails obvious implications for the organization of religious life. Jewish religion is not an "endowing" religion, promising redemption and tranquility. It is a "demanding religion" that imposes duties on human beings. Redemption is not concretized in the world beyond, nor is it linked to some eschatological event. Human redemption lies in the heroic effort to comply with religious obligations in this world.[15]

Like Camus, Leibowitz attaches no religious meaning to worldly events. Understanding of the world is not based on information available from the Torah or from any particular religious system: "The great principle — which is also a great religious principle — of 'the world follows its course' applies to history as it applies to nature."[16]

Leibowitz, then, acknowledges only a "neutral world," devoid of religious meaning, knowable only through rational scientific means.[17] In sum, neither Camus nor Leibowitz accept the ontological assumption about a true reality beyond the empirical human reality open to human cognition.

(2) Normative commitment without transcendence

When Camus and Leibowitz assume that concrete reality is the ultimate reality, they must confront the problem of normative commitment without a transcendent foundation: for Camus — *ethics* without a transcendent basis, and for Leibowitz — *religion* without a transcendent foundation.

Camus contends with this problematic in his various works: *The Plague*, *The Fall*, and *The Rebel*. In a sharp formulation of this question, he asks: "It is essential for us to know whether man, without the help either of the eternal or of rationalistic thought, can unaided create his own values."[18]

Another question, which Camus finds no less troublesome, concerns the nature and the focus of these values — the individual or the society. As for the meaning of this ethic, Camus offers more than one answer. *The Myth of Sisyphus* presents a quantitative, solipsistic ethic, striving for awareness of experience in its entirety.[19] By contrast, in later works, and particularly in *The Rebel*, he rejects this solipsistic ethic on the grounds that it ultimately cancels out the distinction between just and evil acts. In the absence of any basic values, "everything is possible and nothing has any importance."[20] Contrary to this quantitative ethic, the ethic Camus proposes in *The Rebel* is founded on human solidarity as the new metaphysical starting point of human existence. Yet, and despite this significant shift, both trends still share a common denominator: contrary to the Kantian position, the transcendence that has been removed from the metaphysical world cannot reenter it through the ethical dimension.

Leibowitz's religious-ethical world view is not founded on a transcendent basis either. God is the *purpose* of the religious act but not the basis of the obligation. Even the Sinai theophany, which Jewish tradition considers constitutive, plays no role for him in the religious obligation: "Even if one could be absolutely certain that...He revealed Himself to them on Mount Sinai, and that the Torah was given from Heaven, one may still refuse to serve God."[21] Rather than representing a misunderstanding of the obligation that this event imposes on human beings, this refusal is definitely justified given that worldly facts, including the fact of revelation, lack any religious meaning. In line with this trend, Leibowitz posits a value reversal in Judaism. The foundation of the halakhic system is not the Torah, which reflects revelation, but the halakhic system: "The religion of Israel, the world of Halakhah and the Oral Law, was not produced from Scripture. Scripture is one of the institutions of the religion of Israel. ...the Halakhah of the Oral Teaching, which is a human product...determines the content and meaning of Scripture."[22]

Halakhah as a human creation, then, is the very embodiment of the religious act. It is meaningful because it is "for the sake of Heaven" not because it is "from Heaven." What makes this value system compelling? If not anchored on a "religious" fact, on the divine command, its sole basis is faith: "It is rather an *evaluative decision* that one makes, and, like all evaluations, it does not result from any information one has acquired, but is a *commitment to which one binds himself.*"[23] The normative system, then, is binding because of a human decision, and the status we ascribe to human freedom and autonomy is therefore crucial.

(3) The shift to praxis

The problem of normative commitment points to another element stressing the closeness between these two thinkers — the shift from theory to praxis. Camus and Leibowitz thereby remain in the path chosen by many other existentialist thinkers, beginning with Kierkegaard, who shifted the focus of the philosophical discussion from the question of "what must I know" to that of "what must I do."[24] For Camus, accepting the absurd is only the beginning of a process, which will end with a concrete act: "The realization that life is absurd cannot be an end, but only a beginning... It is not this discovery that is interesting, but the consequences and rules for action that can be drawn from it."[25]

The stress on the practical dimension comes to the fore in the way Camus contends with the problem of evil. Evil is a given to be fought with action, not with theoretical or metaphysical solutions. The plague is a concrete enemy that threatens human existence. According to Rieux, the protagonist of *The Plague*, we must fight disease and death, but this is not a struggle for "salvation."[26] Indeed, theological-metaphysical solutions might even hinder action against evil. Evil, after all, has an explanation. In this sense, argues Rieux, "mightn't it be better for God if we refuse to believe in Him, and struggle with all our might against death?"[27]

For Leibowitz, the shift to praxis is anchored in the very fact that at the center of his thought is Halakhah rather than theoretical speculation, a digression I called above "the Copernican revolution of Jewish thought."[28] Classic Jewish thought had dealt with epistemological and ontological issues, focusing on metaphysical speculation and on the concept of God. For Leibowitz, however, Halakhah and the religious obligation are the central axis for the understanding of the religious world. This digression means giving clear preference to praxis as the dimension exhausting the meaning of Judaism: "The Mitzvot are a norm for the prosaic life that constitutes the true and enduring condition of man."[29]

Leibowitz's view of human reality as the only one possible leads him to the claim that "the first mark of the religion of Halakhah is its realism,"[30] and the way to contend with this reality is through action, that is, through the halakhic norm. Like Camus, Leibowitz argues that the theodicy problem does not have theoretical solutions: "Creation, insofar as it is divine, is entirely without meaning; all its occurrences and phenomena are absurd."[31] Hence, the question of evil becomes the test of the believers' faith, of their readiness to comply with the religious demand and worship God, even barring a metaphysical solution to the problem of evil. Leibowitz too, like Camus, saw evil in all its aspects as part of reality's basic givenness, irremovable through metaphysical-theological solutions. These parallels in the work of these two thinkers reflect a similar response to the challenge of modernity.

Beyond these similarities, however, these two philosophies engage in a fascinating dialogue that at times brings them closer and at times draws them apart, culminating in the tension between faith and the absurd. Below is a detailed comparison of several of their basic theses.

CHAPTER THREE

(4) *Human reality as rift and crisis*

Leibowitz and Camus propose a similar structure for human reality. Both reject the harmonious ontology and endorse one of rift and crisis. I open with the philosophy of Leibowitz, who proposes several formulations of this predicament in his writings:

(a) *The human being as an entity that transcends natural reality.* The rift between givenness and subjection to nature as opposed to its transcendence is formulated as follows:

> Faith is the antithesis of human harmony. From a faith perspective, man does not and cannot accept natural reality, although he himself is part of it. He cannot transcend it, whether believer or heretic... But the religious man differs from one who has not assumed the yoke of the heavenly kingdom... because he does not accept the fact that he is part of the natural reality and cannot transcend it. The faith that constitutes his psychic experience does not fit the objective reality of which he is part, and never will.[32]

According to this description, the source of the rift is the basic ontological datum of human reality. The human being is an entity bound by the natural order on the one hand, but yearns to go beyond nature on the other. This deviation, or this trend toward transcendence, shows that human beings are not entirely part of nature. For Leibowitz, as for Pascal[33] and for Camus,[34] this trend is evident in consciousness and volition, which do not operate by virtue of the natural order. Leibowitz, therefore, holds that human history is the clear embodiment of human transcendence:

> History is an arena for the operation of human consciousness, which does not operate in natural reality and is not subject to its laws. Natural reality has no consciousness, and functions

> according to its immanent laws, whereas human history is created by human beings…in natural reality there is no will either, whereas history is an expression of human volition.[35]

Had Leibowitz remained at the theoretical-phenomenological level, this formulation would not have been particularly original. In the previous passage, however, Leibowitz raised another claim that is not part of human ontological phenomenology and begins in the value world of faith. His claim is that non-believers, even if they do not accept that they are part of the natural reality, have no way of transcending nature. By contrast, the very essence of faith as a system of Torah and commandments that is not fitted to the needs of humans as natural creatures succeeds in transcending nature. Thus, only faith can fully express basic human ontology; only through faith do human beings transcend nature, are not bound by its laws, and become free. Without faith, human will would be merely natural will.[36]

Against the trend that creates a value-religious based hierarchy in its very characterization of human reality, however, Leibowitz proposes an alternative trend in his later writings. This trend is reflected in the second cited passage. If human history realizes the consciousness and the will that cannot be derived from natural reality and are an expression of human transcendence, believers do not differ from non-believers. Transcendence is realized through the basic human "datum": will and consciousness. Elsewhere, Leibowitz views even scientific activity, which enables human beings to control nature and subdue it for their purposes, as an expression of transcendence from nature.[37] Leibowitz's philosophy, then, reflects a tension between phenomenological and value judgments characterizing thinkers whose phenomenological stance is part of their value-religious world.

(b) *Human beings in the world and before God*. "Crisis...is the essence of religious faith, the essence of the fear of God. It negates the superstitious belief in the harmony of human existence. It exposes the contrast between the standing of man in nature — his physical and psychic nature — and his standing before God."[38] This is a vague formulation of the rift, since it does not clarify the essence of the contrast between the human standing in nature and before God. But if we consider this passage in the context of the paragraph it is meant to summarize, the opposition is between the values we hold as human creatures and the obligation of obedience and renunciation. As creatures, human beings have natural feelings, aspirations, and values that reflect their world. Believers are required to renounce all these values, because "God, may He be blessed, appears before man not as a God *for* him, but as a God demanding everything *from* him."[39] But why are human values related to "man's standing in nature" and to the essence of his existence as a psycho-physical creature? Here we return to the first dimension of the rift. Leibowitz's starting assumption is that feelings and values originate in the self-perception of human beings as creatures bound by the laws of nature. Hence, the demand to renounce these values creates the dyadic contrast between "nature and God."[40] As opposed to the first meaning of the rift, then, which had relied primarily on a phenomenological datum, the rift is now identical to faith itself. The non-believer, from whom no renunciation is demanded, does not sense a rift.[41]

(c) *The crisis of "the death of God" — the alienness of the world.* One meaning of modern consciousness is God's irrelevance to existence. For Leibowitz, this irrelevance has special meaning. It does not mean that God is entirely removed from human life, since the religious deed is *per se* is an expression of worship. Rather, God's irrelevance is another facet of his transcendence —

since God is a sublime and supreme entity, we cannot expect the divine to be present in natural reality.[42] Human beings, however, cannot reconcile themselves to a meaningless world; they cannot accept unexplainable suffering: "Job's suffering is no longer the focus of his protest; rather, it is his inability to comprehend the meaning of his suffering, which is but one detail within an incomprehensible world."[43] What anguishes the suffering man, Job, is his sense of alienation from the world which stems from his inability to understand it.[44] Individuals are ready to accept suffering as long as they can understand it as part of a world guided by God. They are prepared to settle for the certainty that the order of the world has some kind of meaning, that innocent suffering can be explained, even if not justified. But this is precisely the nature of faith in a transcendent God that does not intervene in the world: "Job held that some hidden meaning attaches to the Creation and sought to know it, whereas God shows him that Creation, insofar as it is divine, is entirely meaningless; all its occurrences and phenomena are absurd."[45]

The absurd is now the contrast between the expectation of meaning and the failure to fulfill it.[46] But this use of Camus terminology here should not mislead us. The failure to realize this expectation is neither a factual matter nor the result of some epistemological flaw, but an expression of God's transcendence. Believers, therefore, do not find themselves within the absurd but, through their very faith, decide to live within the absurd. The absurd challenges man to decide "whether to commit himself to believe in God and serve him in the world as it is."[47] The fact of the absurd thus becomes the believer's test: "Is he ready to believe in God, not because of God's function in creation — his wisdom or his justice — but because of his divinity?"[48] Alienation from the world is thus no longer a fact. The ability to affirm this alienation and bear this estrangement from the world is the believer's test, and Leibowitz thereby continues Kierkegaard's tradition.[49]

The common denominator of these three aspects of the crisis is that they reflect a relationship unable to balance between two elements: between natural givenness and transcendence, between nature and God, and between the expectation of meaning and its absence. Human ontology amounts to a perception of human beings as creatures in the midst of two contradictory elements. In this light, Leibowitz justifiably notes that the crisis is not a "special situation or event,"[50] and reflects something essential to human reality or faith, according to the various trends in his thought.

Faith also enables human beings to reach conscious transparency, at least concerning the first dimension of the crisis. Through faith, they fully realize the dichotomy of human existence. The diagnosis of the crisis as hinting at a relationship between two elements, and the identification between endorsement of the absurd and conscious transparency, are also at the basis of the Camus' thesis analyzed below.

In a move typical of phenomenological-existentialist tradition, Camus draws a distinction in *The Myth of Sisyphus* between two levels of the absurd: the absurd as a datum of human experience and the absurd as a concept, which in the process of its conceptualization re-explicates the human experience. Through this explication, "the feeling of the absurd becomes clear and definite."[51]

The basic data of the sense of the absurd are: (1) The loss of a sense of continuity in the sequence of daily gestures, which acts as a unifying element (2) The experience of real time as a sequence of events, leading us to lose our sense of the present.[52] (3) The presence of death. (4) Alienation from the world. The world becomes strange and threatening because we cannot truly understand it. Precisely because cognition is "too human," it creates a sense of detachment from the world, since the world becomes known to us only through "the images and designs that we had attributed to it beforehand."[53]

This cluster of feelings is organized in the concept of the absurd, which reflects their shared structure. In *The Myth of Sisyphus*, Camus suggests various formulations of the term such as, for instance: "This world in itself is not reasonable, that is all that can be said. But what is absurd is the confrontation of the irrational and the wild longing for clarity whose call echoes in the human heart. The absurd depends as much on man as on the world."[54]

Unlike Sartre, Camus argues that the absurd is not founded on a specific sense — the contingency of existence.[55] The absurd is based on a comparison[56] between what is and what is expected. Human beings encounter an incomprehensible world, but the absurd emerges because of the yearning for clarity and understanding.

The structure of the rift, then, is the same for both Leibowitz and Camus, and derives from the lack of correspondence or from the contradiction between opposite elements. Indeed, the first and third meaning that Leibowitz ascribes to the rift resemble the meanings of the rift in Camus. Our going beyond nature, our difference from the world, this is the primary datum giving rise to the absurd: "If I were a tree among trees, a cat among animals, this life would have a meaning or rather this problem would not arise, for I should belong to this world. I should *be* this world."[57]

The third meaning of the rift according to Leibowitz — the human estrangement from the world — is also one of the basic sources of the absurd for Camus. Beyond it, however, two fundamental differences separate these two approaches.

Although my analysis so far showed that both Camus and Leibowitz consistently support a theory of rift, the first difference between them relates to the status of the rift in their thought. For Leibowitz, the rift reflects only human existence, or at least the believer's existence. Camus, however, beside the rift that is prominent mainly in *The Myth of Sisyphus*, offers two other patterns presenting a harmonious model of human existence. In some of his Mediterranean essays, Camus describes an experience of unity with nature. Descriptions and symbols of mingling with, and even of communion with the world, abound in "Nuptials at Tipasa," often symbolized by immersion in the sea. In another essay, "The Wind at Djemila," Camus writes: "The violent bath of sun and wind drained me of all strength. …Soon, scattered to the four corners of the earth, self-forgetful and self-forgotten, I am the wind and within it… And never have I felt so deeply and at one and the same time so detached from myself and so present in the world."[58] At times, Camus also uses the Plotinian model of unity: "What is strange about finding on earth the unity Plotinus longed for? Unity expresses itself here in terms of sea and sky."[59]

After Camus presents the rift that subverts the possibility of harmony in the world, he returns in later works, and particularly in *The Rebel*, to present human harmony, solidarity, and a sense of basic cooperation that prevails even between victim and executor.[60] This sense of solidarity does not find the unity cognition longs for and, therefore, is not a metaphysical harmony. It does, however, pave the way for a human life of partnership in the struggle for the shaping of a new society. This approach is not a retreat from the achievements of the absurd but it does involve new movement — a rebellion in Camus' terminology — and a struggle for a world that is fairer and hence ethically harmonious.[61]

This tension between rift and harmony, present in Camus and ignored by Leibowitz, marks the second difference between them. For Leibowitz, the rift is primarily a characteristic of the religious decision. Although Leibowitz's rift includes, as noted, a phenomenological-descriptive element, the main trend of his thought conveys the claim that the rift is constituted by faith itself. In other words, the very act of the religious decision is what shapes the rift as a permanent condition and makes retreat from it impossible, since it would imply retreating from faith. Given that Leibowitz characterizes human reality in terms he views as the essence of faith, no room is left for an alternative description.

By contrast, the rift for Camus is primarily an explication of human reality. The basic datum of human existence is the sense of the absurd, which reaches clear formulation in its descriptive explication. This sense, as well as its explication, is not a matter of a voluntary decision but part of the thrownness of human existence, to use Heidegger's terminology. Since this is a value-based rather than a phenomenological characterization of human reality, others descriptions are also possible. The rift orientation could be contradicted by presenting another experience of unity with the world. An alternative view suggesting ways of contesting with the rift and the absurd could also be offered, and this is the approach developed in *The Rebel*.[62]

(5) Between faith and acceptance of the absurd

The dialogue between the two thinkers culminates in the parallel between faith and a life of faith in Leibowitz's thought, as opposed to the absurd and the acceptance of the absurd in Camus. Faith and the acceptance of the absurd express conscious transparency and self-affirmation, and both are based on a decision.

First, Leibowitz. The analysis has so far shown that opting for faith conveys transcendence beyond nature, reflecting our actual existence as human creatures. At least according to one trend in Leibowitz's thought, as noted, only the believer realizes this transcendence, meaning that only the believer's existence embodies conscious transparency. But even according to the second trend, whereby transcendence is embodied in consciousness and volition, faith is certainly one of this transcendence's distinct expressions.

This conscious transparency is also the individual's self-affirmation as a free creature, in several ways. First, the believer realizes negative freedom, "freedom from" in Nietzsche's terms.[63] The believer is liberated, or at least struggles for liberation, from the bonds of nature. For Leibowitz, assuming the yoke of the Torah and the commandments is the sole embodiment of faith, since faith is the decision to assume it. The contents of the Torah, according to Leibowitz, neither do nor can correspond to the needs and the interests of human beings as natural creatures. If this correspondence were a goal of the normative system, it would not express the worship of God but the worship of humanity; Jewish religion is a "demanding religion," which imposes a yoke on human beings rather than gratifying their needs. Clearly then, "by observing the Mitzvot, one in a sense subdues nature and frees himself from subjection to it. 'No one is free except he who occupies himself with Torah.'"[64]

Second, through the religious decision we activate our autonomous will, which Leibowitz does not see as deriving from an external source; will is the first and independent element through which we concretize our existence as human creatures. Hence, faith also embodies positive freedom or, in Nietzschean terms, "freedom to," meaning the freedom to realize our autonomy.

Although the religious decision represents an affirmation of our existence as free creatures, freedom is the product rather than the purpose of the religious decision:

> The religious decision has no other purpose beyond itself, and a religion perceived as a means for an end and explained through this end is no religion. The religious decision is self-sustaining but has further implications, not only for the believer's way of life but also for his spiritual and psychic existence, and one of them is his freedom. Freedom is a side-effect of assuming the yoke of the Torah and the commandments, but not its reason or its purpose.[65]

For Camus too, adopting the absurd means conscious explicitness or, in his terms, "lucidity."[66] The negation of the absurd and the choice of suicide or of philosophical suicide — that is religion. In some way, it involves renouncing the epistemic clarity of human existence's very meaning as absurd. Renouncing the absurd involves a renunciation of the human consciousness that, according to Camus, is the source of the rift and sparks the sense of the absurd.[67]

The decision required from the individual facing the absurd is what Camus calls "metaphysical rebellion." This concept, which Camus uses mainly in *The Rebel*, appears also in *The Myth of Sisyphus* in another sense. In *The Rebel*, metaphysical rebellion is the refusal to accept the conditions of life: "Metaphysical rebellion is the movement by which man protests against his condition and against the whole of creation. It is metaphysical because it contests the ends of man and of creation... The metaphysical rebel declares that he is frustrated by the universe."[68]

The metaphysical rebellion is mainly the rejection of reality. Camus indicates that the origin of this refutation is another positive value proposed by the rebel, who demands a non-existent "unity" and a "justice" not to be found, expressed above all in negation and refutation. By contrast, "metaphysical rebellion" in *The Myth of Sisyphus* implies a rebellion against the vagueness of consciousness threatening to overwhelm us. Human beings must fight for conscious transparency: "One of the only coherent positions is thus revolt. It is a constant confrontation between man and his own obscurity. It is an insistence upon an impossible transparency."[69]

From this perspective, faith in Leibowitz's sense also conveys a kind of "metaphysical rebellion" because, as natural creatures, we are tempted to transform the meaning of faith and adapt it to human existence. According to Leibowitz, faith "for its own sake," meaning genuine faith, is a refusal to accept this vagueness and is synonymous with self-transcendence. Above all, however, this is the denotation of rebellion adopted in *The Rebel*.

For Camus, as for Leibowitz, the decision process also involves corroboration and self-affirmation, which come to the fore in happiness: "One must imagine Sisyphus happy."[70] Happiness is not the purpose of accepting the absurd but, as Leibowitz described freedom, its "side effect." Just as for Leibowitz freedom as a product of the religious decision confirms the existence of human beings as transcendent entities, so happiness constitutes the absurd person's self affirmation.

What is this happiness? Does it amend the threat and despair of life? Does it remove absurdity? Happiness in Camus' thought has indeed been interpreted as an expression of those random moments granting an illusion of unity with nature.[71] But this approach has no support in *The Myth of Sisyphus*. Indeed, Camus explicitly argues: "Happiness and the absurd are two sons of the same earth."[72] Rather than replacing the absurd, happiness is a kind of affirmation of the absurd in the person's inner existence. In John Cruickshank's elegant formulation:

> He defines happiness as a simple harmony relating the individual to his existence. What more sure basis can there be for happiness, then, than recognition by the individual of that insoluble paradox which constitutes his position in the world? Happiness will follow from a relationship in which the individual accepts the eternal antagonism between his desire for life and the inevitability of his death.[73]

This harmony of human beings with their absurd existence reflects their liberation from hopes and illusions. We become aware of the full meaning of our existence as human creatures, and this awareness fill our hearts with happiness.

But this happiness is inseparably related to freedom in both its negative and positive meanings. One who endorses the absurd is free of illusions and expresses "the return to consciousness, the escape from everyday sleep."[74] Although this liberation appears to be confined to the conscious realm, it has the power to generate in us a new attitude to our existence because it liberates us to live and exhaust the given. We are liberated from the future in favor of experiencing the present or, in sum, to realize our existence as human creatures. In other words, liberation from illusions enables freedom in its positive sense. Happiness as self affirmation thus expresses these two meanings of freedom.

The chasm between Leibowitz and Camus is now obvious. If the purpose of faith is to worship God, the purpose of accepting the absurd is conscious transparency of our existence as human creatures. This issue is itself related to a more primary question: the meaning of the decision.

According to Leibowitz, the religious decision reflects the absolute human transcendence of natural existence: freedom is an expression of the person's detachment from all world objects. Leibowitz's anthropology expresses the absolute separation between the cognitive and conative dimensions.[75] Freedom, then, neither is nor can be derived from a specific datum. It is self-generated, without any other context. In other words: the religious decision is a "leap."

For Camus, however, the decision to endorse the absurd is not a decision of this kind, and Camus does not accept the dichotomy between the cognitive and conative levels. To clarify the nature of this decision, I will briefly consider a riddle puzzling Camus scholars. Cruickshank notes that reading *The Myth of Sisyphus* evokes discomfort because "A sudden twist in the argument changes the absurd into a solution...a kind of salvation."[76] The question of how the absurd turned from a problem into a solution is related to a deeper problem, formulated by Hochberg:

> Camus has leaped from the factual premise that the juxtaposition of man and the universe is absurd, to the evaluative conclusion that this state ought to be preserved...For this transition, we have no justification. Without such justification, Camus has not...made his point. He has simply begged the question.[77]

These problems arise from the assumption that Camus' thought proceeds from factual hypotheses to value conclusions. But is this indeed the direction of this thought? Should it be understood in the context of an ethics of obligation? Or is it perhaps closer to the Aristotelian tradition that views ethics as a kind of self-realization on the one hand, and to the phenomenological tradition that posits an explication course on the other? The latter option appears to be the one supported by Camus.

The starting point of *The Myth of Sisyphus* is the transition from the factual data of the sense of the absurd to its conceptualization. This transition reflects, according to Camus, the spirit's immanent passion for clarity and self awareness: "The will is only the agent here: it tends to maintain consciousness."[78] In other words, the primary situation of consciousness is lack of clarity: consciousness is unaware of the structure and meaning of reality. The consciousness sunk in its slumber awakens through the sense of the absurd, which "inaugurates the impulse of consciousness. It awakens consciousness and provokes what follows."[79] This awakening of the mind is the mind's voyage to itself. This is a process of self-explication driven by the mind's immanent demand. Camus explicitly describes this process as "the mind that studies itself,"[80] portraying the explication course in classic Husserlian terms: "Up to now we have managed to circumscribe the absurd from the outside. One can, however, wonder how much is clear in that notion and by direct analysis try to discover its meaning on the one hand and, on the other, the consequences it involves" (33).

As in the Husserlian explication, so in the process of accepting the absurd, going inwards into the human experience does not detract from it; rather, it results in the "profound enrichment of experience and the rebirth of the world in its prolixity" (45).

The ending of the explication process is lucidity and the clear acknowledgement that reality is split between finality and a yearning for absolute clarity. In light of this ending, we face a question: do we reject reality or do we endorse it? Contrary to Nagel's claim, however, Camus' endorsement of reality does not follow from a romantic stance,[81] but reflects a readiness to accept human existence as is. In other words, this decision is not a consequence of the explication but is taken in light of the explication. In Camus' formulation: "Living an experience, a particular fate, is accepting it fully. Now, no one will live this fate, knowing it to be absurd, unless he does everything to keep before him that absurd brought to light by consciousness."[82] In this sense, the decision Camus speaks of has only one meaning: a readiness to acknowledge the character of human existence exposed in the explication.[83]

Ostensibly, the difference between Leibowitz and Camus reflects the difference between two alternatives in existentialist philosophy, one represented by Kierkegaard and the other by Heidegger. According to this interpretation, Leibowitz continues the Kierkegaardian tradition of the "leap" springing from nowhere and reflecting "direct voluntarism."[84] By contrast, Camus continues the Heideggerian tradition, whereby the human decision is in a process of continuous transition from explication to decision. I do not accept this distinction. As I showed in my work, Kierkegaard does not detach the decision from the cognitive context that serves as its background.[85] Leibowitz's position, therefore, reflects a rare dichotomy and, on this count, he is far removed from Camus.

(6) The believer and the absurd person

The focus of the discussion, so far fixed on faith vis-à-vis the absurd, will now shift to the world of the believer as opposed to that of the absurd person, concentrating on three aspects: (a) The attitude to the transcendent. (b) The meaning of the rebellion. (c) The infinity of the task.

(a) *The attitude to the transcendent.* Camus' philosophy, as noted, leaves no room for God. Immanent reality is the absolute reality, and individuals cannot return to the transcendent without blurring their consciousness as human creatures. Camus is not an atheist, but primarily an anti-theist.[86] He is not driven by the metaphysical approach claiming that God does not exist, and he explicitly emphasizes: "The history of metaphysical rebellion cannot be confused with that of atheism."[87] His refusal of the transcendent suggests that faith, more than the actual existence of an entity called God, enables human beings to escape the absolute freedom and responsibility incumbent on them.[88]

The assumption about the existence of an active God rewarding human beings and promising hope implies a renunciation of the present: "If I obstinately refuse all the 'later on's' of this world, it is because I have no desire to give up my present wealth."[89] The absurd individual therefore lives with the "total absence of hope,"[90] and it is this absence that fully exhausts our existence as creatures whose only reality is ourselves.

Leibowitz's position is a kind of response to Camus' challenge. Leibowitz, as noted, accepts the position that this reality is the one absolute and inescapable reality available to human beings. In his view, however, this position is not supposed to deny the possibility of religious life; quite the contrary, faith and Halakhah reflect this realism, since human reality is the only arena for concretizing religion. Believers acknowledge their obligation to realize the Torah in this world rather than hope for redemption in the next. The value of this reality determines the clear advantage of the present over another future in the next world. Contrary to Camus' perception, human redemption according to Leibowitz takes place in this world, and is identical with liberation from the bonds of nature: "Religion as Torah and commandments redeems man from the bonds of nature. It is not redemption in the Christian sense — where man is redeemed through his consciousness of being redeemed — but actual redemption, release from the bonds of meaningless natural causality."[91]

This conceptual transmutation of redemption to the realm of existential being is a radical turning point in Jewish tradition,[92] and reflects the "inner worldly" digression in Leibowitz's thought.

What place, then, is left for God in this world? This question emerges even more sharply because, from a religious point of view, Leibowitz supports God's absolute transcendence. The answer to this question appears in what could be called "the subjective digression." Religious existence is not defined through the individual's association with a transcendent God but through a subjective decision to accept the Torah and the commandments: "The believer...makes an effort to direct his religious consciousness to himself as recognizing his duty to his God."[93]

In *The Plague*, Tarrou reveals his concern: "What interests me is learning how to become a saint...Can one be a saint without God?"[94] In a way, this is another version of the question troubling Leibowitz. If God is indeed transcendent, and if no worldly fact or event is holy, can one become holy? Or is this category doomed to be banned from the world? Leibowitz's answer is that the adjective holy cannot be employed to describe anything in this world because doing so would be "utter idolatry."[95] Only God is "holy," human beings are not holy. They are "called upon to be holy."[96] The meaning of this holiness is the realization of self-transcendence, the liberation from the bonds of nature, which takes place here and now in this world. Camus is mistaken — Leibowitz would say — if he assumes that a life of faith subverts the meaning of human reality, and he is mistaken if he holds that religious life is "other worldly." The place for a life of faith is this world, and individuals realize their relationship with God in this transcendence. The transcendent God is not the basis of values or even of hope, but the object of the religious decision. God is the noematic pole of the religious decision, and is not found anywhere else in a religious life.

(b) *The meaning of the rebellion* — Camus, as noted, offers two models of "metaphysical rebellion." One rebels against lack of clarity, and the other against the conditions of reality. Since Leibowitz's concern is religious praxis, his adoption of the metaphysical rebellion endorsed in *The Rebel* could be expected. In Leibowitz's view, Halakhah is a clear expression of rebellion against natural reality, since it neither follows from this reality nor is it built to fit it:

> [The world of Halakhah] is man's rebellion against the rule of blind natural elements in his body and his soul. In the shape of laws, rulings, and commandments, religion ceases to appear as an auxiliary tool for man's adjustment to life and for finding happiness within it — which is the essence of idolatry — and becomes a rebellion against life's natural reality.[97]

Whereas Camus' metaphysical rebel defies God,[98] for Leibowitz rebellion is the meaning of religiosity. For him, as for Kierkegaard, religiosity means the victory of the "spirit" over nature and the flesh.[99]

For Camus, the metaphysical rebellion mirrors an awareness of history as currently devoid of holiness and divine grace.[100] Once history becomes human, the rebellious consciousness is redefined as a "generous act of complicity" (19) with a "natural community" (16). Human beings now strive to reshape the world and return the order and justice that have been lost (103-104). By contrast, Leibowitz's rebellion means coping with the natural givenness without an alternative utopia.

Camus, who removed the transcendent from the world, discovers that the metaphysical rebellion is a constant search for this transcendence. Instead of the traditional transcendence of the divine, human beings strive for a world that will embody what this transcendence had represented. For Leibowitz, however, rebellion does not assume another positive value. It is not a yearning for utopia but a classic expression of the human creature as an exceptional entity, whose exceptionalism is concretized in the acceptance of the Torah and the commandments.

(c) *The infinity of the task — the Sisyphean struggle.* The idea of an infinite human struggle is a leit-motif of Camus' thought, while changes in his approach are reflected in the different meanings he ascribes to this struggle. In *The Myth of Sisyphus*, the infinite struggle is the struggle for "lucidity." This struggle is infinite because of the constantly lurking danger of entrapment in the "hope" to escape human destiny. Sisyphus is the human hero because, faced with the tragedy of despair and pain, he does not surrender to hope; quite the contrary, the very acceptance of tragedy is an expression of his lucidity:

> If this myth is tragic, that is because its hero is conscious. Where would this torture be, indeed, if at every step the hope of succeeding upheld him?…Sisyphus…knows the whole extent of his wretched condition; it is what he thinks of during his descent. The lucidity that was to constitute his torture at the same time crowns his victory. [101]

The infinity of the task, then, denotes the intensity of the endless temptation compelling us to struggle for lucidity.

Contrary to this solipsistic stance that makes the "self" and the self's consciousness the focus of the struggle, in his later works Camus makes the character and infinity of the struggle contingent on life's concrete conditions. Tarrou, Rieux's partner in the fight against the plague, says to him: "Your victories will never be lasting." And Rieux answers: "Yes, I know that. But it's no reason for giving up the struggle."[102] The two protagonists of the story share an understanding: "Plague is here and we've got to make a stand" (112). But no "final victory" is possible, and he will always have to struggle "against terror and its relentless onslaughts" (251–252). The rebel, then, acknowledges the dreadful reality as a *fait accomplie* but refuses to endorse it as absolute, as evident in his infinite metaphysical and historical struggle against it:

> The rebel, far from making an absolute of history, rejects and disputes it, in the name of a concept that he has of his own nature. He refuses his condition, and his condition to a large extent is historical. Injustice, the transience of time, death — all are manifest in history. In spurning them, history itself is spurned.[103]

The refusal of reality is not only a negative position. Its first meaning is actually positive, and implies a human struggle to reshape it: "But confronted with it [with history], he feels like the artist confronted with reality; he spurns it without escaping it (290). Camus, like Nietzsche before him, recognizes that the deep power of freedom does not lie in its negative denotation — "freedom from,"[104] but in its positive meaning: "freedom to": "Liberty coincides with heroism."[105]

Leibowitz also recognizes that the struggle is infinite. He does not endorse the version of infinity adopted in *The Myth of Sisyphus*, however, since the purpose of his philosophy is not the attainment of lucidity but the clarification of the religious obligation. The digression to praxis, then, brings Leibowitz extremely close to the model of *The Plague* and *The Rebel*. According to Leibowitz, this infinity rests on both existential and religious grounds. Existentially, the concrete individual lives in a natural reality and not in a reality of redemption in the Christian sense, since Judaism does not believe in "extricating man from the human condition."[106] The believer struggles with reality and transcends it by observing the commandments, but this transcendence does not imply detachment from natural reality. Therefore, "the project it sets for man is permanent and endless. No religious attainment may be considered final; the project is never completed."[107]

The endless struggle thus reflects the permanent dichotomy between factual givenness and its transcendence, between causality and freedom. Since we are dichotomous entities, the struggle is infinite. In other words, the infinity of the task is not necessarily related to the religious dimension but to the dichotomy between freedom and the spirit as opposed to reality. Leibowitz's formulation presents this idea in clear terms: "The essence of a value attitude to man's problems...is that human beings, facing a goal that is not anchored in reality, are still required to strive toward it from reality and transcend it, even though the goal is infinite and can never be accomplished."[108] This picture, however, is incomplete, since the dichotomy is never between nature and spirit, between the human world and the divine demand.[109] The endlessness of the task reflects the infinite gap between human and divine:

> Performance of the Mitzvoth is man's path to God, an infinite path, the end of which is never attained and is, in effect, unattainable. A man is bound to know that his path never terminates. One follows it without advancing beyond the point of departure...The aim of proximity to God is unattainable. It is infinitely distant, "for God is in heaven and you on the earth" [Ecclesiastes 5:1].[110]

Whereas the existential dimension emphasizes the gap within man, the gap is now between man and God. In this light, the Torah is perceived as eternal, not because its instructions cannot be changed, but "because it is divine, not human."[111]

The assumption that the task is infinite turns the effort into the actual meaning of the religious act, and Leibowitz emphasizes this in many places in his work.[112] At one point, he traces a pessimistic picture of human reality that emphasizes the effort even more strongly:

> Man may not be free in the sense of being able to choose between good and evil, but he is free to strive for this choice... The ability to worship God may not be part of man's nature — and is it not the case that "nature" is precisely that which cannot be transcended? Nevertheless, it is incumbent on man to be "brave as a lion" — to make a supreme effort to do what cannot be done... The depth of religious faith may indeed be fully revealed in man's acknowledgement of the task that is incumbent on him — to worship God — a task he must never desist from.[113]

In this passage, a far greater heroism is expected from believers. They are not only required to struggle to realize the norms, but they must also engage in a struggle, perhaps a losing one, against their own nature. The hopelessness of this struggle stresses the power of faith. Making faith the antithesis of the possible and the rational brings Leibowitz closer to formulations in Christian tradition, from Tertullian to Kierkegaard, stressing the overlap between faith and decisions without any rational meaning in Tertullian's perception, or hopeless decisions in Kierkegaard's perception. The believer is now a Sisyphean hero living "a heroic life."[114] The believer's heroism, however, does not invoke human solidarity and is a gesture of faith.

Chapter Three

What can be learned from the comparison between Camus and Leibowitz? Can any conclusions be drawn from it, beyond that of Camus' influence on Leibowitz? Even if Leibowitz strongly admired Camus,[115] it is questionable whether he was influenced by him. Beyond the personal dimension, the source of this admiration is probably related to the similarities in their thinking. Thus, two worlds appearing as parallels that cannot meet are found to be deeply associated and conceptually close in their perceptions about the meaning of human existence. One element substantiating this resemblance is the similarity in their responses to the modern world and particularly to the status of immanence, although one of them removed God from the world and the other centered immanence on a commitment to God.

Notes

1. Scholars have questioned whether Camus can be considered a philosopher. For a discussion of this issue, see Avi Sagi, *Albert Camus and the Philosophy of the Absurd*, trans. Batya Stein (Amsterdam-New York: Rodopi, 2002), ch. 2.
2. Albert Camus, *The Plague*, trans. Stuart Gilbert (Harmondsworth, England: Penguin Books, 1960), 107–108.
3. For a critique of this issue, see Yaakov Yehoshua Ross, "Anthropocentrism and Theocentrism" (in Hebrew), in *The Yeshayahu Leibowitz Book: An Anthology of His Thought and in His Honor*, ed. Asa Kasher and Jacob Levinger (Tel Aviv: Tel Aviv University Students' Union, 1977), 56–65.
4. See Albert Camus, *The Myth of Sisyphus*, trans. Justin O'Brien (Harmondsworth, England: Penguin Books, 1975), 35.
5. Ibid., 23.
6. Ibid., 53, 62 (note).
7. Albert Camus, *Lyrical and Critical Essays*, trans. Ellen Conroy Kennedy (New York: Vintage Books, 1970), 101. Note that "The Desert" abounds with transmutations from religious to secular language. Religious concepts such as "revelation," "eternity," "salvation," assume new meaning: revelation is the exposure of the eternal meaning in the present, and salvation, as opposed to its religious

meaning, is salvation from hope. Faith is "the loving understanding between the earth and a man" (100). The gospels too are "gospels of stone, sky and water" showing, as opposed to the original gospels, "that there are no resurrections" (101)

[8] See, for instance, John Cruickshank, *Albert Camus and the Literature of Revolt* (New York: Oxford University Press, 1960), 50; Patrick Henry, *Voltaire and Camus: The Limits of Reason and the Awareness of Absurdity* (Banbury, Oxfordshire: The Voltaire Foundation, 1975).

[9] In a seminal article, Herbert Hochberg points out that, for Camus, the ideal explanation of reality is the Platonic model. See Herbert Hochberg, "Albert Camus and the Ethic of Absurdity," *Ethics*, 75 (1965): 78–102.

[10] Camus, *The Myth of Sisyphus*, 42.

[11] Ibid., 25–26.

[12] Ibid., 38. See also Dean Vasil, *The Ethical Pragmatism of Albert Camus: Two Studies in the History of Ideas* (New York: Peter Lang, 1985), ch. 2.

[13] Yeshayahu Leibowitz, *Judaism, Human Values, and the Jewish State*, trans. Eliezer Goldman et. al. (Cambridge, MA: Harvard University Press, 1992) (henceforth *Judaism*), 12.

[14] Ibid., 19.

[15] Ibid., 70. See also 45–46.

[16] Yeshayahu Leibowitz, *Judaism, the Jewish People, and the State of Israel* (in Hebrew) (Tel Aviv: Schocken, 1976) (henceforth *Yahadut*), 91.

[17] Ibid., 340.

[18] Albert Camus, *Resistance, Rebellion and Death*. trans. Justin O'Brien (New York: Alfred A. Knopf, 1966), 58.

[19] Camus, *The Myth of Sisyphus*, 60.

[20] Albert Camus, *The Rebel: An Essay on Man in Revolt*, trans. Anthony Bower (New York: Alfred A. Knopf, 1956), 5. See also ibid., 6.

[21] *Judaism*, 75.

[22] Ibid., 12. In the lines I omitted, Leibowitz states that the Torah is the source for the authority of the Oral Law. In his earlier works, some of which were published in the German version of *Zion*, Leibowitz adopts the traditional starting point about the centrality of the Sinai theophany, but he changes his mind in his later works. This passage appears to be a remnant of his early thought, which

23 *Judaism,* 37 (emphasis in original). See also *Yahadut,* 345.
24 See Avi Sagi, *Kierkegaard, Religion, and Existence,* trans. Batya Stein (Amsterdam-Atlanta, GA: Rodopi, 2000), ch. 1.
25 Camus, *Lyrical and Critical Essays,* 201–202; cf. 159; Camus, *The Rebel,* 8, 10. See also, Sagi, *Albert Camus and the Philosophy of the Absurd,* ch. 10.
26 Camus, *The Plague,* 178–179.
27 Ibid., 106. See also Camus, *Resistance, Rebellion and Death,* 73.
28 See above, p. 46.
29 *Judaism,* 12.
30 Ibid.
31 *Yahadut,* 397.
32 Yeshayahu Leibowitz, *Faith, History, and Values* (in Hebrew) (Jerusalem: Academon, 1982) (henceforth *Faith*), 57.
33 See Blaise Pascal, *Pensées* (London: J. M. Dent & Sons, 1932), 96–97.
34 See Camus, *The Myth of Sisyphus,* 51–52.
35 Yeshayahu Leibowitz, *People, Land, State* (in Hebrew) (Jerusalem: Keter, 1992), 28
36 *Judaism,* 21–22. This notion of faith as the supreme manifestation of human ontology appears already in Kierkegaard, who even stated: "religion is the true humanity" (see Sagi, *Kierkegaard, Religion, and Existence,* 89). For further clarification of Kierkegaard's position, see ibid., ch. 5, particularly section 3.
37 *Judaism,* 51.
38 *Faith,* 58.
39 Ibid., emphasis added.
40 *Judaism,* 22.
41 According to the contrary trend, the opposition is not between nature and God but between spirit and nature, a version he rejected in his early writings.
42 In this sense, Leibowitz returns to the course adopted in Protestant tradition.

43 *Judaism*, 50.
44 Cf. *The Rebel*, 100.
45 *Yahadut*, 397.
46 Cf. Thomas Nagel, "The Absurd," in *The Meaning of Life*, ed. E. D. Klemke (New York: Oxford University Press, 2000), 178.
47 *Faith*, 50.
48 *Yahadut*, 397.
49 See Sagi, *Kierkegaard, Religion, and Existence*, chs. 5, 6, 9.
50 *Faith*, 58.
51 Camus, *The Myth of Sisyphus*, 26.
52 Ibid., 19–20.
53 Ibid., 20. Despite these expressions of the absurd in *The Myth of Sisyphus*, Camus suggests other expressions of alienation in other works. See Sagi, *Albert Camus and the Philosophy of the Absurd*, ch. 5.
54 Camus, *The Myth of Sisyphus*, 26.
55 See Jean Paul Sartre, *Nausea*, trans. Lloyd Alexander (Norfolk, CT: New Directions, 1959), 174–183.
56 Cf. Camus, *The Myth of Sisyphus*, 33.
57 Ibid., 51 (emphasis in the original). Note a distinction between consciousness and full awareness of the absurd. The sense of the absurd indeed rests on a person's transcendence of the world through consciousness. But awareness of the significance of consciousness emerges only through the explication process of the sense of the absurd. The explication does not create the absurd. It describes and clarifies the original datum of the opposition and the rift between the individual and the world. See Sagi, *Albert Camus and the Philosophy of the Absurd*, chs. 5, 7.
58 Camus, *Lyrical and Critical Essays*, 75.
59 Ibid., 90.
60 Ibid., 346.
61 Cf. also G. G. Hardy, "Happiness Beyond Absurd: The Existentialist Quest of Camus," *Philosophy Today* 23 (1979), 368–369.
62 In this sense, Camus is actually close to Kierkegaard's thought, who presents both the model of the rift and the model of harmony. From both a religious and an existentialist point of view, see Sagi, *Kierkegaard, Religion, and Existence*, chs. 5, 6, 9.

63 See Friedrich Nietzsche, *Thus Spoke Zarathustra: A Book for Everyone and Nobody*, trans. Graham Parkes (Oxford: Oxford University Press, 2005), 54.
64 *Judaism*, 74.
65 *Faith*, 49.
66 Camus, *The Myth of Sisyphus*, 26, 109. Camus also uses other equivalent terms, such as "clarity" (23) and "transparency" (53).
67 Ibid., 51–52.
68 Camus, *The Rebel*, 23.
69 Camus, *The Myth of Sisyphus*, 53. Obviously, these rebellions have several features in common. First, both reflect opposition and refusal. Second, both reflect the tension between negation and an ideal affirmation that cannot be realized. Nevertheless, the difference is sufficiently clear to enable their characterization as two different types of rebellion. In *The Rebel*, the rebellion is against the conditions of existence and, therefore, is also related to historical rebellion. In *The Myth of Sisyphus*, the rebellion is one of consciousness.
70 Ibid., 111.
71 See Serge Doubrovsky, "The Ethics of Albert Camus," in *Critical Essays on Albert Camus*, ed. Bettina L. Knapp (Boston, Mass.: G. K. Hall, 1988), 151–164.
72 Camus, *The Myth of Sisyphus*, 110.
73 Cruickshank, *Albert Camus and the Literature of Revolt*, 38–39. Cf. also J. David Newell, "Camus on the Will to Happiness," *Philosophy Today* 23 (1979): 380–385; Robert S. Tate, "The Concept of Equilibrium in the Early Essays of Albert Camus," *The South Atlantic Quarterly* 70 (1971): 377–385.
74 Camus, *The Myth of Sisyphus*, 58.
75 Based on Leibowitz's writings and speeches, we may assess that this dichotomy is based mainly on the strange phenomenology he proposes for a situation of moral dilemma. In his view, the decision in this situation is neither the product of an empirical evaluation nor can it logically follow from factual data or from any type of knowledge. Rather, it is evidence of the absolute separation between these two levels. He is obviously not considering options linking

these two levels such as, for instance, the status of moral cognitions in the shaping of motivation and will, or the fact that human will is conscious volition.

76 Cruickshank, *Albert Camus and the Literature of Revolt*, 63.
77 Hochberg, "Albert Camus and the Ethic of Absurdity," 92.
78 Camus, *The Myth of Sisyphus*, 61, note †.
79 Ibid., 19. Cf. 46–47. Note that the sense of the absurd functions in ways similar to Heidegger's conscience in *Being and Time*. As conscience awakens and directs the *dasein* to the possibility of its authentic existence, so also the experience of the absurd. Just as conscience is perceived as compelling the person from outside (*es rauft*), so the sense of the absurd entraps him. Conscience, like the sense of the absurd, is a midway phenomenon, between an inauthentic existence where the meaning of existence lacks any transparency and an authentic existence of self-transparency. For Heidegger's stance, see Martin Heidegger, *Being and Time*. trans. John Macquarrie and Edward Robinson (Oxford: Blackwell, 1962), § 54–60. Pointing to the proximity between the two is significant for an understanding of Camus' sources of inspiration. If Heidegger is one of them, it is hard to see how the problem of the transition from facts to values is in any way relevant to him.
80 Camus, *The Myth of Sisyphus*, 22.
81 Nagel, "The Absurd," 185.
82 Camus, *The Myth of Sisyphus*, 53.
83 At least in this sense, then, Nagel's response to the endorsement of the absurd (see "The Absurd," 185 in particular) strongly resembles Camus' view.
84 Louis P. Pojman, *Religious Belief and the Will* (London: Routledge and Kegan Paul, 1968), 143–148. This interpretation of Leibowitz appears in Ran Sigged, "Leibowitz and Kierkegaard" (in Hebrew), in *The Yeshayahu Leibowitz Book: An Anthology of His Thought and in His Honor*, ed. Asa Kasher and Jacob Levinger (Tel Aviv: Tel Aviv University Students' Union, 1977), 42–46.
85 The terms "absurd" or "leap" should not mislead us in this context. Indeed, Kierkegaard's stance resembles that of Heidegger, who views the decision as another step after reflection and as

a shift from theory to praxis. Yet, he does not adopt the dichotomy ascribed to it. See Sagi, *Kierkegaard, Religion, and Existence*, ch. 3, section 4.

86 See Sagi, *Camus and the Philosophy of the Absurd*, ch. 10.
87 Camus, *The Rebel*, 25. Note also that religious dimensions are evident not only in his Mediterranean writings but in his other works as well. See, for instance, Camus, *Lyrical and Critical Essays*, 364; Sagi, *Camus and the Philosophy of the Absurd*, ch. 10.
88 See, for instance, Albert Camus, *The Fall*, trans. Justin O'Brien (London: Hamish Hamilton, 1957), 99–101; Camus, *The Plague*, 106–107.
89 Camus, *Lyrical and Critical Essays*, 76.
90 Camus, *The Myth of Sisyphus*, 34.
91 *Yahadut*, 60.
92 The only thinker who has suggested a similar intuition is Joseph B. Soloveitchik.
93 *Judaism*, 76. Obviously, this is another symptom of modernity because, in the modern world view, religiosity becomes a personal matter. See Peter Berger, Brigitte Berger, and Hansfried Kellner, *The Homeless Mind: Modernization and Consciousness* (New York: Vintage Books, 1974), 80.
94 Camus, *The Plague*, 208.
95 *Faith*, 142.
96 *Yahadut*, 117.
97 Ibid., 60.
98 Camus, *The Rebel*, 25.
99 But while Kierkegaard also suggests other options, for Leibowitz this is the only one. On Kierkegaard's position, see Sagi, *Kierkegaard, Religion, and Existence*, ch. 9.
100 Camus, *The Rebel*, 20–22.
101 Camus, *The Myth of Sisyphus*, 109.
102 Camus, *The Plague*, 108.
103 Camus, *The Rebel*, 289–290.
104 Nietzsche, *Thus Spoke Zarathustra*, 54.
105 Camus, *The Rebel*, 72.
106 *Judaism*, 15.
107 Ibid.

108 Yeshayahu Leibowitz, *Conversations on the Ethics of the Fathers* (in Hebrew) (Jerusalem: Schocken Books, 1979), 106.
109 *Judaism*, 21–22.
110 *Judaism*, 15–16. See also Leibowitz, *Conversations on the Ethics of the Fathers*, 106.
111 *Judaism*, 28.
112 See, for instance, *Judaism*, 15–16.
113 Leibowitz, *Conversations on the Ethics of the Fathers*, 106.
114 *Yahadut*, 61.
115 In an interview with David Ohanah, Leibowitz said: "Camus is a great figure...I admire Camus very much" (*Ma'ariv*, "Arts and Literature," 22 January 1993, 26).

Chapter Four

JEWISH RELIGION WITHOUT THEOLOGY

In *Der Philosophische Gedanke und seine Geschichte*, Nicholai Hartman offered his well-known distinction between "systematic thinking" and "problem thinking": whereas systematic thinking begins from a series of assumptions and proceeds to offer all-encompassing solutions, problem thinking begins from a problem and considers it in depth, without striving for comprehensive systems. Problem thinking is dialectical — it appraises the boundaries of the problem and the limitations of its solutions. According to Hartman, a typical instance of a systematic thinker is Spinoza, who founded an inclusive metaphysical system based on primary and irrefutable assumptions. A classic example of problem thinking is the philosophy of Plato, which is more intent on clarifying the predicament than on offering solutions, and hence its dialectical character.

Yeshayahu Leibowitz obviously belonged to the species of problem-thinking philosophers. As other distinctions, however, Hartman's too is overstated, and many thinkers focusing on problems transcend the dialectical move and go on to create a reasonably coherent system. Two renowned instances are Kierkegaard and Nietzsche. Both transcended the critical, "negative" stage and offered daring, "positive" solutions to the problematic raised by their work. Although these solutions were not articulated systematically, they do develop into extensive and coherent philosophies.

This is also true for Leibowitz, who went beyond problem analysis to create an integrated system leading to a profound transformation in Jewish thought. In many regards, his trailblazing endeavor can be compared to that of Maimonides. In this chapter, I analyze the problem raised by Leibowitz and the solution he suggested, paying special attention to a comparison between him and Wittgenstein. The similarities between them do not necessarily reflect Wittgenstein's influence on Leibowitz. Although Leibowitz had high respect for Wittgenstein's work, his basic theses were framed long before the publication of Wittgenstein's writings.[1] The comparison will thus reveal the extent to which Leibowitz's philosophy is uniquely and radically Jewish.

One basic question occupied Leibowitz mainly since the early 1950s, when he published "Religious Praxis": Is religious commitment possible without metaphysical and theological assumptions? As a scientist nurtured in the tradition of Popper, Wittgenstein, and logical positivism, he was aware of the epistemic difficulty entailed in all attempts to justify metaphysical claims regarding God, the world, or historical events. To say that God's revelation took place at a specific historical time, or that God functions in a particular fashion, compels us to apply to God categories drawn from our concrete experience. The very act of using our own experience to describe God, however, is invalid and tantamount to idolatry, since God is precisely the transcendent entity beyond our cognition:

> Faith in God approached from his divine dimension, which is ungraspable through the categories of human thought, as opposed to faith in God from the dimension of the attributes

and functions ascribed to him, which due to the limitations of human consciousness necessarily involves objectification. Our human consciousness contains no features or functions that are not derived from the natural reality known to human beings. Hence, whoever ascribes one of these to God...sinks into idolatrous faith: he worships God in the image of man.[2]

The everyday language we use in regard to God, then, contradicts what we think or can think about God, and believers should direct their theological efforts to the removal of natural and ordinary meanings from religious language: "If, however, a religious person's thought turns to theological reflection, he is not at liberty to forego analysis and criticism of theological terms and concepts and must master their meanings which are necessarily different from their meanings when they are used in discoursing of nature and man."[3]

Like Maimonides, Leibowitz endorsed a radical theory of divine transcendence, based on the character of human cognition and warranting the conclusion that "God is not an object of religious thought."[4] Similarly, nothing can be said about the world as such, neither that it precedes creation nor that it was created, because "the concept of 'creation' does not resemble anything in our own experience, or any concept derived from our perception of reality. Hence, this concept too is meaningless to us when used to describe reality."[5]

Like Wittgenstein, Leibowitz held that science can help us understand processes unfolding in the world but not the essence or the very existence of the world. This is a question beyond our cognitive powers. He also rejected, like Wittgenstein, the possibility of riddles, namely, questions that science cannot answer. Wittgenstein wrote: "When the answer cannot be put into words, neither can the question be put in words."[6] Likewise, Leibowitz wrote: "Science answers every question that can be formulated in the language of scientific methodology — and only science answers it. No scientific question remains as a 'riddle' in science, its solution to be sought elsewhere."[7]

If we are indeed limited and bound by our concrete, day-to-day experience, we cannot ascribe meanings that transcend our cognition to actual historical events. Classic religious concepts reflecting a metaphysical interpretation of historical events, such as "providence" or "redemption," now become unintelligible, since they are based on "factual information" that fails to match our empirical cognition.

The tendency of religion to rely on arguments drawn from the factual and metaphysical realms had bothered religious thinkers such as Pascal and Kierkegaard, who understood that religion is thereby made contingent on the validity of these arguments. In logical terms, this reliance implies that religious truths are contingent rather than necessary. As believers, however, they refused to endorse this conclusion. Wittgenstein too understood that believers do not approach their religious beliefs as they do other factual truths: "Those people who had faith didn't apply the doubt which would ordinarily apply to any historical propositions."[8] On these grounds, Wittgenstein and other thinkers in his wake concluded that religion does not compete with metaphysics or science and offers something else altogether — faith. Faith is not contingent on any outside factor. It is the primary foundation, not grounded on truth claims, through which the believer perceives the world. Faith, then, is not the sum of truth claims about the world; rather, in the terminology of post-Wittgenstenian philosophy, faith is the believer's absolute disposition toward the world, which shapes an entire "form of life."[9]

Leibowitz's thought strongly resembles that of some of these thinkers, but his approach rests on a consideration present in an early work of Wittgenstein, the *Tractatus Logico Philosophicus*.

According to Leibowitz, the problem with metaphysical and factual religious truths is not their logical status, namely, the possibility that they might be refuted, but their meaninglessness. The key question for Leibowitz, then, is the following: Is Judaism based on meaningless claims or can it be championed on other grounds? Rejecting metaphysics as meaningless is thus an expression of critical thinking, but dismissing metaphysics is not enough — Judaism now needs a new justification. Here we reach the essence of the Leibowitzian revolution, whereby the meaning of Judaism shifts away from the metaphysical-theological realm and is perceived as a system of values. My analysis will trace in greater detail the two stages of this revolution — the negative, entailing the removal of metaphysics from Jewish existence, and the positive, establishing Judaism as a system of values.

The removal of metaphysics from religion is manifest at two levels in Leibowitz's thought: first, in the denial of theology, and second, in the denial of "religious facts." Theology, meaning the detailed and precise concern with God's attributes, is a classic area of religious thought. Monotheistic traditions deal at length with God as source and creator, as a perfect entity describable in terms of one or another attribute. Even ordinary believers, who are not interested in God as an object of philosophical contemplation, do make theological assumptions in their ways of life and in their religious language about God's goodness and concern for his creatures. All propositions regarding God, however, are actually committed to assumptions that Leibowitz considers epistemologically meaningless and thus religiously unacceptable. Leibowitz knows that traditional religious language is loaded with theological statements, but does not consider this a special problem. He recurrently emphasizes Maimonides' doctrine of "negative attributes" as a unique contribution, key to the eradication of positive statements about God. According to this theory, all positive statements about God — "wise," "powerful," and so forth — are to be understood not as the ascription of positive attributes to God but as indicating that these attributes are not absent: "wise" means that God is not foolish, "omnipotent" means that God is not limited. When dismissing these flaws, human beings do not gain a better understanding of God but a perception of God as a supreme entity, different from any other known to them. Leibowitz argues that only through this theory can religious individuals be released from mistaken religious perceptions and worship God, meaning that only by endorsing this approach can they accept divine sovereignty and not be like "he who worships God in the image of man."[10]

The removal of theology from Jewish religion does not follow only from systematic critical reflection. Leibowitz argues that, at the concrete level of Jewish religion, theology is entirely irrelevant: "Religious faith can be pure and profound without the believer engaging in theological reasoning."[11] Like Wittgenstein, Leibowitz understood that using the word "God" does not require a full grasp of what this word represents. Leibowitz would certainly agree with Wittgenstein's statement concerning the word God whereby, primarily, we understand "what it didn't mean."[12] For Leibowitz, this understanding is the most believers will ever attain and, beyond it, they do not need theology to live as believers.

Similarly, Leibowitz removes "religious facts" — such as creation, the Sinai revelation, and providence — from the realm of religion. Facts are determined only by what takes place in reality and can be verified by our standard epistemic tools. Although none of the religious facts mentioned is amenable to such validation, Leibowitz cannot deny their significant role in the prevalent religious language. His contribution, then, is to offer a new and daring interpretation of them, guided by the following principle: "Historical facts are...*per se* religiously indifferent. No historical event assumes religious meaning unless it expresses religious consciousness, namely, unless it reflects the religious consciousness — knowledge and worship of God — of the event's participants."[13]

Although Leibowitz formulated this principle in regard to historical facts, he actually applies it to facts in general — historical, natural, or metaphysical. A "religious fact" derives from the religious-normative system — only from and within this system does it acquire meaning. "Religious facts" are one type of normative claims. The religious meaning of creation can thus be summed up in the claim that the "universe ('Heaven and Earth') is not God — the great refutation of idolatry, pantheism and atheism."[14] The Sinai revelation is not the name of yet another past event, but one of the institutions that shaped Jewish religion. The role of this institution is to endow the halakhic system as a whole with the force of a command incumbent on everyone or, in Leibowitz's pointed formulation: "The meaning of Sinai is accepting the command we have been commanded."[15] In religious language, the concept of "revelation" does not point to a fact in the world or to a norm within the system; rather, it indicates our judgment of the system *in toto*. Therefore, revelation makes a meta-normative or second order statement, which determines the status of the Torah: "It has divine authority."[16]

Prima facie, this approach marks a dramatic revolution in the perception of the Sinai revelation. In classic Jewish tradition, the Sinai revelation as an incontrovertible historical fact is the cornerstone of Jewish faith. The commitment to observe the Torah and the commandments derives from the Sinai revelation, which took place at a particular place and time. Moreover, after Judah Halevi, the overwhelming sense was that this was a demonstrated fact because it was witnessed by a multitude and transmitted by tradition over many generations: "Those who have handed down these laws to us were not a few isolated individuals, but a multitude, all learned men who received them from the prophets. And in the absence of prophecy, they received them from the bearers of the Torah...and the chain beginning with Moses has never been interrupted."[17]

For Judah Halevi, the empirical validity of the Sinai revelation is far higher than the validity of religious facts in other religions, both because it took place in front of a multitude and because of the continuity of the tradition. Halevi seems to have reflected a basic religious intuition of Jewish tradition as perceived in his time and by believers over many generations up to the present day. But is this perception of the Sinai revelation as part of the current commitment to Jewish tradition still possible? The traditional view of the Sinai theophany as the cornerstone of the obligation to assume the yoke of the Torah and the commandments could be hindered by several obstacles.

First, this view involves *petitio principii* circularity. The claim that the Sinai revelation was an event that took place before a multitude and was faithfully transmitted through the generations is not a consensual fact. Revelation is a fact only if we presume that the claim that Jewish tradition is embodied in the biblical text is reliable. But the reliability of this tradition is precisely the fact that needs to be demonstrated. Without independent faith in the biblical text, we cannot rely on it and on the Jewish tradition that embraces this text as a factual report in order to claim that this was indeed a fact. The "fact" is a fact only if we believe in it, but if we believe in it, how can we see it as a datum that substantiates faith itself?

This problem did not trouble medieval philosophers because all — Jews, Christians, and Moslems — agreed that the Sinai revelation had indeed occurred and that the tradition relying on it was valid. Within these parameters, Halevi's argument sounds plausible. If all agree on a fact as described, its validating power is far stronger than that of "religious" facts occurring before a limited audience. But medieval discourse is blocked to us, since what is in question is the actual reliability of religious texts, and what was possible in a medieval context becomes highly problematic in our times. Eliezer Goldman, who continued the Leibowitzian tradition, formulated this claim with his proverbial clarity:

> Certainty in this form [as reflected in medieval Jewish tradition] is not possible today, for two reasons. One, the prevailing critical approach toward the tradition and the literary sources. The difficulty does not lie in the particular circumstances of biblical research, of the history of faith, or of Halakhah. The question is one of principle: is there room for the critical research of Scripture or of halakhic tradition? A negative response cannot be based on the reliability of the tradition. This is precisely the issue at stake...For us, the accepted criteria for determining the reliability of traditions are the criteria of critical research. The argument that a specific tradition is reliable in ways that exclude the application of critical criteria must substantiate this reliability on a criterion other than the continuity of tradition. The epistemic certainty that R. Judah Halevi, for instance, could ascribe to the tradition of the Sinai revelation, is no longer possible for us.[18]

Second, as noted, facts are logically contingent. All that we assume as fact could turn out to be a fiction or a deception. The validity of a fact is merely contingent and, in principle, could be refuted. The believer's disposition, however, is entirely different. The believer endorses faith unconditionally and is entirely unwilling to assume the possibility of its refutation. Hence, religious commitment could not possibly rely on fact.

Third, even if do assume a fact's actual occurrence, how does the believer's obligation to observe the Torah and the commandments follow from it? One of the most important distinctions in the theory of values is that between "is" and "ought," and the determination that "is" does not follow from "ought": normative value conclusions cannot be derived from factual data. How, then, does the obligation to observe the Torah and the commandments follow from the very occurrence of the Sinai theophany? A typical response to this problem is that, since the commander is the good God, we are obliged to obey his commands. This answer, however, does not anchor the obligation in the fact of the Sinai commandment but on our faith and our judgment about the nature of the commanding God. In Jewish tradition, this conclusion has been formulated by Simeon Shkop who writes: "The obligation and the imperative to worship God and fulfill his will, may He be blessed...is an obligation and a necessity according to the laws of reason."[19] Several aspects of the distinction between facts and values have indeed been questioned in the philosophical literature, but the attempt to ground belief in the Sinai revelation on a critique of the distinction between facts and values would anchor faith on shaky foundations.

Fourth, theophany as fact assumes that time and place categories apply to God: revelation occurred at a particular time and place, meaning that God operates in place and time. This perception, however, refutes the view of God as transcendent. It is also incongruent with the understanding of revelation as a subjective experience unfolding in the individual's personal life that William James, for instance, describes as "conversion."[20] In this description, revelation is not a nomistic experience with a universally valid legal system as its object, but an internal private experience. This experience unfolds in the depths of an individual's being, its contents are personal, and its object are the values, approaches, and existence of the person rather than anything beyond it. This concept, however, though compatible with Christian — mainly Protestant — approaches, is incompatible with Jewish religion.

Attempts to contend with these obstacles allow for a range of answers. One extreme response is to negate the existence of any problems and cling to a simple faith. Another is to dismiss Jewish religion as groundless. The first option strives to preserve the traditional Jewish intuition that ascribes crucial weight to the Sinai revelation. The will to retain the specific *contents* that Jewish tradition ascribed to this event deserves respect, and should not be scorned because rationally unacceptable, since religion cannot be based solely on rational contexts. The price of this outlook, however, is obvious. Its supporters must renounce the notion that the Sinai revelation serves as a justification for something else. The Sinai revelation now becomes an "inner" fact of Jewish religion rather than the prooftext of its truth. Although this is a modest price for those seeking a share in their ancestors' tradition, it is still quite high, from two perspectives. First, at least in classic Jewish philosophy, the Sinai revelation was the datum that substantiated the overriding certainty of Jewish religion. Second, preserving the traditional outlook that views the Sinai theophany as a religious fact still leaves several questions unanswered: In what sense is the Sinai revelation a fact? What do we mean when we say it is a "religious fact"? What is the meaning of this religious fact?

The contrary option comes to the conclusion warranted by this argument: since the Sinai revelation cannot substantiate Jewish religion, Jewish faith should be relinquished. This conclusion is indeed possible but not imperative, and alternative interpretations of the Sinai revelation could also be suggested. Abandoning religion would then be the result of endorsing a particular interpretation of the Sinai revelation. In other words, the conclusion was chosen a priori, when choosing an interpretation.

A third and indeed particularly fruitful option rests on a new interpretation of the Sinai revelation as a normative rather than a factual landmark. The term does not relate to an event that occurred in the past but expresses an act of judgment about the

Torah. According to this interpretation, the attributes ascribed to the historical fact of the Sinai revelation are displaced to the judgment of the Torah *per se*. As a factual event, the Sinai revelation marked the Torah's divine source, in an act of judgment that ascribes it transcendent validity. This transcendence is the basic paradox of religious life: through an act of judgment that is by nature immanent, believers ascribe transcendent status to their object of judgment — the Torah. As a factual characteristic, the Sinai revelation expresses the fact that the Torah is from heaven, that it is not a human product. As a normative characteristic, believers accept the Torah unquestioningly and unreservedly. In judging the Torah in these terms, believers assume its absolute authority and acknowledge its divine source.

The religious intuitions expressed through the term "Sinai revelation" when referring to a factual characteristic are definitely preserved when it is transformed into a normative characteristic. Indeed, it is only through this transformation that revelation preserves its "inner" religious meaning. The Sinai revelation denotes the believer's act of acceptance, the decision to assume the yoke of the heavenly kingdom; it is no longer a factual event that may or may not have taken place in the world. As a factual characteristic, the Sinai revelation relates to the distant past; as a normative characteristic, the Sinai revelation relates to the present and to the believer's concrete life. In sum, the Sinai revelation as a fact relates to the act of giving, whereas the Sinai revelation as a normative characteristic expresses the believer's act of acceptance and decision.

Shifting the center from the divine act of giving the Torah to the individual's act of accepting it can also trace its precedents to Jewish sources. Thus, for instance, R. Johanan says: "Whoever performs one commandment truly is accounted as though he had enacted it from Mount Sinai, for it is said 'You shall therefore keep and do them' (Deuteronomy 26:16). What is the meaning of the words 'do them'? It means that whoever observes the Torah and performs it truly is accounted as though he had enacted it from Sinai."[21]

Another text suggesting such a shift is BT Shabbat 88a. The Talmud cites a homily by R. Avdimi bar Hama bar Hasa, claiming that the Holy One, blessed be He, forced the Jewish people to accept the Torah by tilting the mountain and threatening them to cover them with it, as though it were an upturned vat. R. Aha bar Yaakov was critical of this homily: "This is a powerful protest against the Torah." If the Torah was indeed forced upon the people of Israel, they are free not to observe it on a claim of duress. Rabba accepts this argument but goes on to say, "Nevertheless, they accepted it again in the days of Ahashverosh." For Rabba, the autonomous acceptance of the Torah is the basis for the obligation it creates.[22] Although these homilies do not significantly transform the term "Sinai revelation" from a factual into a normative characteristic, they do stress the centrality of human freedom as the constitutive validation of the Sinai revelation.[23]

In this context, note the use of the term *de-oraita* [from the Torah] in halakhic literature. This term appears to denote a fact: a norm defined as *de-oraita* is a norm transmitted at the time of the Sinai revelation. But the characterization of norms as either *de-oraita* or as enacted by the sages — *de-rabanan* — is a bone of contention between Maimonides and Nahmanides. Maimonides holds that the term *de-oraita* refers only to what is explicitly written in the Torah or what halakhic tradition states was given to Moses at Sinai.[24] According to this view, most of the talmudic literature conveying statements founded on the sages' discretion or on exegeses of the written text is not *de-oraita*. Indeed, in the Second Root of *The Book of the Commandments*, Maimonides writes: "It is not admissible to include in this Classification [*de-oraita*] (a commandment) that is derived by any of the Thirteen Principles of Exegesis by which the Torah is expounded."[25]

Nahmanides categorically rejects this stance. In a sharp formulation, he states: "This Principle and this Root [Maimonides' Second Root] dismisses and abolishes many roots in the Talmud...and our principle, the roots of our tradition, are the thirteen principles for the exegesis of the Torah, and most of the Talmud is based on them."[26] According to Nahmanides, the basic assumption of talmudic discourse is that a conclusion reached by the sages through the implementation of the thirteen principles of exegesis is identical to the text of the Torah "because the principles are for them as explicit words of Torah."[27] The reason is that the principles of exegesis were given to Moses exactly as the Torah itself. Contrary to Maimonides, Nahmanides holds that a halakhic norm is defined as legislation enacted by the sages only if they state so explicitly: "Therefore, the proper understanding is the opposite [of Maimonides' view]: everything expounded in the Talmud through one of the thirteen rules of exegesis is *de-oraita*, unless they say it is an *askmakhta* [meaning that the homily was used only for illustration]."[28] According to Nahmanides, the norm is valid because it is based on a rabbinic legislative act and, barring such an explicit statement, all halakhic inferences from the Torah have *de-oraita* status.

The dispute between Maimonides and Nahmanides, then, concerns the use of the term *de-oraita*: Maimonides holds that this term denotes the norms explicitly issued at the Sinai revelation, be it in the text of the Torah or through the chain of tradition, when the sages of Israel attest so explicitly.[29] Whatever is not part of this corpus, is not part of the revelation event or of the Torah *per se*. Both the place (Sinai) and the actual occurrence play a crucial role in the constitution of a norm as part of the Torah. By contrast, Nahmanides holds that revelation as it actually took place at a particular place lacks this status. The term *de-oraita* indicates, above all, the status of the halakhic norms themselves rather than what happened at the revelation. In his critique of

Maimonides, Nahmanides adduces strong evidence to support his claim. Hanania Kazis, a Maimonides' advocate who responds to this critique, writes as follows:

> He [Nahmanides] also cites several commandments that were not given at Sinai in an attempt to show that it is not necessarily Sinai…I hold that the rabbi's [Maimonides] words below, in the Third Root, will suffice to answer this objection. And this is what he says: "And they indeed meant 'at Sinai,' since the gist of the Torah was given at Sinai." The rabbi explicitly says "the gist of the Torah," because rabbinic statements were not included in the Torah. Hence, the word Sinai is not meant to point to a place but to denote the notion of *de-oraita*, since the gist of the Torah was given at Sinai. He therefore relied on the phrase "at Sinai" to allude to the Torah as a whole.[30]

In defending Maimonides, Kazis argues that Maimonides too accepts the assumption that the term *de-oraita* does not denote only what was given at Sinai. Rather, it denotes the norms enjoying the special legal status indicated by the term *de-oraita*, which are legally different from norms enacted through rabbinic legislation. For instance, when in doubt concerning a norm *de-oraita*, the call is for greater stringency, but when a rabbinic norm is at stake, further leniency is advised. Whether or not Kazis is right in his interpretation of Maimonides' approach, he brings Maimonides' position closer to that of Nahmanides: the term *de-oraita* does not indicate only the norms issued at the actual Sinai revelation.

This analysis shows that, at least implicitly, Jewish tradition assigns greater importance to the determination of the norms' status than to the factual question of what precisely was given at Sinai. Although the views of Nahmanides and Kazis are not identical to Leibowitz's, their approaches do convey the original digression in the discussion about the Torah, which shifts from the factual question to the issue of assessment and judgment. In this sense,

Leibowitz's interpretation of the Sinai revelation as a normative characteristic continues a hermeneutical discourse within Jewish tradition. It points to a desire to preserve traditional constructs as conveyed in specific wordings while pouring new meanings into the claims expressed through them.[31] This hermeneutical innovation, then, is a continuation of Jewish tradition rather than a deviation. The paradigm that Maimonides presented in the *Guide of the Perplexed* is a fascinating instance of the immanent religious need for an innovative interpretation that balances religious and intellectual commitments. The *Guide of the Perplexed* has by now become a legitimate part of the Jewish canon. Hermeneutically, however, very little in this essay remains relevant to our generation, since Maimonides' horizons differ from ours. What does remain alive in this book is the very legitimacy of reinterpreting tradition.[32] Interpretation and renewed interpretation reflect the permanent dialogue of believers with their tradition. Through this dialogue, a "fusion of horizons" emerges between the legacy and the cultural value horizons of the person turning to the tradition.[33]

This conceptual transformation is an innovation that becomes significant for believers who affirm their religion as well as a set of cognitions and insights deeply entrenched within a specific culture. Individuals who do not wish to renounce their religious commitment must embark on this hermeneutic voyage, a voyage that endows the statements of religious tradition with new meaning. The seeds of this innovation lie within Jewish tradition, as does the renewed meeting with the tradition that takes place through the horizons of the present and sheds light on aspects included in the horizons of the past.[34] Can a religious commitment based on human autonomy encompass the full range of this commitment's meanings? All the possible answers to this question share a common characteristic: the alternative of anchoring religious commitment in historical facts is even less satisfactory.

This renewed interpretation of the Sinai revelation, which neutralizes its factual dimension, is compatible with the removal of all mythological meanings from Scripture, again pointing to the illuminating similarity between Leibowitz and Wittgenstein:

> Christianity is not based on historical truth; rather, it offers us a (historical) narrative and says: now believe! But not, believe this narrative with the belief appropriate to a historical narrative, rather: believe, through thick and thin, which you can do only as the result of a life. *Here you have a narrative, don't take the same attitude to it as you take to other historical narratives*! Make a *quite different* place in your life for it.--There is nothing *paradoxical* about that![35]

The factual story thus assumes its meaning from the believer's life context. For Wittgenstein, the fact that the "historical narrative" becomes meaningful through faith was not paradoxical. Leibowitz, in his distant dialogue with Wittgenstein, argued that "this is a logical paradox but not a religious paradox."[36] In other words, it is paradoxical that halakhic Judaism, which draws its authority from Scripture, is also the one that determines the meaning of Scripture. Asa Kasher, however, a prominent neo-Leibowitzian thinker, showed that no logical paradox is present here,[37] and Leibowitz agreed with him,[38] thus reaffirming his support for Wittgenstein.

If we dismiss theology, it appears we must also dismiss God, turning it into a meaningless concept. Had Leibowitz endorsed such a move, however, the gap between his approach, which strives to describe "empirical-historical" Judaism as is, and conventional religious language, would have become unbridgeable. Rather than offering an entirely new "language game," Leibowitz strives to preserve the old "language game" while offering a new interpretation when he interprets *de-oraita*, a central metaphysical concept in Halakhah, *within* the language game of Halakhah rather than as a metaphysical claim. In this light, eradicating God from the religious realm becomes inconceivable. Leibowitz thus suggests a solution composed of two elements. The first, as noted, is to turn God into a transcendent entity of which nothing can be said.[39] The second is to interpret statements about God that are necessary for the perception of religion as a normative system as pointing to the *relationship* between the individual and God. Thus, for instance, the statement "God commands" means that individuals take upon themselves this command as divine: "In reflecting and speaking about man's standing before God, the believer...tries to refer minimally to God, who has no image at all, and makes an effort to direct his religious consciousness to himself as recognizing his duty to his God."[40]

Leibowitz knows that the metaphysical meaning of religious language cannot be fully translated according to his suggestions. In fact, the statement that God is a necessary entity, which Leibowitz endorses, entails a specific metaphysical commitment requiring God's very existence and even characterizing his mode of existence. Furthermore, the claim that individuals acknowledge their obligations toward God makes God, if not the object of this knowledge, at least an entity toward which one has obligations.

Leibowitz disregards most of this metaphysical language by resorting to a sharp distinction between two types of faith that recurs pervasively throughout his writings: *lishmah* (for-its-own-sake) and *lo-lishmah* (not for its own sake), a means for realizing human ends.[41] The religious language that tends to make frequent use of metaphysics is idolatrous and not-for-its-own-sake. The struggle against idolatry is indeed a crucial element of Leibowitz's thought, essentially implying the eradication of metaphysics from the religious realm. Continuing the passage above, Leibowitz notes: "The pagan...and he who serves God not-lishmah direct their attention to an imaginary notion of their god and to the understanding of his attributes and actions. This is the mystical approach which is represented in Judaism by the Kabbalah."[42]

This move, which purports to dismiss theology while leaving room for a relationship with God, might seem unsatisfactory because, as noted, relating to God entails more than a hint of ontological commitment. No wonder, then, that Asa Kasher suggested the hermeneutical technique of "denying the elements."[43] According to this technique, any theological proposition ascribing a certain attribute to God will be transmuted into a new proposition in which the subject is "all things in the world." In the new proposition, the attribute ascribed to God is denied in regard to the world. Thus, for instance, the proposition "God is inevitable" is translated as "every single thing in the world is not inevitable." In this translation of religious language, it is forbidden to ascribe absolute value to anything in the world since, according to Leibowitz and Kasher, doing so is tantamount to idolatry. Despite its elegance, however, this sophisticated move is not an interpretation of Leibowitz but goes a step beyond him, because faith for Leibowitz is still an intentional act directed toward an "object" — God. If religion is reduced to being a war against idolatry, prayer and other religious phenomena lose all meaning. Prayer and other religious phenomena can still be meaningful, however, on the basis of Leibowitz's perception of them as intentional activities addressing God, although this is not a simple matter.

These statements may appear somewhat vague as long as we have not considered the positive meaning of the Leibowitzian revolution — the perception of religion as a normative system. Wittgenstein closes the *Tractatus* with an evocative statement: "What we cannot speak about we must pass over in silence."[44] Leibowitz concurs unquestionably; we must not speak about God or about metaphysics. But he transcends the young Wittgenstein when he writes, specifically addressing this statement: "This is true only so far as philosophical contemplation is concerned...but does not apply to religion as embodied in the Torah and in the commandments. That which cannot be said is said by the religion of the Torah and the commandments."[45]

The religion of the Torah and the commandments speaks in the language of values rather than of facts, and Leibowitz claims that things one is forbidden to say in the epistemic realm do have a place within a system of values. This is the essence of Leibowitz's radical positive innovation which, following the term coined by Kant regarding his own thought, can be viewed as the "Copernican revolution" in Jewish thought.

In his terse prose, Leibowitz traces the contours of this revolution as taking a step beyond the young Wittgenstein. As shown below, however, the parallels between the Leibowitzian revolution on the one hand, and the late Wittgenstein and the philosophy influenced by him on the other, are quite striking. The current task is a clearer presentation of Leibowitz's Copernican shift.

The first step in this shift is in the clarification of what we can think and say. If we remain within the frame of our conventional cognitions, most metaphysical-theological propositions become groundless. More precisely, like Wittgenstein before him, Leibowitz argues that these statements are meaningless rather than false. This is the critical-negative stage, preparing the second and more important shift in Jewish religion — from theory to praxis, from metaphysics to Halakhah or, essentially, from the realm of facts to the realm of values: "There is no other content to the faith in God and the love of God than the assumption of the yoke of the Kingdom of heaven, which is the yoke of Torah and Mitzvoth."[46]

These pointed phrases sum up the Leibowitzian revolution: Halakhah is the embodiment of faith, and its meaning is the understanding that the human obligation is to worship God.

In this approach, religious obligations cannot be derived from any factual datum found in a socio-historical or anthropological context, or from any "religious fact." Jewish religion is "an institutional religion, but not in the sense that it comprises institutions... The description is intended to reflect the peculiarity of Judaism, for which the institutions of halakhic practice are constitutive. Apart from them, Judaism does not exist.[47]

If Judaism is constituted by halakhic law, and if this law is neither conditioned by nor derived from any outside datum, the meaning of the halakhic system is "intrinsic." In Wittgenstein's terms, religion is an autonomous "language game," with its own rules, open to its participants. Even if the meaning dimension is intrinsic, however, it is open to cognitive understanding from the outside, since the meaning of the system is the worship of God.

The link between Leibowitz's approach to Jewish religion and John Searle's notion of "constitutive rules" is worth noting.[48] Nothing precedes this legal system; rather, the law constitutes itself and defines a new realm of activity. For Searle, the notion of "rules of the game" is an instance of such a system. Thus, chess or basketball would not exist were it not for a system of laws that defines them and determines their purpose.

The antithesis of a constitutive system of laws is a system of regulative rules, of which traffic laws are a classic example. Traffic is not constituted by the rules of traffic, and the purpose of traffic laws is determined by the fact that there is traffic. Since the purpose of these laws is given, they can indeed be criticized and compared to other legal systems meeting similar needs, and even replaced by other laws that might serve this purpose better.

Leibowitz thus claims that Halakhah is a constitutive system. Halakhah, therefore, creates an autonomous world of meaning or, in Wittgenstein's terms, a "form of life" or an independent "language game," without reflecting meanings outside it.

If institutionalized Jewish religion is a constitutive system, it is not judged by its match to some extrinsic datum but is actually coextensive with its intrinsic activity. Jewish religion then, is primarily a form of life rather than a metaphysical doctrine. This claim is strikingly similar to that found in Wittgenstein's later writings, where he strongly emphasized that religion does not compete with our standard consciousness concerning truth claims but, instead, offers faith, meaning it is a form of life rather than a "doctrine." In one of his most poignant and deepest religious insights, Wittgenstein writes:

> I believe that one of the things Christianity says is that sound doctrines are all useless. That you have to change your *life*. (Or the *direction* of your life).
> It says that wisdom is all cold; and that you can no more use it for setting your life to rights than you can forge iron when it is *cold*.
> The point is that sound doctrine need not *take hold* of you...But here you need something to move you and turn you in a new direction...Once you have been turned round, you must *stay* turned round.
> Wisdom is passionless. But faith by contrast is what Kierkegaard calls a *passion*.[49]

Both Wittgenstein and Leibowitz claim that the contrast between theory and faith as a form of life is manifest in the believers' readiness to shape their lives according to faith. Wittgenstein speaks of religious faith as "unshakeable belief," the peculiar faith shown not "by reasoning or by appeal to ordinary grounds for belief, but rather by regulating for all in his life."[50] He then points to the essential feature of religious life: the readiness of believers to assume risks they would not have taken without faith. Leibowitz too describes faith as the individual's decision to assume the yoke of Torah and the commandments, a decision that neither follows from any external context nor can it be inferred from it:

> I, however, do not regard religious faith as a conclusion. It is rather an *evaluative decision* that one makes, and, like all evaluations, it does not result from any information one has acquired, but is *a commitment to which one binds himself*. In other words, faith is not a form of cognition; it is a conative element of consciousness.[51]

Through this decision, according to Leibowitz, believers take no risks regarding their cognitive world, but renounce their non-religious values because of their love and fear of God. The paradigm of religious life is the sacrifice of Isaac, "in which all human values capable of being subsumed under the categories of human understanding and feeling were set aside before the 'glory of the majesty' of God."[52]

The comparison with Wittgenstein on this point is revealing because, in his later writings, Wittgenstein clarifies that believers do take risks and forsake their standard epistemic world. He sees the believer and the atheist at odds over a world picture:

> But what men consider reasonable or unreasonable alters. At certain periods men find reasonable what at other periods they found unreasonable. And vice-versa. But is there no objective character here? Very intelligent and well-educated people believe in the story of creation in the Bible, while others hold it as proven false, and the grounds of the latter are well known to the former.[53]

The different language games of the believer and the atheist, then, relate to the factual world. The believer offers an unshakable world view, antithetical to that of the atheist. The evidence supporting this world view is not, as noted, better than that of the atheist, but mirrors precisely the world picture of religion itself. Leibowitz, however, does not endorse this view and remains loyal on this point to the younger Wittgenstein — whatever is groundless, or false, does not change its status within a religious world view. Religion does not compete for recognition by offering a different *factual* picture but is rather a system of *values*, which only assumes meaning within a context of values. Hence, believers make concessions and assume risks within a world of values rather than within a world of facts.

The question, however, remains open: can religion, defined as a commitment to a legal system, successfully avoid all metaphysical claims while ultimately addressing God as its supreme object? Leibowitz seems to follow Wittgenstein here, who writes on this point: "The way you use the word 'God' does not show whom you mean — but rather what you mean."[54] The key question concerning God, then, is not his objective character, his existence or identity, but the way in which human beings, in their language and in their lives, use the concept of God. The examination of the uses and the function of the concept of God in a particular life context must precede any a priori analysis of it.

This Wittgenstenian principle wholly coincides with Leibowitz's position. Leibowitz claims that the meaning of the concept "God" must be inferred from the concrete form of life espoused by Judaism as a religion constituted by Halakhah rather than from an isolated conceptual-theological analysis. In Leibowitz's analysis, God functions within religious faith as the supreme concept, unifying the system and endowing it with religious significance. Neither the divine *source* of religion nor the believer's immediate experience of the transcendent God, which is impossible for Leibowitz to construe, endow the system with religious value; rather, the system is made religiously meaningful by the believers' perception of it as concerned with the worship of God.

All metaphysical statements must therefore be translated into normative language. Of all the propositions that need to be clarified within the new value system, the one pertaining to the Sinai revelation seems to require it most urgently. As noted, Leibowitz does not view the Sinai revelation as pointing to a fact or as the metaphysical basis of the religious obligation, but as one of the institutions of religion. Religiously, the "raw" fact of revelation is meaningless; in religious language, revelation expresses the attitude of believers to norms they view as God's command and to which they are committed.

Generally, the statements in which God is the subject are translated into statements where the individual is the subject and God is the object. Thus, the proposition "God gave the Torah" means that the individual assumes the yoke of the Torah so as to worship God, and "God's command" means the obligation compelling the individual to worship God. Leibowitz illustrates this technique well regarding the concept "God's will":

> As a category applicable to man, willing does not refer to what already exists, but is rather an aspiration, an inclination, an intention towards something that should or ought to be. Conversely, "He has done whatsoever has pleased"; we are in no position to distinguish His will from given reality. It thus follows that in its profound sense, the expression "to do God's will" asserts nothing about God, but is rather an expression of the believer's recognition of his duty to serve God.[55]

Since religious language is metaphysically overloaded, the act of translation will not be seamless. Nor can Leibowitz's various distinctions between different types of religiosity — for-its-own-sake v. not-for-its-own-sake, demanding v. endowing, and so forth — ensure the removal of all metaphysical traces, as the above passage, where Leibowitz assumes that will and reality are identical for God, goes to prove: Is this not a metaphysical statement?

Dismissing these traces entirely is indeed impossible, because religion is an intentional activity that ultimately addresses God. The task of translating a metaphysical language into a value language requires from the faithful a religious-critical levelheadedness, which Leibowitz may view as the believer's endless test. Although believers will always fail at it, they will persist in this Sisyphean endeavor: "The project it [Jewish religion] sets for man is permanent and endless. No religious attainment may be considered final; the project is never completed."[56]

This is one feature distinguishing the levelheaded believer from what Leibowitz calls the idolater: whereas the latter rests in the serenity of his metaphysical world, the former contends with the remnants of metaphysics, powerless to eliminate them.

These metaphysical remnants, however, neither express nor pretend to offer any metaphysical claims apart from the normative context, according to Leibowitz. Leibowitz proposes what we might call a "value metaphysics," meaning one that is meaningful only within a value context. Within it, God is only the commander, and the meaning of this concept is itself determined by the value system. God is the commander in the sense that believers acknowledge their obligation toward him. This is a minimalist metaphysics whose meaning fundamentally lies in the interpretation of the religious obligation, which is its sole original datum: "The essence of Jewish faith is consistent with no embodiment other than the system of halakhic praxis."[57]

Leibowitz, however, is clearly inconsistent in this approach, and more than once resorts to classical metaphysics and to the claim that God is necessary. This flux between classic and value metaphysics is important because it points to the difficulty of applying a "value metaphysics" to the *lebenswelt* of Jewish experience.

Structurally, Leibowitz's thought is remarkably similar to Kant's thought. Kant, who removed God from the *Critique of Pure Reason*, returned him in the *Critique of Practical Reason*, that is, in the normative realm. In the *Critique of Pure Reason*, cognition discovers it cannot say anything about God because it is conditioned by sensorial raw material in which God has no part. God does have a place, however, in the *Critique of Practical Reason*, which is determined by the "needs" of the practical system. Kant argues in the *Critique of Practical Reason* that God guarantees the fit between the moral obligation and the concretization of the supreme good in reality. Kant views God's existence as a "postulate" or a demand that must be imposed on the value system; the meaning of this system and the obligation it conveys are not conditioned by God, but God is "demanded" by the concept of the good as such. Similarly, Leibowitz removed God from the metaphysical discourse but returned him as the purpose of the value system and as its metaphysical postulate. Individuals view their endeavor as a religious obligation imposed by God; human autonomy compels heteronomy — God's external command. Without this "postulate," the entire system would become idolatrous.

The question that remains open concerns the reasons for endorsing this system. According to Leibowitz, we cannot explain the adoption of any value system, not only one specifically Jewish, as derived from any external context. Believers become what they are only because of a deliberate decision that is impossible to justify. Leibowitz engages what could be called the "subjectivist digression." Religion is borne by the individual, who decides on its very existence, and its meaning is embodied in the believer's self-relation to his duties. Kierkegaard endorses this response when he writes that "religiousness is inwardness, that inwardness is the individual's relation to himself before God."[58] Like Leibowitz, Kierkegaard locates religiousness in the subject's inwardness, as a kind of self-relatedness ultimately directed toward God. For Kierkegaard, the subject is involved in the process of self-knowledge as related to God. For Leibowitz too, the bearer of religion is the individual who decides to adopt it, and its meaning is embodied in the believers' approach to their obligations. Unlike Kierkegaard, however, Leibowitz does not view religiosity and the norms in which it is embodied as part of a believer's direct address to God. Such an address is, after all, impossible. Rather, the norms reflect a commitment undertaken by the believer as an obligation "toward God." The most salient difference between Kierkegaard's model and Leibowitz's models of the subjective digression reflects the profound chasm between Protestantism and Judaism. Whereas Protestantism views faith as an emotional and reflective relationship with God, Judaism is normative and thus conveys this emotional and reflective dimension less successfully. The subjective relationship with God is thus shaped by Halakhah, and only by Halakhah.

Through his comprehensive analysis, Leibowitz concludes the revolution he initiated in traditional Jewish thought. Rather than relying on truth claims, religiosity expresses the believer's primary decision. Similarly, Judaism as a religion does not make any claims about the world but creates a normative system shaping a form of life, in light of the demand to worship God.

Notes

1. A programmatic article where he first suggested the theses that were to become the backbone of his approach is a transcription of a lecture he delivered in 1953. See Yeshayahu Leibowitz, "Religious Praxis: The Meaning of Halakhah," in *Judaism, Human Values, and the Jewish State*, trans. Eliezer Goldman et. al. (Cambridge, MA: Harvard University Press, 1992) (henceforth *Judaism*), 3–29.
2. Yeshayahu Leibowitz, *Conversations on the Ethics of the Fathers* (in Hebrew) (Jerusalem: Schocken, 1979), 20.
3. *Judaism*, 75–76.
4. Yeshayahu Leibowitz, *Judaism, the Jewish People, and the State of Israel* (in Hebrew) (Tel Aviv: Schocken, 1976) (henceforth *Yahadut*), 362.
5. Ibid., 340.
6. Ludwig Wittgenstein, *Tractatus Logico-Philosophicus* (London: Routledge, 1974), 149. See also Alan Keightley, *Wittgenstein, Grammar and God* (London: Epworth Press, 1976), 67.
7. *Yahadut*, 364.
8. Ludwig Wittgenstein, *Lectures and Conversations on Aesthetics, Psychology, and Religious Beliefs* (Oxford: Basil Blackwell, 1970) 57.
9. Keightley, *Wittgenstein, Grammar and God*, 73–87; D. Z. Phillips, *Faith After Foundationalism* (London: Routledge, 1988).

[10] Yeshayahu Leibowitz, *The Faith of Maimonides*, trans. John Glucker (Tel-Aviv: Mod, 1989), 95.

[11] *Judaism*, 75. Compare Peter Winch, *Trying to Make Sense* (Oxford: Basil Blackwell, 1987) 114.

[12] Wittgenstein, *Lectures and Conversations*, 59.

[13] *Yahadut*, p. 92.

[14] Ibid., 341.

[15] Yeshayahu Leibowitz, *Faith, History, and Values* (in Hebrew) (Jerusalem: Academon, 1982), 154–155.

[16] Yeshayahu Leibowitz, *Conversations about Moshe Hayyim Luzzato's "The Path of the Upright"* (in Hebrew) (Jerusalem: n. p., 1995) 228.

[17] Judah Halevi, *The Kuzari*, trans. Hartwig Hirschfeld (New York: Schocken Books, 1964), III: 53 (with modifications). See also I: 25.

[18] Eliezer Goldman, "Revelation in Philosophical Discourse" (in Hebrew), *De'ot* 46 (1977), 64.

[19] Simeon Shkop, *She'arei Yosher*, vol. 2 (New York: Hava'ad Le-Hotsa'at Sifre Ha-Gaon R. Shimon, 1980), 4. For a detailed analysis of Shkop's approach, see Avi Sagi, *Judaism: Between Religion and Morality* (in Hebrew) (Tel Aviv: Hakibbutz Hameuchad, 1998), ch. 16.

[20] See William James, *The Varieties of Religious Experience: A Study in Human Nature* (London and New York: Longmans, Green 1928), 189–258.

[21] *Tanhuma, Ki Tavo*, 1.

[22] For further analysis, see E. E. Urbach, *The Sages: Their Concepts and Beliefs*, trans. Israel Abrahams (Jerusalem: Magnes Press, 1979), 328–330.

[23] Ibid., 329.

[24] See Maimonides, *The Book of Divine Commandments (The Sefer ha-Mitzvoth of Maimonides)*, trans. Charles B. Chavel (London: Soncino Press, 1940), First Root. For an extensive discussion of Maimonides' position, see Jacob Levinger, *Maimonides' Techniques of Codification: A Study in the Method of the Mishneh Torah* (in Hebrew) (Jerusalem: Magnes Press, 1965), ch. 2.

[25] Maimonides, *The Book of Divine Commandments*.

[26] Maimonides, *The Book of Divine Commandments with Nahmanides' Glosses*, ed. Hayyim Dov Chavel (in Hebrew) (Jerusalem: Mosad Ha-Rav Kook, 1981), 30–31.

27 Ibid., 32.
28 Ibid., 34.
29 Ibid., Third Root.
30 Maimonides, *The Code of Maimonides, The Book of Divine Commandments* (in Hebrew) (Jerusalem: Am Olam, 1968), *Kin'at Soferim*, p. 6, s.v. *ve-'od hevi*.
31 On this question, see an insightful analysis in Eliezer Goldman, *Expositions and Inquiries: Jewish Thought in Past and Present* (in Hebrew), ed. Avi Sagi and Daniel Statman (Jerusalem: Magnes Press, 1996), 340–345.
32 On this question see Avi Sagi, "Religious Language in the Modern World: An Interview with Eliezer Goldman" (in Hebrew), *Gilayon* (August 1995), 12–13.
33 For these terms, see Hans Georg Gadamer, *Truth and Method* (New York: Harper, 1962), 269–274.
34 On the meeting with tradition, see Avi Sagi, *Tradition vs. Traditionalism: Contemporary Perspectives in Jewish Thought*, trans. Batya Stein (Amsterdam-New York: Rodopi, 2008), ch. 1.
35 Ludwig Wittgenstein, *Culture and Value*, trans. Peter Winch (Oxford: Basil Blackwell, 1980), 32e (emphasis in original).
36 *Judaism*, 11.
37 Asa Kasher, "Paradox--Question Mark" (in Hebrew), *Iyyun* 26, 4 (1975), 236–242.
38 *Yahadut*, 277.
39 In stressing God's transcendence, Leibowitz continues a central line of argumentation in Maimonidean tradition, and Leibowitz's particular attachment to Maimonides might be related to this dimension.
40 *Judaism*, 76.
41 See *Judaism*, 61–78.
42 *Judaism*, 76.
43 Asa Kasher, "Theological Shadows" (in Hebrew) in *The Yeshayahu Leibowitz Book An Anthology of His Thought and in His Honor*, ed. Asa Kasher and Jacob Levinger (Tel-Aviv: Tel Aviv University Students' Union, 1977), 67.
44 Wittgenstein, *Tractatus*, 151.

45 *Yahadut*, 343.
46 *Judaism*, 44.
47 *Judaism*, 4.
48 See John Searle, *Speech Acts* (Cambridge: Cambridge University Press, 1994), 50–53.
49 Wittgenstein, *Culture and Value*, 53e (emphasis in original).
50 Wittgenstein, *Lectures and Conversations*, 54.
51 *Judaism*, 37 (emphasis in the original).
52 Ibid., 22–23.
53 Wittgenstein, *On Certainty*, ed. G. E. M. Anscombe and G. H. von Wright; trans. Denis Paul and G. E. M. Anscombe (New York: Harper and Row, 1972), 43e.
54 Wittgenstein, *Culture and Value*, 50e; Ludwig Wittgenstein, *Remarks on the Philosophy of Psychology*, ed. G. E. M. Anscombe and G. H. von Wright, trans. G. E. M. Anscombe (Oxford: Blackwell, 1980), 91e.
55 *Judaism*, 76.
56 *Judaism*, 15. See also Leibowitz, *Conversations on the Ethics of the Fathers*, 142–152.
57 *Judaism*, 8.
58 Søren Kierkegaard, *Concluding Unscientific Postscript to "Philosophical Fragments,"* edited and translated by Howard V. Hong and Edna H. Hong (Princeton, NJ: Princeton University Press, 1992), 436–437.

Chapter Five

THE CRITIQUE OF THEODICY: FROM METAPHYSICS TO PRAXIS

SINCE the dawn of religious thought, theodicy has been a paramount problem. The significance of this question is quite obvious: if we assume that God is good, and if a good God can do no evil, the existence of evil refutes the existence of God. Classic philosophical traditions have confronted this question through a series of explanations that deny evil its unique character, either by denying the reality of evil or by providing teleological or causal explanations for its existence. Causal explanations show that, even if evil exists, it is justified. God, then, does not operate arbitrarily but as a good and rational entity. The assumption of God's goodness also allows for a solution of the theodicy problem that rests on the infinite gap between human beings and God, which prevents them from understanding God's actions. Recognition of this epistemic gap enables human beings to go on believing in God's goodness, even if it cannot provide an acceptable explanation for the existence of evil.[1]

Beyond the differences between the various explanations, all assume that not only is the theodicy question legitimate but also that failing to solve it constitutes a refutation of God's existence and results in religious life losing its meaning. Contrary to this stance, a widespread approach in contemporary Jewish thought casts doubt on both the gravity of this question and on the classic approaches to its solution. From a crucial theological question, theodicy turns into a kind of litmus test of the believer's stance in the world. The shift from a theological concern to the individual's religious disposition reflects a wider trend in contemporary Jewish philosophy, focusing on religious life rather than on classic theological issues.

Two trends can be discerned in this philosophy — one is sharply critical of classic theodicy's basic assumptions, while the other formulates a social-existential critique of it. The first is represented by Yeshayahu Leibowitz and Eliezer Goldman and the other by Joseph B. Soloveitchik and David Hartman.

The Critique of Classic Theodicy

Goldman and Leibowitz negate the legitimacy of the theodicy question outright resting on two mutually complementary elements: the first is God's absolute transcendence, and the second is the neutrality of historical events. The assumption of God's transcendence in the work of both these thinkers is not only epistemological, confined to the claim that God is not amenable to human knowledge, but also ontological, claiming an infinite, unbridgeable gap between God and human beings. The latter, complementary claim, states that human history is religiously neutral. After discussing Leibowitz's formulation of these claims in previous chapters, this chapter will focus mainly on Goldman's articulation of these two assumptions.

Goldman engages in a critical dialogue with Leibowitz and draws a distinction between illusory and non-illusory faith, both of which contend with the fundamental problem of an imperfect human reality:

> The consciousness of the religious person is generally sensitive to flaws in human reality. Even when the contemplation of human reality does not necessarily highlight these flaws, its contrast with the description of divine perfection must evoke reflections about its failings. These flaws — death, sin, dark inclinations, the flimsy foundations of human knowledge, the inevitable confusion between good and evil...appear to cast doubt on the possibility of any association between humanity and its Creator.[2]

Given these problems, argues Goldman, two opposite "typological" reactions are possible. One, the "redemptive religiosity that Leibowitz calls illusory religion," assumes that religion promises to amend the world, bringing release from reality's flaws and true closeness to God. Goldman then adds: "In its most developed forms, this religiosity aspires to liberation from the bonds of reality up to its elimination. Religion thus redeems human beings from the fundamental flaws of their reality."[3]

According to Goldman, illusory religiosity has two main manifestations — an eschatological view of reality and "the ontological perception of reason" (362). The eschatological view assumes several modes, "from magic to contemplation" (361), which must be addressed because Jewish literature includes several variations of what appears to be an eschatological perception such as, for instance, the widespread use of the term "redemption" in biblical literature. To reject this approach, Goldman argues that the biblical concept of redemption "does not relate to man's fundamental conditions of existence, but to specific historical conditions. This is redemption from political subjugation and at times from wicked government" (361–362). Goldman is aware that recourse to miracles involving supernatural elements is a widespread characteristic of Jewish literature. His response to them is: "Even the descriptions of miracles including an expectation of change in the natural order do not redeem man in the sense we are using this term here. Hence, eschatological visions do not prove that Judaism is a redemptive religion" (362). In other words, even if the natural order changes, the real character of human existence will not; according to Jewish sources, no "transformation of human reality, releasing it from its flaws," is to be expected (361).

Goldman's analysis, however, seems questionable. To claim that Jewish sources do not include transformational perceptions of human nature is an exaggeration. Goldman's critique of eschatological outlooks appears to rely on halakhic tradition on the one hand, and on an epistemological critique of the assumptions underlying the eschatological outlook on the other. The latter are my concern in this chapter.

Both Goldman's and Leibowitz's main claim is that God's ontological transcendence precludes claims about changes in human reality. This, according to Goldman, is the "non-illusory religion": "In non-illusory religion, the essence of the religious stance is the contrast between the Creator and the created reality, and the unbridgeable gap between the human and the divine. Human reality must be accepted as is, without any illusion of escape" (361).

According to the view both these thinkers share, real history is a neutral arena from a religious perspective. In Leibowitz's formulation:

> The whole of natural reality is religiously irrelevant — "the world pursues its course"...God is not revealed in natural reality, and the claim of "God's hand" in a natural event bears traces of pantheism or polytheism...No meaning should be

sought in history that, like nature, is meaningless...and no religious aura should be attached to the course of history.[4]

This neutrality is the antithesis of eschatological, illusory religion.

Another, different mechanism is also part of this type of religiosity: "the ontological perception of reason." Contrary to the previous approach, this one does not cope with the incongruity between reality's flaws and God's perfection by offering eschatological hope. Instead, it attempts to decode the rational character of human reality. Whereas eschatology rejects human reality, the ontological perception of reason reaffirms it through a rational explanation that mediates between reality and God. This perception dismisses the gap between the divine and the human and assumes that human beings, through their cognition, can understand the rationality of this ostensibly irrational reality. Through theodicy, for instance, human beings can understand that what appears to be evil is actually good or, at least, is a means for attaining the good.

Goldman's rejection of this trend fits his assumption about God's transcendence. But Goldman, as a critical thinker, is reluctant to rely on this perception to reject another view because such a move would lead him to a *petitio principii* fallacy. His rejection is based on his critique of human cognition: "The question of human wisdom is not religious but philosophical. Only in light of our philosophical perception of wisdom can we adopt a religious attitude toward it."[5]

This link between religion and human cognition again points to Goldman's unique position. Though he shares Leibowitz's rejection of a special religious epistemology, he is not a partner to Leibowitz's thesis on compartmentalization.[6] Goldman rejects the thesis that religion creates a separate, autonomous world. Instead, he holds that, after a critical analysis of human cognition, one can again determine a religious stance toward it. Goldman's argument is that an epistemological critique of the ontological view of reason could be the catalyst for rejecting the religious world. Furthermore:

> Many who follow such an epistemology are driven by an antireligious motivation. For them, it is part of the ideology that ascribes importance only to human values and scientific cognition and refuses to acknowledge relevance or "meaning" in anything beyond this frame of reference, which human beings could sense they have transcended. (363)

This approach, however, is not the necessary conclusion of rejecting the ontological view of reason. Another option is that the rejection of ontological rationalism constitutes an amendment of religion and a removal of illusory elements from Judaism (363). The critique of reason, which is religiously neutral, is thus an efficient means for amending religion even if this had not been its goal. What, then, is the critique of ontological rationalism?

> As is well known, the perception of reason as an ontological element of which human reason is part has long been questioned. Many epistemologies reject it, among them not only those known as positivistic or pragmatic but even some of those known as idealistic. According to this view, what is known as the rational structure of the world is merely the structure of its thinking tools, of language and of consciousness, as well as our experimental tools. We discover order in the world because of the selective way in which we arrange it in our understanding. (362–363)

These general statements, formulated in Goldman's programmatic article "On Non-Illusory Faith" published in 1960, appear in far greater detail in an obscure critique he had published five years previously entitled "Divine Good and Human Good."[7] This is a particularly interesting piece because it focuses precisely on the problem of theodicy and, in fascinating ways, applies the general insights presented above to a set of claims leading to a negation of classical theodicy.

Goldman's first critique relates to what might be called "lack of moral symmetry." This argument assumes: "If God planted in us specific moral feelings, the contents of these feelings apply to God as well...[According to this claim], a belief in Providence is ultimately identical to a belief that the world behaves as it should have behaved according to his [the believer in symmetry] view" (15).

But this symmetry, based on the assumption that man is created in God's image, is not logically substantiated and reflects what Goldman calls a type of "primary experiences" (15). These experiences reflect our basic perceptions about existence. The fundamental experience of the supporters of moral symmetry is manifest in the immanent perception of God: human beings and God belong to the same moral community and this is why we can judge God's goodness and providence. Yet, argues Goldman:

> By contrast, another religious consciousness is built upon a sense of the absolute asymmetry of creation in God's image. God's seal is imprinted upon us, but even the mere thought of attempting to imprint our seal upon God seems a type of idolatry. If our day-to-day life as his worshippers is determined by the rule "Dismiss your will before His [Avot 2: 4]," I find it hard to understand a problematic resting on the assumption that God must direct his actions according to our will. (15)

By pointing at different primary experiences, Goldman shows that the theodicean discourse cannot be conducted as a rational discourse involving decision-making rules; these experiences are

CHAPTER FIVE

not "a subject of theoretical discourse" (15). Endorsing or negating the theodicy discourse, then, is no more than a confession about, or an explication of, primary religious experiences. Goldman thereby dramatically minimizes the role and the meaning of theodicy in religious life, no longer viewing it as its constitutive basis and turning it instead into a personal, random matter. Indeed, Goldman goes even a step further. He seeks to re-examine to what extent supporters of the theodicean discourse reflect a logical discourse that is not self-contradictory:

> At this point, there is room for showing to what extent we succeed in consistently clinging to our primary experiences and to what extent they lead us to contradictions. Furthermore, it sometimes appears to us that our primary experiences can be expressed in a statement that seems a logical conclusion of other statements we have accepted. Here too, there is room for considering whether these seemingly logical contexts do indeed exist. (15)

This move is even more radical than the previous one and, through it, Goldman points out not only the contingent and episodic nature of the theodicean discourse but also several of its fallacies.

The starting assumption of the theodicean discourse is God's characterization as a good God. Since God is perceived as morally good, an evil reality is perceived as a contradiction to God's existence. In this discourse, the good is apprehended as a "common attribute" of God and humanity, and this partnership enables the theodicean discourse. Goldman, however, argues that the good is not necessarily a common feature:

> When we speak of a red house, a red book, red wine, and so forth, the term "red" appears as a common attribute of various

> objects...By contrast, when we speak of a good book, a good cobbler, or a good teacher, the attribute leading us to claim that a particular one is good is different in each case. The term "good" is evaluative. In each of the contexts we use it, we assume a criterion that we generally use in that particular context and serves us to evaluate objects or actions positively or negatively. The use of the term "good" in two different contexts does not prove that we are using the same criterion in both cases. (15)

This analysis attests that the shared component of these modes of use in the term "good" is merely formal and therefore entirely empty: "good" is an expression of judgment and evaluation but not necessarily *moral* judgment and evaluation.[8] What, then, is the meaning of the term good in regard to God? Is it a moral evaluation? Goldman answers: "In the context of metaphysical methods used by classic theologians, the term [good] was intended as some kind of unique metaphysical perfection in God. Classic theology always stresses the metaphorical character of the term 'good' in reference to God" (15). Indeed, the use of the concept good in the sense pointed out by Goldman is prominent already in Platonic tradition: good is self-containment and independence from external elements. Plato formulates this as follows: "The good differs from everything else in a certain respect...A creature that possesses it permanently, completely, and absolutely, has never any need of anything else; its satisfaction is perfect."[9]

This analysis, however, does not entirely undermine the theodicean discourse because religious traditions in general, and Jewish ones in particular, abound with moral value statements about God. Even if Greek tradition and classic theology used "good" concerning God as denoting perfection and wholeness, we could still claim that religious traditions use "good" concerning God in its common moral denotation. To reject this option, Goldman engages in a series of moves. First, if we do indeed adhere to the language of Jewish tradition, assigning God only the quality of moral goodness would not fit the tradition itself:

> This is a matter of choosing the convenient verses. Other descriptions could be cited — "jealous and vengeful" "full of wrath" "puts no trust in his servants" — showing an entirely different attitude of the Creator to his creatures. A suitable choice of biblical verses could even support a description of a cruel despot that Christians and liberal critics sometimes wish to present as the prophets' description of God.[10]

Second, according to Goldman, Jewish tradition rejected "simplistic" theodicy as a response to the problem of "divine justice." Goldman illustrates this view with several examples, such as, for instance: "Isaiah ascribes to the Creator the proclamation 'I make peace and create evil,' which was imperative to eradicate idolatry and instill faith in the unity and uniqueness of God" (16). Relating to his general stance, Goldman then proceeds to claim: "I think this conclusion is unavoidable if we wish to preserve faith in God's uniqueness and, at the same time, arrive at a realistic evaluation of man's fate as a natural creature" (16).

Nevertheless, Goldman does understand that gross displays of evil could threaten religious faith and that the Holocaust, for instance, could lead to the negation of God's existence. Goldman's answer is that this inference from the Holocaust "is one-sided and subjective." Someone with a different "temperament" may not conclude from the Holocaust that "God is dead," but something entirely different:

> He might be so enthused by the miracle of the establishment of the State of Israel that the tragedy of European Jewry might sink in his eyes to a third or fourth level, by contrast with the

great salvation. Such a person would be amazed of how one fails to see the hand of God and his great rescue, so to whose temperament should the Creator adapt his qualities? (16)

These considerations void the theodicean discourse from meaning and portray it as merely an individual's confession about his world, his expectations, his insights, and his values. The fit between a "religious criterion" and the "criterion of 'a man of the world'" (16) is hard to substantiate.

Goldman knows that religious tradition includes statements that seem to contradict his position, and he contends with them:

> How, then, should we understand the end of Genesis 18 and Abraham's claim, "Shall not the judge of all the earth do right?" It seems nothing could be added to Maimonides' explanation of the Thirteen Principles. The attempt to understand God's attributes from his actions could even lead to contradictory results and meanings. He appears merciful and gracious and also vengeful and full of wrath. When the Torah describes his qualities, it does so in order to teach us what are the qualities we must see as divine in order to adhere to them. For us, this is also the meaning of the dialogue between Abraham and his God about Sodom. (16)

This interpretation of the biblical text is highly questionable. Goldman is indeed careful in his formulations, since he writes: "*For us*, this is also the meaning of the dialogue..." In other words, textual hermeneutics does not disclose the meaning of the text but its significance for us.

Through this view, Goldman hints at a more fundamental stance concerning the meaning of the canonical text, which he developed in several of his writings. In his programmatic article, "Scientific Statements and Religious Statements: Several Fundamental Differences," Goldman draws a distinction between religious and scientific statements. He points out, for instance, that affirming a scientific statement means affirming both the linguistic phrase and its contents. Affirming a religious statement, however, means affirming the statement but not necessarily the contents it expresses,[11] which may no longer be considered valid in light of cultural, historical, and personal changes. A claim that believers might affirm in certain cultural circumstances, could become unacceptable and even false in others. Advocates of the religious statement will then have to propose another interpretation.

Goldman reiterates this view of text in a general hermeneutical context, not necessarily a religious one:

> We are attentive to a text when seeking in it its message to us rather than viewing it merely as an object of philological-historical research. The text expresses a religious idea through concepts and metaphors germane to the culture and the environment where it was written. This message was transmitted in the context of the day-to-day life of its original recipients. An attentive interpretation is an attempt to decode the message in the concepts of our own *lebenswelt*.[12]

This view of the text points to Goldman's closeness to Rudolf Bultmann. Like Bultmann, Goldman recognizes the importance of demythologizing the text. Contrary to Bultmann, however, who proposes a hermeneutics where myth functions as a window that serves to expose the divine message or *kerygma*, Goldman views the hermeneutical process as the application of the text to the actual world. Goldman thereby suggests, as noted, an approach that balances the concrete and the religious contexts of human life. This distance between Goldman and Bultmann is also the distance between Goldman and Leibowitz, since Leibowitz interprets

Scripture statically, resting on his assumptions of correct and incorrect from the perspective of Judaism.[13]

Goldman's approach to theodicy, then, reflects a combination of analytical criticism and religious considerations, an attempt to offer an alternative reading of the biblical text, which suggests a classical theodicy, without contradicting critical assumptions. The very option of an alternative reading suffices to dismiss the use of the biblical text to support or reject the theodicy discourse.

Both Goldman and Leibowitz offer an alternative reading of classical sources and challenge traditional views, and both must therefore contend with the question of whether Jewish tradition fosters this alternative reading. Both claim it indeed does and, moreover, both claim that the rejection of theodicy represents a higher religious stage than its acceptance. Following is Goldman's formulation:

> One of the most important aims of religious education must be to raise popular religious consciousness to the level endorsed by deeper thinkers. This is not impossible. To us, the idea of repentance seems obvious, part of every religious Jew's fundamental assumptions. But what efforts did the prophets invest until the people came to this understanding! When Isaiah says that God will have mercy upon the wicked who forsakes His way, he is forced to add: "For my thoughts are not your thoughts." Ezekiel engages in the same debate: "Yet you say, The way of the Lord is unfair... Is my way unfair? Surely your ways are unfair!" Even among the prophets, some did not accept the notion of "repents of evil."[14]

According to Goldman, raising religious consciousness is tantamount to repentance: it is the amendment of religious life itself. Goldman, therefore, seeks in canonical religious sources the demand to change the original disposition, and renouncing the theodicean discourse is a change of this kind. Leibowitz's formulations on this count are even sharper. In his view, the theodicy problem is the believer's constant test. Passing this test means negating theodicy, since affirming theodicy means putting God to the human test. Leibowitz views Job as the paradigm of the believer who gradually changes his religious disposition because he understands God's absolute otherness and the gap that separates him from God. Leibowitz returns to this comparison between the sacrifice of Isaac and the Book of Job in several of his writings.[15] Despite this comparison, however, he points to one important difference between Abraham and Job that is relevant to our present discussion. Contrary to Abraham, Job undergoes a transformation process that turns him into a believer: "And if Job was a parable, what is the moral? The moral is the return to the sacrifice of Isaac and to faith for its own sake. Except that, in Job, faith for its own sake is a conclusion reached after a huge struggle, while Abraham reached a decision to believe in God because of his sheer divinity without any discussion, debate, or hesitation."[16]

What is the nature of Job's struggle? Leibowitz leads us through its various the stages and points to its significance. Job contends with the suffering and the pain that afflicts him:

> The argument rises to a level which becomes both loftier and more profound...It begins with Job's cry of protest against the iniquity in the governance of the world by its Creator, and his urgent demand for justice. Gradually, a new note is insinuated, which becomes more and more explicit as the argument proceeds. Job's suffering is no longer the focus of his protest; rather it is his inability to comprehend the meaning of his suffering...Job demands that God reveal to him why the world is as it is. The inscrutability of the creation, and of human fate in general and Job's in particular, has become a source of anguish deeper than the torment of the sense of iniquity.[17]

Job's friends suggest theodicy as a solution to his problem: "The three friends...deal with theodicy, that is, with the attempt to justify God, saying to him, you are forbidden to cast doubt on the fairness of divine judgment. Maybe you were not as righteous as you thought...and maybe you do not understand divine justice, the wisdom embodied in the way God conducts the world."[18]

Job rejects their view, not because he understands that theodicy is not a legitimate position but because it fails to answer his urgent questions.[19] At this stage, Job and his friends agree that theodicy is a legitimate assumption. Only God's answer out of the whirlwind results in Job's awaited religious transformation. He had so far held that faith means assuming that God works for human beings and that, therefore, their circumstances must be related to God's direct action. Now, Job understands that God does not work for human beings, and "that he must decide whether to commit himself to faith in God and to His service in the world as it is, to believe in Him and to serve Him not for his (Job's) benefit, but because of His divinity."[20] Job now realizes what Abraham had realized at the outset: theodicy is not a legitimate assumption, because it erodes the foundations of faith.

When Leibowitz discuses the interpretation that denies theodicy in Job's story, he generally appears to be insensitive to the hermeneutical problematic. The denial of theodicy is, as it were, the only meaning of Job's story. In one place, however, he does show awareness of this question and formulates it in terms of hermeneutical circularity. Leibowitz juxtaposes Karl Barth's interpretation, which resembles his own, to that of Iris Murdoch, which states we must do the good for its own sake and not for any ulterior end, an interpretation Leibowitz describes as atheistic. Facing these contradictory views, Leibowitz writes: "This fact confirms the rule that interpretation does not follow the text; instead, the meaning of the text follows its interpreter."[21]

Leibowitz is again revealed as close to Bultmann, who also assumes that the approach to the biblical text is guided by religious presuppositions.[22] Bultmann, though, assumes that textual interpretation is existential and the believer's individual and historical meaning is therefore significant. By contrast, Leibowitz perceives the believer in ahistorical and a-concrete terms. The believer is all believers, and Job's answer is therefore the answer of all believers: theodicy is an illegitimate element in the world.

Based on this assumption, Leibowitz returns repeatedly to the Sodom story. Goldman approaches this text aware of his hermeneutical tools, that is, of the interpreter's disposition as conferring meaning upon Abraham's story in Sodom. By contrast, Leibowitz tries to read events differently: "As the advocate of Sodom's defendants, Abraham adduces claims of justice, fairness, and compassion, which are human categories about which he 'kindly' concedes to argue with God. But when his faith is put to the test — he remains silent."[23]

Beyond these differences, however, both thinkers agree that theodicy is a problem of the *faithful*, not of *faith*. Indeed, it is the faithful's supreme test: will they believe in God as God, whose role is to regulate human life. "Genuine" believers know that evil and suffering are not a religious problem but part of the natural reality. Even if they find it hard to reach this insight, this is indeed the concern of faith and this is the challenge it poses to human beings. Changing the believer's dispositions is thus an expression of actual faith.

The Social-Existentialist Critique

Joseph B. Soloveitchik devoted two essays to the theodicy question: "*Kol Dodi Dofek*,"[24] and a later one, "A Halakhic Approach to Suffering."[25] In "Kol Dodi Dofek," Soloveitchik argues that evil and suffering can be discussed at two levels of existence: the "existence of fate" and the "existence of destiny." Soloveitchik describes a fate existence through a terminology drawing on existentialist tradition as one in which individuals perceive themselves as objects: "His being is empty, lacking any inwardness, any independence, any selfhood."[26] In a destiny existence, people will perceive themselves as dynamic, influential creatures:

> It is an active mode of existence, one wherein man confronts the environment into which he was thrown, possessed of an understanding of his uniqueness, of his special worth, of his freedom, and of his ability to struggle with his external circumstances without forfeiting either his independence or his selfhood... Man is born like an object, dies like an object, but possesses the ability to live like a subject, like a creator, an innovator, who can impress his own individual seal upon his life and can extricate himself from a mechanical type of existence and enter into a creative, active mode of being. (54)

Soloveitchik argues that the question about the existence of evil cannot be detached from the individual's mode of conscious existence: consciousness will shape a person's attitude towards suffering and evil. People who perceive their existence in terms of fate will contend differently with this question than those who perceive their existence in terms of destiny. One who perceives existence in terms of fate contends with the problem of evil in two stages. The first stage is marked by confusion: "Man the object, bound in the chains of an existence of compulsion, stands perplexed and confused before that great mystery — suffering... his being, shattered and torn, contradicts itself and negates its own value and worth." (52)

After the deep psychological upheaval, the sufferer strives to find a rational explanation to suffering and evil, to return the shattered psychological harmony. The yearning for a rational explanation engenders what Soloveitchik terms the "metaphysics of evil" (53), which enables the person to reach an accommodation with evil through "the denial of the existence of evil in the world" (53).

The link that Soloveitchik traces between the conscious disposition and the way of contending with suffering and evil is particularly illuminating. People who perceive themselves as objects thrown into existence cannot strive for change in existence itself, since the object is a final given. Their only course, then, is metaphysics, which does not demand action and does not impose responsibility because it explains what already is. This analysis is thus a conscious critique of the history of our contest with the problem of evil. According to this critique, posing the question in a classic metaphysical context blurs the character of human existence. In existentialist terms, the traditional discussion of theodicy is not an authentic human stand.

But Soloveitchik's critique is not confined to the conscious disposition. In his view, the classic approach to evil is based on an ethical-social mistake: "the denial of the existence of evil." Prima facie, this claim is exaggerated, since purposeful or causal explanations do not question the very existence of evil but place it within a broader conceptual framework. Only neo-Platonic metaphysical theories denied evil's very existence. This critique requires a clarification of Soloveitchik's argument. In his view, every explanation of evil implies a denial of the negative, destructive dimension of evil, since the explanation that makes evil understandable incorporates it into the rational conceptual framework of the divine good. Soloveitchik therefore argues that the fundamental features of evil as negation and destruction are denied in the metaphysical explanation. Accepting evil means accepting it as a non-reductive datum exposed in reality. This critique originates in a realistic orientation toward reality: "Judaism, with its realistic approach to man and his place in the world, understood that evil cannot be blurred or camouflaged...Evil is an undeniable fact. There is evil, there is suffering, there are hellish torments in this world... It is impossible to overcome the hideousness of evil through philosophico-speculative thought" (53).

Contrary to this approach to the problem of evil, Soloveitchik presents the concept of destiny. As opposed to the "man of fate," whose own self-perception is as a finished object, the "man of destiny" diverts the question away from metaphysics. A consciousness of destiny enables one to accept evil as is and to cope with it:

> In the realm of destiny man recognizes the world as it is and does not wish to use harmonistic formulas in order to gloss over and conceal evil. The man of destiny is highly realistic and does not flinch from confronting evil face to face. His approach is an ethico-halakhic one, devoid of the slightest speculative-metaphysical coloration...In this dimension the center of gravity shifts from the causal and teleological aspect of evil...to its practical aspect...We ask neither about the cause of evil nor about its purpose, but rather about how it might be mended and elevated. How shall a person act in a time of trouble? What ought a man to do so that he not perish in his afflictions? (55–56)

From this perspective, the question of theodicy ceases to be legitimate and the ethical question arises instead: what should a person do given that evil actually exists? Whereas the answer to the former question is metaphysical theory, the answer to the latter one is action. Failure to measure up to the challenge posed by evil and the return to metaphysics imply the return to a non-authentic consciousness. Diverting the problem of evil from metaphysics to ethics reflects a subjective shift typical of contemporary Jewish thought. Through this shift, not God but individuals and the concrete reality within which they live become the bearers of religious experience and consciousness.[27]

This change in Soloveitchik's thought originates in two sources: Hermann Cohen's legacy and existentialist tradition. Cohen vehemently rejects recourse to metaphysics as a way of contending with suffering:

> The metaphysics of suffering, which considers suffering as the fate of mankind, or even more ambiguously, as the fate of all living creatures, does not belong to an earnest religion: its earnestness has nothing to do with the play of poetry and art. Suffering only reaches ethical precision as social suffering...Only the religion of reason is moral religion, and only moral religion is truthful and true religion.[28]

Cohen's discussion of suffering highlights the social dimension of suffering as related to reciprocity in human relations. For Cohen, true religiosity contends with this social reality and not with the metaphysics of suffering. Soloveitchik, who dealt at length with Cohen's philosophy and was influenced by it,[29] took from him the shift from metaphysics to practice and translated it into existentialist terminology. The categories of "fate" and "destiny" are a translation of the conventional existentialist analysis about authentic and unauthentic ways of life. Soloveitchik does not eschew Heideggerian terminology, which expresses the relationship between the two ways of life. Though thrown into existence, we are not denied our freedom.[30] In Heidegger's term, the person is a "thrown possibility." When faced with suffering, confidence in our existence collapses. In existentialist terms, this is the experience of anxiety. Suffering shatters the harmony of human existence and forces us to face its anxiety, and the reaction should not be a denial of reality but a return to contend with it. Finally, contrary to Hermann Cohen, Soloveitchik does not formulate the problem of suffering as a social issue pivoted on interpersonal relations but as an oppressing personal question: "What ought a man to do so that he not perish in his afflictions?"[31]

For Leibowitz, the meaning of suffering is a stage in the education toward faith but not part of faith itself, which overrides the meaning of suffering. Soloveitchik turns the tide: the meaning of suffering becomes the heart of the drama in religious life. He agrees with Leibowitz's rejection of metaphysics, but he does not agree with the rejection of the question; rather, this question will become the catalyst of the shift from metaphysics to praxis.

On closer scrutiny, it appears that Soloveitchik does not exhaust this shift. He chooses the practical shift as a default option — given the human inability to understand suffering, all that is left is to contend with it:

> Only if man could grasp the world as a whole would he be able to gain a perspective on the essential nature of evil. However, as long as man's apprehension is limited and distorted, as long as he perceives only isolated fragments of the cosmic drama and the mighty epic of history, he remains unable to penetrate into the secret lair of suffering and evil...We, alas, view the world from its reverse side. We are, therefore, unable to grasp the all-encompassing framework of being. And it is only within that framework that it is possible to discern the divine plan, the essential nature of the divine actions.[32]

From this perspective, the shift from metaphysics to praxis reflects the limitations of human cognition rather than the acceptance of metaphysics' fundamental irrelevance. David Hartman formulates this critique as follows:

> Although Maimonides and Soloveitchik evidently gave up hope of making sense of God's justice, their explanation of human history still operates with this model. While Soloveitchik does not suppose that we shall ever achieve a full rational comprehension of God's actions in history, he does believe that, in principle, were we able to look at the world from God's vantage point, we would understand how all of human suffering is compatible with the belief in God as a loving Creator and just Lord of History…believing in principle that events in history are the carriers of God's will, Soloveitchik looks forward to the eschatological moment of unity between nature and history, when the God of Creation will be manifestly mediated in His full loving justice in historical reality. In the meantime, however, the manner in which His justice operates is partly or largely inscrutable.[33]

This critique, which emphasizes the fact that the shift to practice does not entirely replace metaphysics, returns in Soloveitchik's attempt to answer the question he had posed, "What ought a man to do so that he not perish in his afflictions?" We would expect a practical answer to this question, pointing to the person's obligation to act in the world, yet his answer is:

> The halakhic answer to this question is very simple. Afflictions come to elevate a person, to purify and sanctify his spirit, to cleanse and purge it of the dross of superficiality and vulgarity, to refine his soul and to broaden his horizons. In a word, the function of suffering is to mend that which is flawed in

an individual's personality. The Halakhah teaches us that the sufferer commits a grave sin if he allows his troubles to go to waste and remain without meaning or purpose. Suffering occurs in the world in order to contribute something to man, in order that atonement be made for him...From out of its midst the sufferer must arise ennobled and refined, clean and pure.[34]

Soloveitchik offers a teleological answer to this practical question. In this world, suffering has a purpose. Indeed, this purpose is not part of the purpose of universal or Jewish history but part of a series of conditions through which individuals amend and refine their being. The difference between this response and the traditional teleological response ultimately rests in the identification of a specific purpose for the existence of evil.

"Kol Dodi Dofek" shows Soloveitchik oscillating between metaphysical and practical language. The metaphysical language features in the text cited above and in the essay's general plan, intended to point out that Jewish history has a purpose. Contrary to traditional teleological approaches claiming that history realizes a given purpose, Soloveitchik offers a more complex version whereby God provides opportunities, to which human responses are expected. These opportunities are hints, as it were, of God's desirable goals. Interpreting and applying these hints is incumbent on human beings. In this sense, this approach assumes that the teleological movement of history is contingent on humanity. History, then, is a synergistic event unfolding as a partnership between God and the divine ends on the one hand and the human ability to respond to God's hints on the other. Suffering plays a significant role in God's hints, as an opportunity through which God suggests a new possibility. In the context of this approach, argues Soloveitchik, the Holocaust is a kind of occurrence that produced the State of Israel (69).

CHAPTER FIVE

Contrary to this metaphysical language, the text includes many expressions reflecting the adoption of a practical language. This is prominent in Soloveitchik's analysis of God's response to Job's suffering. Soloveitchik holds that Job's suffering is a test that will show whether he is still immersed in his egoism or will turn his gaze to the other and share in his suffering. Job, argues Soloveitchik, passed the test:

> In a moment he discovered its plural form, he descried the attribute of *hesed* which sweeps the individual from the private to the public domain. He began to live the life of the community, to feel its griefs, to mourn over its calamities, and to rejoice in its happiness. The afflictions of Job found their true rectification when he extricated himself from his fenced-in confines, and the divine wrath abated: "And the Lord turned the captivity of Job, when he prayed for his friends" (Job 42: 10).[35]

This is a particularly prominent illustration of this trend because it inadvertently combines metaphysical and practical language. God's initiative — a test that Job passes — has a purpose, but this purpose is translated into the practical-interpersonal field.

This opaqueness gradually disappears in Soloveitchik's second essay, where he again contends with the question of suffering and evil. In "Kol Dodi Dofek," as noted, Soloveitchik assumes that "Judaism, with its realistic approach to man and his place in the world, understood that evil cannot be blurred or camouflaged" (53). Now, Soloveitchik seeks to draw a distinction between two different contexts for approaching suffering and evil: "topical Halakhah" and "thematic Halakhah." Topical Halakhah focuses on concrete reality. It does not offer a conceptual framework for a cognitive interpretation of reality, but a system of positive and formalistic attitudes for approaching reality in order to shape it:

"The Halakhah does not venture outside of the human world, and the human world is a very small world. Whatever is relevant to man, to his interests, to his self-fulfillment and his self-realization is relevant and pertinent to the Halakhah. Whatever is irrelevant to man is irrelevant to the topical Halakhah."[36] Topical Halakhah is not interested in understanding the human creature in metaphysical terms, as an idea, but rather as an individual entity: "The Halakhah insists that nothing, not the idea nor the collective, should supplant the single transient and frail individual" (94).

Contrary to topical Halakhah, the concern of thematic Halakhah is the general, conceptual value system. This conceptual framework, which Soloveitchik leaves somewhat vague, can be understood through its contrast with topical Halakhah. Whereas topical Halakhah focuses on concrete existence and relates to it through a normative system of duties, thematic Halakhah creates a cohesive conceptual system of immanent meaning. This system exceeds the concrete and encompasses totality, "thematic Halakhah extends into infinity and eternity" (95). This difference between the two models comes to the fore in the attitude to suffering. According to Soloveitchik, thematic Halakhah enables and affirms theodicy: "Within the thematic Halakhah, we find a theodicy or, to be more precise, a metaphysic of suffering. Judaism, at the level of axiology or at the level of transcendental reference, did develop a metaphysic of evil, or, I would rather say, of suffering, of the passional experience" (95).

Soloveitchik argues that theodicy developed by drawing a distinction between suffering and evil. Suffering is perceived as a subjective experience, a kind of feeling, whereas evil describes an objective reality (95). This distinction enables to separate human suffering from concrete reality. We tend to ascribe suffering and pain to the objective existence of evil. Thematic Halakhah does not deny suffering, but claims that its source is not any objective evil: "This sharp distinction between evil and pathos opened up to the thematic Halakhah new vistas which explained suffering. It did so by denying the reality of evil in a twofold way, by introducing transcendentalism and universalism" (96).

Soloveitchik claims that evil is removed in two moves: the first, which he called the transcendental principle, is based on the expansion of ontological consciousness. If reality begins and ends with the concrete experience, the presence of evil undermines order and justice. But "evil vanishes as soon as the threshold of man's ontological consciousness is raised from the order of the sensible, phenomenal, and transient to a higher order of the absolute and eternal" (94). Soloveitchik illustrates this approach through several sources. Thus, for instance, he quotes the Talmud: "Thus the Holy One brings suffering upon the righteous in the world in order that they may inherit the future world... (*Kiddushin* 40b)" (97). By including the world to come within the concept of reality, evil is removed altogether (97).

Another source that Soloveitchik quotes is the *Guide of the Perplexed* III: 51, where Maimonides contends with the most dreadful of all evils — death — by idealizing old age as a reality that, together with a decaying body, brings with it a strengthened consciousness: "His joy is that knowledge grows greater, and his love for the object of his knowledge more intense, and it is in this great delight that the soul separates from the body" (98). Thematic Halakhah, then, neutralizes the terror of death by glorifying the rational element as the basis for the process of the soul's separation from the body. Since reality is not identical to sensorial bodily reality but to the rational reality that we approach as we approach death, its evil is removed.

The second principle in disposing of evil is the universalistic principle: "Thematic Halakhah maintains the universal doctrine of suffering that evil as a universal entity does not exist, that it is nothing but a chimera, just a figment of our fantasy. Suffering and misery are due to the accidental and contingent character of our existence, which is confined to a narrow segment of being" (98).

Indeed, not only does suffering reflect human contingency but "sufferings of the individual are ministerial to a higher good within a universal order...Evil is not an essential part of being if the latter is placed in the perspective of totality" (98).

In "Kol Dodi Dofek," Soloveitchik rejects these approaches by invoking halakhic realism. In "Approach to Suffering," he withdraws from this position because thematic Halakhah, which is part of Judaism, contends with suffering and evil by endorsing a metaphysical approach, to which theodicy provides the main access. Soloveitchik rejects this view through an argument combining existentialist and modernist outlooks, and claims that thematic Halakhah cannot console human suffering:

> Can such a metaphysic bring solace and comfort to modern man who finds himself in crisis, facing the monstrosity of evil, and to whom existence and absurdity appear to be bound up inextricably together? Is there in the transcendental and universal message a potential of remedial energy?...I can state with all candor that I personally have not been successful in my attempts to spell out this metaphysic in terms meaningful to the distraught individual who floats aimlessly in all-encompassing blackness...I tried but failed, I think, miserably, like the friends of Job. (99–100)

This text represents the radical turnabout in Soloveitchik's position: the criterion for evaluating the metaphysical theory is not the measure of its rationality or sophistication, but its ability to respond to true human needs. Its acceptance is contingent on its therapeutic powers, its "remedial energy."

Soloveitchik's use of this criterion, however, is problematic. This criterion allows him to claim that thematic Halakhah could provide an answer, at least in principle. The preliminary condition for this is "indomitable faith and a passionate transcendental experience." Thematic Halakhah, then, has lost its comforting power only within the confines of modern life, where people are detached and alienated. This approach not only minimizes but entirely cancels out the religious meaning of the alternative approach to suffering and evil. On the other hand, Soloveitchik identifies thematic Halakhah (in this text as well as in "Kol Dodi Dofek") with Job's friends, who offer theodicy as the response to Job's suffering. The problematic of thematic Halakhah, then, is not contingent on modern reality, and reflects the gap between Halakhah and the angst of concrete existence. This trend fits in with the fact that contending with evil in the context of topical Halakhah does provide an answer to distress. Since topical Halakhah could not possibly be viewed as modern, the human distress to which this Halakhah is responding is not an expression of detachment and alienation from religious tradition but the basic human stance vis-à-vis existence. This ambivalence vis-à-vis modernity is indeed a permanent component of Soloveitchik's thought.

Contrary to thematic Halakhah, the attitude of topical Halakhah to evil and suffering is entirely different. The realism of "Kol Dodi Dofek," which was a typical characteristic of Judaism, is now confined to topical Halakhah: "Realism and individualism, ineradicably ingrained in the very essence of the topical Halakhah, prevented it from casting off the burden of the awareness of evil" (100).

Topical Halakhah sees concrete reality in all its manifestations as the ultimate datum, which cannot be explained through a metaphysical theory:

> The topical Halakhah lacked neither the candor nor the courage to admit publicly that evil does exist, and it pleaded ignorance as to its justification and necessity. The topical Halakhah is an open-eyed, tough observer of things and events and, instead of indulging in a speculative metaphysic, acknowledged boldly both the reality of evil and its irrationality, its absurdity. (100)

The assumption that evil is absurd eliminates the option of contending with it through the "metaphysic of suffering" (102). Instead, topical Halakhah develops an "ethic of suffering" (102). This ethic is not meant to confer ontological meaning on suffering but to develop a human approach toward it. An ethic, contrary to a metaphysic, requires that we deliver ourselves to suffering. We need not surrender to evil, but we must accept it exists and engage in a ceaseless struggle with it.

In "Kol Dodi Dofek," the main way of contending with evil is through reflection — we turn inwards and see suffering and evil as a voyage of self-improvement, in which suffering redeems and refines. In the later essay, the contest with suffering unfolds by turning outwards to existence itself. Adopting topical Halakhah leads to a practical struggle with suffering and evil.

With great sensitivity, Soloveitchik recognizes that this approach to suffering "differs little from the attitude usually adopted by modern man toward evil. Modern man...is sensitive to the disorder and disharmony with which the universe is paced, and he is far from indulging in a happy-go-lucky contentment...Otherwise, he would not work so hard in order to find cures for some incurable diseases" (104).

Topical Halakhah, then, is compatible with the modern stance vis-à-vis the world, which refuses to surrender to the conditions of reality and constantly strives to amend it and reshape it. In this sense, thematic Halakhah is an obstacle to the amendment of reality. A theodicy that reconstructs harmony in theory makes the actual struggle against evil redundant.

Soloveitchik's outlook on this count resembles that of Camus, who also refuses to accept an other-worldly interpretation of the question of evil. Rieux, the doctor in *The Plague*, rejects Tarrou's attempts to explain evil. For Camus, the assumption about a metaphysical-transcendent order hinders the struggle against evil and leads to passivity. Rieux, who speaks for Camus, states: "Mightn't it be better for God if we refuse to believe in Him, and struggle with all our might against death, without raising our eyes towards the heaven where He sits in silence?"[37]

According to Camus, the struggle against suffering should be a driving force for humanity. Rieux claims that metaphysics should be rejected in favor of compassion and openness to suffering: "For the moment I know this; there are sick people and they need curing. Later on, perhaps, they'll think things over, and so shall I."[38] Both Camus and Soloveitchik agree that we contend with evil through ethic. They disagree regarding the relationship between ethic and the religious stance. Camus holds that an ethic placing the suffering human being at its center must dispose of God and religion, which hinder practical action. Soloveitchik, by contrast, holds that this ethic can be a religious gesture of faith. Indeed, human beings should not turn to transcendence, but normative action per se is an affirmation that transcendence is present in this world.

In sum, Soloveitchik offers a complex model for coping with suffering and evil. He recognizes evil as a concrete given and, therefore, tends to reject theodicy as a way of contending with it. Whereas in "Kol Dodi Dofek" he rejects theodicy entirely, in "Approach to Suffering" he recognizes the presence of a theodicy trend in Jewish tradition. And yet, precisely in his attempt to deny the theodicy trend, Soloveitchik fails to displace the struggle against evil and suffering to the socio-political arena. The language of "Kol Dodi Dofek" points to personal fulfillment rather than to praxis, contrary to "Approach to Suffering," where Soloveitchik presents a practical blueprint for contending with suffering. Hence, whereas in "Kol Dodi Dofek" Hermann Cohen's influence translates into existentialist language, in "Approach to Suffering" he returns to Cohen's social approach.

Soloveitchik's approach to evil and suffering is that of a believer, so that the questions related to the religious meaning of this approach require further consideration. If the existence of evil should indeed be admitted, and if Jewish tradition, or at least its main stream, demands the adoption of a practical approach toward suffering and evil, what theology could substantiate this outlook? The fact that topical Halakhah is part of Jewish tradition raises the question: how to understand the fact that the giver of the Torah allows a reality of evil and suffering and establishes a Halakhah that acknowledges this reality? Soloveitchik's philosophy provides no answer to the contradiction between a reality of evil and God's goodness. Concern with this missing theological project is a unique feature of the philosophy of David Hartman, Soloveitchik's student. A hallmark of his philosophical endeavor is the removal of the theodicy trend beside the substantiation of a theology that enables this removal.

Hartman's main innovation is a renewed analysis of the religious-psychological role that theodicy had played in religious life. Hartman thereby reframes the theodicean discourse. A philosopher or a theologian dealing with the problem of theodicy is troubled by the contradiction between God's goodness and omnipotence versus the existence of evil in the world. In the context of religious life, however, the problem is entirely different:

> How do we respond to events that can call into question our whole identity as God's relational partners? Can we allow ourselves to embrace a personal God, knowing that chaos can at any moment invade our reality and arbitrarily nullify all our efforts and expectations? Do we have the strength to open ourselves to a personal God in a world filled with unpredictable suffering? When her child dies, the question a mother faces is less how to explain the logic of Torah's omnipotence than whether she has the strength and emotional energy to love again.
>
> From the anthropological perspective on the problem of evil, therefore, the prime concern is not so much to defend the notions of divine justice and power. It is rather, as in other personal relationships, to determine what measure of continuity, stability, and predictability can enable the relationship with God to survive all shocks.[39]

Hartman's philosophy, therefore, replaces the question of theodicy, which is metaphysical, with the question of existentialism: how and whether believers can maintain their religious identity given the existence of evil and suffering. This shift follows from an understanding of the destructive role of evil and suffering in human life. Suffering erodes human confidence in existence: "One of the dimensions of suffering that often makes it unbearable is its arbitrariness. Suffering may involve not only physical pain, but also the disorienting terror resulting from the sufferer's belief that he is the victim of blind and irrational forces."[40]

In *Crisis and Leadership*, Hartman holds that a person can contend with suffering "if he is convinced of some underlying purpose that gives meaning and order to his world."[41] The metaphysical explanation of theodicy could meet this need by placing "a person's immediate experience within a broader framework, such as a grand plan or dramatic story spanning all of history."[42]

In this text, Harman lays the foundation for what will become a dominant element of his philosophy — the test of theodicy is not theoretical but practical. Theodicy cannot provide an absolute speculative solution to the problem of evil in the world; its ability to provide an answer is contingent upon the particular disposition of those who need it. Theodicy, then, has a socio-political rather than a metaphysical role. Hartman illustrates this approach with an analysis of various solutions that Maimonides proposes for suffering and pain. In his view, Maimonides was aware of the socio-political role of theodicy. Therefore: "In addressing the sufferer, one must be sensitive to the specific needs of the person in question. Because Maimonides [in the "Epistle to Yemen"] is trying to comfort and encourage a suffering community, he uses multiple models and suggestions directed at the different types of people comprising his audience."[43] This functional perception of theodicy enables Hartman to make two moves. The first is to explain the existence of a tradition endorsing theodicy in Judaism, and the second is to dismiss the metaphysical value of this approach and reexamine it. His conclusion is that theodicy is a cognitive answer to the problem of evil, whose sole test is the measure of its acceptance:

> A constant gap between our perception of our relationship to a personal God and the reality of the world that we believe He created and rules is liable to give rise to repeated frustration. The question then is: How long can any attempt to cope with the frustration succeed in containing it? How long is it before we decide that the relationship no longer exists or that it is not worth having? To this question there is no single universal answer applicable equally to all human beings.[44]

Hartman can now argue that the various rabbinic responses to suffering, relating to it as "chastenings of love" or calls to repentance,[45] can hardly be considered decisive answers to this question. In principle, we can hardly predict what response will comfort a suffering soul, and this is a matter contingent on the difference between human dispositions:

> Some find the unpredictable dimensions of reality to be [so] overwhelming...For them, suffering is bearable if it results from the limitations of finite human beings, but it becomes terrifying and demonic if it is seen as part of the scheme of their all-powerful Creator. Others would find life unbearably chaotic if they could not believe that suffering, tragedy, and death were part of God's plan for the world feeling that there is meaning and order in the world and that God in His wisdom decided to terminate the life of their loved ones makes their tragedy bearable. (202)

This approach continues the programmatic line that Soloveitchik had set originally, but is expressed more coherently in Hartman's thought. From a pragmatic-empirical vantage point, the traditional theological discussion of the problem of evil is merely a "disruption," since human beings do not opt for faith (or the alternative) as a function of theological or theodicean propositions (201-202). We can handle evil only by shifting the center of gravity to a life of actual faith (202). Hartman speaks of this displacement as a transition from "philosophical theology" to "religious anthropology" (187). The crucial question is not the one bearing on theology and theodicy but the religious-existentialist question. In this discussion, the key issue is the person's ability to go on believing when faced with evil, not the justification of God. In Hartman's terms, the main question is not theodicy, but the modes of response to suffering (16).

Existentialist faith assumes that, structurally, the relationship with God resembles human interactions (187, 202). Human relationships are constantly tested and contingent on real events, as well as on the baggage borne by each individual. Individuals have expectations from God, and relate to God as loving and just. The rift of evil casts doubts on the possibility of sustaining this view. People do not ask themselves whether God is right, but "how can I sustain commitment to a way of life predicated on God's covenantal love and justice?" (188). This question is doomed to remain open, since no universal, metaphysical single solution can provide answers to human distress.

For Hartman, the practical-existential shift of the problem of evil and suffering is anchored in two mutually related considerations: one is human responsibility and freedom, and the other is covenantal theology. The theodicean view of suffering could hinder human readiness to act — if suffering, evil and pain are justified, why struggle against them?: "If we are to uphold the dignity implied by the notion of the covenant, with its full respect for ourselves as rational and moral beings, we must reject attempts to see all of nature and history as mediating God's personal will" (276). This consideration is based both on the primary affirmation of human rationality and of our value as human creatures, and on the appropriate theology. The primary affirmation of human value is embodied in the refusal to adopt a disposition of constant guilt. This disposition is imperative for the endorsement of a theodicean view — if the God that is the cause of suffering and evil is right, human beings are guilty. Relentless guilt is a deep injury to a sense of worth, to the possibility of experiencing ourselves as free agents allowed to operate according to our own understanding (276). This theodicy, then, "in no way fits what we know about ourselves in reality" (276). In sum, a theodicy that justifies God humiliates human beings, affronts their dignity, their understanding of reality, and their freedom.

In Hartman's thought, this incongruence between human worthiness and a theodicean viewpoint conveys a deep incompatibility between theodicy and covenantal theology. Hartman's philosophical endeavor is an attempt to reframe covenantal theology, which allows to present evil and suffering in religious-existentialist terms rather than in a theodicean context.

Covenantal theology is based on the assumption that God and human beings act as partners entering a covenant — on the one hand, God as a personality, and on the other, the Jewish collective. Hartman clarifies in his analysis the meaning of this interpersonal partnership. The God of the covenant is not the "Aristotelian God" but a personality, meaning that causality categories are irrelevant: as a personality is multifaceted and unresponsive to this category, so is God (200).

Similarly, the human partner also deserves dignity and respect: "the covenant encourages human dignity and initiative" (187). The covenant, wherein God enters into a partnership with human beings as creatures who are at once limited and free, is an affirmation of human existence in its finitude.[46]

Covenantal theology is based on a limitation of God's role in the natural and historical world on the one hand, and on the imposition of responsibility on human beings on the other. The displacement of the burden of responsibility is evident, above all, in God's removal from nature and history:

> We do not have to seek a personal manifestation of God in the events of nature or of history. Suffering and human tragedy are not signs of divine rejection or punishment. God's providential concern is manifested in the guidance provided by the Torah. God is present as a personal reality through the hearing of *mitzvot*. (17)

The meaning of this displacement implies a recognition of history's and nature's neutral character. Human beings are sovereign agents in history, and historical events are within the realm of human responsibility. The world has the regularity of nature, in which God never interferes. For Hartman, this approach is fully evident in Maimonides' philosophy, which he analyzes at length (232–236). The neutralization of history and of nature is a full affirmation of reality: the only reality is immanent reality. It is neither justified by invoking a theodicy nor is it a stage in an eschatological outlook:

> It does not aim to redeem the creature from creaturely finitude, nor does it point to an existence not shot through by the problematics of human freedom and temporality...the God of Sinai does not promise that history will be secure against the misuse of human freedom. Failure, uncertainty, and unpredictability are permanent features of life under the covenant, since human freedom is constitutive of the covenantal relationship. (261)

This theological framework clarifies the depth of the chasm between Soloveitchik and Hartman. In "Kol Dodi Dofek," as noted, Soloveitchik yearns for a theodicy. This yearning does indeed disappear in his later essay, "Approach to Suffering," but there too he acknowledges the possibility of a theodicean context as a plausible approach for contending with evil. Like Leibowitz and Goldman, Hartman too utterly rejects the theodicean option, and criticizes Soloveitchik because he longs for "the eschatological moment of unity between nature and history, when the God of Creation will be manifestly mediated in His full loving justice in historical reality" (267–268). This criticism does not apply to Soloveitchik's later essay, which was not available to Hartman when writing his critique. But Soloveitchik posits the option of thematic Halakhah, which is rejected in Hartman's covenantal theology. In sum, in Hartman's philosophy, human evil and pain are a constant challenge to human responsibility. As members of the covenantal community, human beings should not expect theodicean explanations or eschatological redemption. They should instead struggle against evil, as a way of realizing their freedom.

The common denominator of all the thinkers discussed in this chapter is the rejection of theodicy as a metaphysical problem and its transformation into a practical question concerned with life itself. Goldman and Leibowitz hold that theodicy is the testing point for the disposition of the faithful and the way they organize their world. By contrast, Soloveitchik and Hartman hold that the theodicy problem is a replacement of the genuine problem: human responsibility for the condition of the world.

Notes

1   For an analysis of this solution and its limitations, see Avi Sagi and Daniel Statman, *Religion and Morality*, trans. Batya Stein (Amsterdam and Atlanta, GA: Rodopi, 1995), 136–138.
2   Eliezer Goldman, *Expositions and Inquiries: Jewish Thought in Past and Present*, ed. Avi Sagi and Daniel Statman (in Hebrew) (Jerusalem: Magnes Press, 1996), 361.
3   Ibid.
4   Yeshayahu Leibowitz, *Judaism, the Jewish People, and the State of Israel* (in Hebrew) (Tel Aviv: Schocken, 1976) (henceforth *Yahadut*), 358–359.
5   Goldman, *Expositions and Inquiries*, 362.
6   See Avi Sagi, *Tradition vs. Traditionalism: Contemporary Perspectives in Jewish Thought*, trans. Batya Stein (Amsterdam-New York: Rodopi, 2008), 43–60.
7   See Eliezer Goldman, "Divine Good and Human Good" (in Hebrew), *News of the Religious Kibbutz* 107 (March 1955). Because of the fragmented, local context of the article, we did not include it in the main anthology of Goldman's writings, and I now correct that mistake.
8   Richard Hare, who may have influenced Goldman, made this claim about moral discourse itself: in moral language, the term good

denotes what is worthy and the term bad what is unworthy, but this language use need not lead us to conclude the existence of one sole moral criterion. See Richard M. Hare, *The Language of Morals* (Oxford: Oxford University Press, 1952), particularly ch. 6.

9   *The Collected Dialogues of Plato*, ed. Edith Hamilton and Huntington Cairns (New York: Bollingen Foundation, 1961), 1108. For a discussion about this perception of the good and its development, see Arthur O. Lovejoy, *The Great Chain of Being: A Study in the History of an Idea* (Cambridge, MA: Harvard University Press, 1970), 39–45.

10 Goldman, "Divine Good and Human Good," 16.

11 Goldman, *Expositions and Inquiries*, 343–345.

12 Avi Sagi, "Religious Language in the Modern World: An Interview with Eliezer Goldman" (in Hebrew), *Gilayion* (August 1995), 13.

13 For further discussion, see Sagi, *Tradition vs. Traditionalism*, 122–125.

14 Goldman, "Divine Good and Human Good," 17.

15 *Yahadut*, 391–394; Yeshayahu Leibowitz, *Five Books of Faith* (in Hebrew) (Jerusalem: Keter, 1995), 36.

16 Ibid., 29–30.

17 *Judaism*, 50.

18 Leibowitz, *Five Books of Faith*, 31–32.

19 Ibid., 32.

20 *Judaism*, 52.

21 Leibowitz, *Five Books of Faith*, 39.

22 Rudolf Bultmann, "Is Exegesis without Presuppositions Possible?" in *The Hermeneutics Reader*, ed. Kurt Muller-Vollmer (New York: Continuum, 1989), 242–247.

23 *Yahadut*, 393. See also Yeshayahu Leibowitz, *Seven Years of Talks on the Weekly Torah Reading* (in Hebrew) (Jerusalem: n. p., 2000), 85; idem, *Notes on the Weekly Torah Reading* (in Hebrew) (Jerusalem: Academon, 1988), 21; idem, *Talks on Maimonides' Eight Chapters* (in Hebrew) (Jerusalem: Keter, 1986), 197; idem, *Five Books of Faith*, 22–23.

24 Joseph Dov Soloveitchik, "Kol Dodi Dofek: It Is the Voice of My Beloved that Knocketh" (henceforth "Kol Dodi Dofek"), in *Theological and Halakhic Reflections on the Holocaust*, ed. Bernhard Rosenberg (New York: Ktav, 1992), 57–117.

NOTES

25. Joseph B. Soloveitchik, "A Halakhic Approach to Suffering," (henceforth "Approach to Suffering") in *Out of the Whirlwind: Essays on Mourning, Suffering, and the Human Condition*, ed. David Shatz, Joel B. Wolowelsky and Reuven Ziegler (New York: Ktav, 2003), 86–115.
26. "Kol Dodi Dofek," 52.
27. For further discussion of the subjective shift, see Sagi, *Tradition and Traditionalism*, 21–24.
28. Hermann Cohen, *Religion of Reason Out of the Sources of Judaism*, trans. Simon Kaplan (New York: Frederick Ungar, 1972), 135.
29. See Aviezer Ravitzky, "Rabbi J. B. Soloveitchik on Human Knowledge: Between Maimonides and neo-Kantian Philosophy." *Modern Judaism* 6 (1986), 157–188.
30. "Kol Dodi Dofek," 54.
31. Ibid., 56. This analysis is opposed to Sokol's interpretation of Soloveitchik's approach. In his view, Soloveitchik endorses Hermann Cohen rather than the existentialist view. See Moshe Sokol, "Is There a 'Halakhic' Response to the Problem of Evil?," *Harvard Theological Review*, 92 (1999), 316–320. Sokol's emphasis on Cohen's legacy is definitely accurate, but he is not persuasive in his attempt to dismiss existentialist foundations from Soloveitchik's thought.
32. "Kol Dodi Dofek," 54.
33. David Hartman, *A Living Covenant: The Innovative Spirit in Traditional Judaism* (New York: Free Press, 1985), 267–268.
34. "Kol Dodi Dofek," 56.
35. Ibid., 62 (emphasis in the original).
36. "Approach to Suffering," 94.
37. Albert Camus, *The Plague*, trans. Stuart Gilbert (Harmondsworth, England: Penguin Books, 1961), 108.
38. Ibid., 107.
39. Hartman, *A Living Covenant*, 187.
40. David Hartman, *Crisis and Leadership: Epistles of Maimonides* (Philadelphia: Jewish Publication Society of America, 1985), 162. See also *A Living Covenant*, 247.
41. Hartman, *Crisis and Leadership*, 163.

[42] Ibid.
[43] Ibid., 164. See also 171.
[44] Hartman, *A Living Covenant*, 200.
[45] Hartman analyzes these and other responses in *A Living Covenant*, ch. 8.
[46] See ibid., ch. 11.

Chapter Six

THE HOLOCAUST: A THEOLOGICAL OR A RELIGIOUS-EXISTENTIALIST PROBLEM?

THIS chapter returns to the theodicy problem, focusing on its application to the Holocaust. Various thinkers have pointed to the Holocaust as a theological turning point, requiring a reconsideration of theological and religious fields of meaning on the grounds that the exceptional evil exposed in its course cannot be approached with conventional standards.

The claim this chapter attempts to substantiate is that the terrifying events of the Holocaust do not constitute a sufficient basis for a theological turnabout. More specifically, my thesis is that the Holocaust does not demand a transformation in the realm of natural theology. In the realm of concrete religious life, however, the Holocaust could involve implications for the organization of religious meaning. At the basis of this discussion is a clear distinction between the theological and the religious fields although, due to their mutual influences, attempts to differentiate between religious and theological language do not seem feasible to many scholars.

My assumption here is that these two languages are independent and not mutually reducible. This assumption can be substantiated through a phenomenological analysis and an analytical critique of the status of theological statements in religious language. Following Wittgenstein, many philosophers[1] have pointed out that believers do not need theological statements in order to believe. Believers do not found their faith on general theological assumptions taken from natural theology. Their faith is primary, unconditioned by external justification contexts, and the meaning of religious language is constituted from "inside," through the complex of religious practices.

This distinction warrants the conclusion that relationships in the theological field do not necessarily involve implications for relationships in the religious field and vice-versa. The discussion about the theological and religious problematic of the Holocaust thus casts new light on the distinction between the theological and the religious fields that, although highly significant for religious life, it is at times ignored.

First Claim: The Holocaust Is Not a Theological Problem

Prima facie, this claim seems unfounded. God's silence vis-à-vis the horrors of the Holocaust poses such a deep problem that many concluded "God died" then. In Richard Rubinstein's formulation: "After Auschwitz many Jews did not need Nietzsche to tell them that the old God of Jewish patriarchal monotheism was dead beyond all hope of resurrection."[2]

Although these formulations reflect the horror evoked by this evil, a distinction is needed between these feelings and the possibility of anchoring them in a coherent theological world view. A structured argument, termed the "argument from evil," will help to clarify the theological problematic of the Holocaust:

(1) There is a good God, omnipotent and omniscient.
(2) God's goodness precludes the existence of evil and suffering.
Therefore:
(3) Evil and suffering do not exist.
But:
(4) The factual truth is that evil and suffering do exist.
Therefore:
(5) God does not exist.[3]

Premise (1) is that goodness is one of God's essential attributes. Without assuming God's goodness, the entity called "God" would be Satan, a wicked creature operating according to its own arbitrary will. This perception of God's goodness is not only an analytical claim but a tenet of Greek philosophy from its very outset as well as of Judeo-Christian tradition.[4]

Premise (2) is based on the claim that evil and suffering are the antithesis of the good and thus warranting conclusion (3) — since God is a good entity, his very existence precludes evil and suffering.

Statement (4) is a factual pronouncement pointing out the existence of evil, which contradicts the assertion in statement (3) that evil does not exist. This is not a trivial contradiction, since statement (3) is a conclusion that follows from the first two premises, so that contradicting statement (3) and recognizing the existence of evil is thus a negation of God's existence. The conclusion that follows from this argument is that the existence of evil not only poses a theological problem but indeed casts doubts on God's very existence.

This formulation of the problem raises the question of whether the evil exposed in the Holocaust requires changing this argument, or the Holocaust should be viewed as another expression of evil that has no effect on it. The analysis of the argument shows the latter to be the correct answer, since refuting the general claim that evil and suffering do not exist only requires proof about the existence of one case of evil. Theologically, then, the evil exposed in the Holocaust is not essentially different from other expressions of evil, such as the death of one innocent creature. Both events raise the same theological problem and, in principle, a solution valid for an isolated event is also valid for the Holocaust.

The extensive literature on the problem of evil in the Holocaust shows that the basic modes of argumentation postulated in its regard are essentially no different from the classic arguments postulated concerning the problem of evil in general. An analysis of various models reflecting the main solutions to the problem of evil in the Holocaust will help to illustrate this point. The models are: (1) The modification of the God's goodness concept. (2) The causal or teleological model. (3) The model of epistemological impairment. (4) The model of freedom as a justification for refraining from intervention. My claim is that these models as well as their shortcomings apply to all manifestations of evil.

(1) The Modification of the God's Goodness Concept

The standard assumption implicit in the "argument from evil" is that the meaning of the concept "good" ascribed to God is identical to the meaning of the concept "good" in human language and practice. In human language and practice, wicked acts causing pain and evil are the antithesis of the concept of good. Similar concepts of good and evil ascribed to God enable the "argument from evil." According to the theory known as "divine command morality," however, morality depends on God, who determines good and evil: good is good because God wanted it and evil is evil because God stated so. There is no autonomous morality.[5] Not only do supporters of this thesis have an obvious answer to the argument from evil, but they can also argue that this argument rests on a false premise — the autonomy of morality. Indeed, in the very midst of the Holocaust, Kalonymus Shapira, the rabbi of Piaseczno, formulates this thesis clearly in his sermons:[6]

> The nations of the world, even the best of them, think that the truth is a thing in itself, and that God commanded truth because the truth is intrinsically true. ...Not so the Jews, who say "You God are truth." He, may He be blessed, is truth, and we have no truth beside Him, and all the truth found in the world is there only because God wished it and commanded it...and stealing is forbidden because the God of truth has so commanded.[7]

Endorsing this thesis enables R. Shapira to offer a radical solution to the argument from evil, by denying the question's very legitimacy: "Not only do we say that this, Heaven forbid, is a problem we do not understand and its justification is beyond our grasp, but we also say there is no truth and justice at all, except for what God commands and does."[8]

This surprising solution to the "argument from evil," however, seldom if ever appears in Jewish texts. In fact, R. Shapira himself offers other answers in other sermons, based on the third and fourth models. The thesis of divine command morality is analytically flawed on several counts,[9] and does not provide a satisfactory solution to the problem of evil in the Holocaust. But if it were an answer to the problem, it could also provide answers to the existence of the most "minor" evil — the death of one innocent child.

(2) The Causal or Teleological Model

This model assumes a need for amending statement (3) in the argument, asserting that God's goodness precludes the possibility of evil and suffering. But this statement could be modified to state that God's goodness precludes the possibility of *morally unjustified* evil and suffering, so that when a sufficient condition for the existence of suffering obtains, God's existence is not refuted.[10] The causal or teleological model proposes a sufficient condition for the existence of suffering. Causal explanations link the occurrence of suffering at a particular point in time to an event or events that preceded it: the present is explained through the past. By contrast, teleological explanations justify present suffering as a condition for attaining valuable goals in the near or distant future.

The problems of this model concern the relationship between evil and worthy purposes: are there causes or purposes that justify performance of, or consent to, morally evil deeds? The problem with teleological explanations lies in the difficulty of accepting that evil is necessary because of its implication that God is not omnipotent, and certain ends can only be attained through evil deeds. Nor can causal explanations avoid this problematic: are there circumstances in the past that compel the performance of moral injustices? If evil is not necessary, then God acts in evil ways and is therefore not God. But if no necessary relationship exists between the circumstances or the purposes on the one hand and evil and suffering on the other, is this not a license to human beings to perform similar deeds? Since human beings and God belong to a community with identical moral rules, why should God be allowed to perform evil deeds forbidden to human beings?

These and other questions are equally applicable to all the answers to evil based on causal or teleological models, but they are equally relevant to all forms of moral injustice — the killing of one innocent child or the murder of millions. In other words, the problematic nature of this solution applies to all manifestations of evil everywhere, and is not aggravated by the Holocaust.

(3) The Model of Epistemological Impairment

According to this model, even if God and human beings are subject to a similar moral order, they are still essentially different. Human cognition is limited and unable to grasp all the relevant facts and all the pertinent moral considerations. Hence, human beings can go on believing in God's goodness even if they do not exactly know how to reconcile it with moral iniquity.

This model might indeed provide answers to individuals who wish to sustain their belief in God's goodness, on two conditions. The first is that the number of instances in which God's commands or God's deeds appear to be immoral is relatively limited — the higher their number, the lower the justification for a continued belief in God's goodness. Second, the model's assumption is that what appears immoral is not really so, only the limitations of the human cognition view it as injustice and evil. In truth, however, what seems immoral is dismissed in favor of a more important moral consideration. If it eventually emerges that some acts are patently immoral, the justification for continued belief in God's goodness will be reduced.[11]

Although this model is rather widespread in the religious literature written in the wake of the Holocaust, its validity in this context is in fact rather weak. What moral consideration could possibly justify the murder of so many? Even supporters of utilitarian theories, who accept as morally justified inflicting a certain injury on some people for the sake of others,[12] will find it hard to endorse this solution regarding the Holocaust. The reason is that no relevant results or moral considerations could possibly be adduced to make the murder of millions permissible.

Moreover, the problems that were noted regarding the causal or teleological model affect this model as well. Even if human beings neither do nor can understand God, they can at least understand that God is a benevolent and omnipotent entity, able to attain worthy results in moral ways. A person's cognition, even if limited, still has some value. The model of epistemological impairment, then, rests on an unnecessary assumption whereby what follows from human epistemological impairment is that we do not understand anything, whereas what follows from the epistemological impairment is that we cannot understand everything, but we do understand something.

To avoid this entanglement, supporters of the epistemological impairment model can endorse the radical claim and argue that we do not understand anything. This claim, however, leads to a series of problems extensively discussed in the history of philosophy. First, if we do not understand anything, how do we know that God's understanding is greater than ours? Second, if we do not understand anything, how can we claim that God is good given that this claim requires some sort of knowledge, both concerning the good and concerning God's attributes? This argument, then, which draws a comparison between us and God — and epistemological limitations are a kind of comparison — must presume some knowledge of the elements compared.

In the current discussion, the claim of epistemological impairment is committed to the following assumptions: (1) God is a good entity that acts rationally; (2) God is an omnipotent entity; (3) God's omnipotence does not contradict his goodness. The omnipotent God acts in the best possible way to attain his aims. Hence, God will not act to attain his aims in a morally despicable way. At most, we do not know God's reasons. Furthermore, supporters of the epistemological impairment model make assumptions about human beings too: (1) Human beings know how to use the terms "good" and "evil" correctly. (2) Human beings know how to apply their insights and concepts in their real judgments. Even if they do not know how to make a correct moral judgment in every context, the distinction between good and absolute evil is definitely clear in some cases. The evil of the Holocaust is a kind of absolute evil, to which the argument of human epistemological limitations does not apply.

(4) The Model of Freedom as a Justification for Refraining from Intervention

The models we have discussed so far tried to deal with the question of evil and suffering in general and in the Holocaust in particular resting on an implicit assumption: what appears as evil is not, in truth, evil. The current model assumes that evil in general and the evil of the Holocaust in particular is indeed evil, unjustifiable through any essential argument or by relying on the epistemological gap between human beings and God. This model, however, claims that the issue of evil should be shifted to the concern with an entirely different question: what is the best of all possible worlds.

As Arthur Lovejoy showed in *The Great Chain of Being*, one of the basic intuitions of Western culture concerning the good is related to plenitude. In the present context, if God is indeed good, no possibility of the good would have remained unrealized. We must therefore assume that our world, which was created by God, is the best of all possible worlds. But how can we assume that this is the best of all possible worlds when it comprises so much evil and suffering?

The answer to this question assumes that a world lacking human freedom is worse than a world enjoying human freedom, making our world, where human beings do have choice, the preferable option. Analytically, the existence of freedom is contingent on the presence of contrary options. Barring choice between good and evil, the concept of choice is meaningless.

Human evil is thus one of the products linked to the very existence of human freedom.

The problem of evil in general and the problem of the Holocaust in particular are particularly troublesome, mainly because they do not reflect a natural event linked to the laws of nature. The more vexing and embarrassing evil is human evil. How can humans, created in God's image, act iniquitously? This evil, however, is evidence of human freedom, since it shows that evil is indeed an available option.

This model is not free of analytical difficulties,[13] but its potential problems are not in any way related to the Holocaust or to any specific historical situation of manifestation of evil.

My review here has not covered all possible answers to the questions of evil in general and the Holocaust in particular, but only to some of the basic ones. Theologically, both the questions and the answers defy the notion of the Holocaust's uniqueness. Hence, the Holocaust neither does nor can require a new theology or a new theological language. A satisfactory theological explanation of human evil in general would also be an adequate explanation of the Holocaust, and the lack of an explanation is not particularly related to the Holocaust. What, then, accounts for the vast body of literature written in the wake of the Holocaust, partly demanding a radical turnabout of theological language?

One answer is that those who demand such a change are indeed wrong, and do not understand that the Holocaust does not pose a unique theological problem. The history of philosophy points to many instances of mistakes that became entrenched and turned into axioms before being recognized as spurious. In this sense, the thesis about the "death of God" following the Holocaust could be considered a further instance of this type of mistake, and if the *ontological* statement about the "death of God" rests on the problematic of the Holocaust, it is groundless.

Second Claim: The Holocaust is a Religious-Existentialist Problem

Formulating the problem of the Holocaust in the language of natural theology conceals an entirely different issue: a religious-existentialist problem. The depth of the distress awakened by the Holocaust is not related to the theological question about God's very existence. Instead, it reflects a disappointed religious expectation. Believers expected God to intervene and not remain silent vis-à-vis the terror of the Holocaust. Given the intimate relationship between God and the faithful, they deserved divine intervention. This expectation is not based on theological assumptions that follow from God's goodness, his providence, and his omnipotence, but on the organization of life according to religiosity per se. The problem of evil in the Holocaust, then, is an inner problem of religiosity. Albert Camus indeed stressed the "internal" religious character in the problematic of evil: "If the rebel blasphemes, it is in the hope of finding a new god. He staggers under the shock of the first and most profound of all religious experiences but it is a disenchanted religious experience."[14]

This statement deserves further analysis. Camus holds that every child's death raises the problem of evil, but what awakens the metaphysical rebellion and subverts the assumption of an ordered world is not "the suffering of a child...but the fact that the suffering is not justified."[15] With wondrous sensitivity, Camus placed the problem of evil in context. This problem is not merely factual. We understand that suffering and pain are part of life, and perhaps even a vital part of life's development, but what bothers us in suffering is that it cannot be justified.

Throughout his *oeuvre*, Camus assumed that justification is tied to a wider metaphysical order — when this order is subverted, persistent adherence to old truths is no longer possible. Camus assumed that religiosity does ensure such an overall order so that, when this order is flawed, religiosity is also flawed. For Camus, a child's suffering and displays of evil toward a child undermine order and supply grounds for our disappointment with religiosity — the greater the expectation, the greater the disappointment. He was wrong, however, on several counts. First, he assumed only one kind of justification for the existence of evil, formulated in general, metaphysical terms. Second, he assumed that this justification is part of the organization of meaning within religiosity. Third, he adopted an absolutist moral approach, which only very few endorse. But Camus' analysis is important because it shows understanding of the link between expectation and disappointment, of how foiled expectations intensify the problematic of evil, and of how expectations are anchored in religious life.

Phenomenologically, an analysis of religious life and the expectations it evokes should not rest on theological assumptions related to God's image but on an analysis of religious practices. These practices assume that God is the "thou" or the other to whom petitioners turn in their prayers. This God is perceived as savior and comforter, forgiving, compassionate, and provident, even when walking through the valley of the shadow of death. A broad context of religious action fosters this expectation: be it festivals marking the memory of God's intervention in reality and the people's redemption, or the emphasis in the prayer book on God's concrete and direct intervention in the world, answering the individual's requests and longings in prayer: this is a God who revives the dead, judges, and heals. The language of prayer and religious practice is a language of turning to an entity that is indeed transcendent, but is also eminently immanent. Religious practice is a living dialogue with a God who has a visage and a personality. The expectation rests on the assumptions developed toward God's personality and visage. The expectation about God's action and direct intervention in the world does not reflect the believer's subjective viewpoint,[16] but surfaces through the very web of religious practice.

This expectation directs the faithful everywhere in their lives, so that evil and injustice pose a problem because they contradict it. Believers can indeed contain a certain measure of evil and injustice on standard theological grounds. As believers, they have also been accustomed to live with the dialectical tension between an immanent perception of God and divine transcendence. They may therefore acknowledge that the expectation of evil's absolute banishment reflects a view that endorses only the immanent dimension of the divinity. Religious practice has taught us to balance between the sense of "thou" in God and the recognition of his transcendent holiness. The fact that we are expected to worship the Creator and renounce autonomy's various dimensions is one of the deepest religious experiences of God's transcendence. As noted, however, all this is limited. Even if the measure of the evil is *theologically* irrelevant, it is *religiously* significant, since extensive evil deals a fatal blow to the religious expectation of banishing evil from the world and also to religious trust: "Even though I walk through the valley of the shadow of death, I will fear no evil: for thou art with me; thy rod and thy staff they comfort me" (Psalms 23: 4). The existence of fundamental evil cannot be reconciled with the image of a personal and comforting God.

On deeper scrutiny, the difference between the theological and the religious perspectives reflects the basic distinction of Judah Halevi and Pascal between "the God of the philosophers" and "the God of Abraham." The theologian's expectations from God differ from those of the religious individual, since each one's God is fundamentally different.

CHAPTER SIX

The Religious Crisis and its Implications for Religious Discourse

In light of the proposed analysis, even if the Holocaust need not be a theological turning point, it could be a turning point for religious discourse, since it threatens to void its basic meaning. Religious responses could vary: one typical response is the absolute rejection of the god that failed. As noted, even if this response is at times formulated in ontological language, stating that this entity called God does not exist, its translation into the religious realm is different. In the religious realm, the rejection of God or the "death of God" means the rejection of religion and of the God represented in religious language — the God as companion, as a 'thou" who turns to human beings and participates in the voyage of history and of existence.

Another typical, opposite, response could be to view the Holocaust as a religious test. A clear distinction separates theological justifications of the Holocaust in terms of a test and the perception of the Holocaust as a religious test. In theological terms, the test category functions as a justification of divine action. In religious terms, however, the test category is an existentialist category applying to human ways of being.

Kierkegaard, who developed the concept of "spiritual test" (*anfaegtelse*), excelled at describing the existentialist meaning of the religious test.[17] This test is the moment at which human beings confront the entire range of their relationship with God — *they* are tested, not God. As human beings, we struggle with ourselves about the nature of the religious demand and its meaning, and our response reveals, above all, something about our own character. We may come out of it stronger or weaker, but we will never go back to be what we were.

Contending with the Holocaust in the context of a test category does not result in an existentialist transformation. At best, we now know something we had not known before. By contrast, the perception of the Holocaust as a religious test reflects the attitude of believers to the situation in which they finds themselves. The Holocaust becomes the decisive dimension in the contest of individuals with their existence, their faith in God, and their attitude to God. One instance of such attempts is the work of Emil Fackenheim.

Fackenheim holds that Auschwitz compels the Jew; it has, in his terms, a "commanding voice." The command, from a religious perspective, is precisely the non-renunciation of faith even if the believer must find a dialectical balance between "continuing to hear the voice of Sinai as he hears the voice of Auschwitz,"[18] that is between faith and defiance. According to Fackenheim, the meaning of religious faith after the Holocaust is witnessing: "We are here, exist, survive, endure, witness to God and man even if abandoned by God and man."[19]

This religious stance means that "they [Jews] are forbidden to despair of the God of Israel."[20] These statements are not part of the natural theological discourse; they do not explain or justify evil. They reflect a religious decision to sustain faith despite religious obstacles, as a kind of persistent testimony of faith.

The central question facing believers endorsing these views is not how to justify God given the horrors of the Holocaust, but how to continue a life of faith given evil. The problem of evil is not one that has God as its object, but a problem expressing the believers' reflections about themselves as believers.

Like all arguments, metaphysical arguments too are either true or false. The span of theological-metaphysical options is not confined to the context of logical inferences from the argument itself but extends to the critique of its assumptions, given that the assumptions of the metaphysical argument, like all assumptions, do not involve necessity. Once these assumptions have been stated, however, options shrink: either the conclusion is correct and the argument is true, or the inference is not necessary, and the argument is false.

In this sense, the theological approach to the question of evil in the Holocaust somehow returns to the classic question about evil and is therefore not particularly interesting. By contrast, the religious reactions to evil in the Holocaust are a fascinating subject because they reveal compelling aspects of religious life from two perspectives. First, they expose the implicit assumptions of religious practice concerning God, assumptions that substantiate the believer's expectations from God. Second, the reactions teach us much about the way in which believers interpret their own religious world to themselves. They expose the fact that, within a given religious practice, more than one reaction is possible to a disturbance as dramatic as the Holocaust for the organization of meaning in religious life. The various reactions, as shown, could extend from an absolute rejection of the religious world to the reinterpretation of this world in a way that dismisses the metaphysical yearning as the constitutive element of religious life.

Is liberation from the metaphysical yearning indeed possible? Can we draw such a sharp separation between natural theological aspects and interpretations of religious life? This is not an easy endeavor. The tendency to shift from religious to theological language evident in many theological discussions about the Holocaust will attest to this. In this sense, the philosophical perspective offers a kind of correction, enabling to refocus the difficulties and the fields of meaning at work in the religious or theological discourses, which are particularly relevant to the study of the Holocaust.

Notes

1. See, for instance, the works of Peter Winch, D. Z. Phillips, Norman Malcolm, and others, discussed in ch. 4 above.
2. Richard Rubinstein, *After Auschwitz* (Indianapolis: Bobbs-Merrill, 1966), 227.
3. The formulation of this argument is proposed by George Schlesinger, *Religion and Scientific Method* (Boston: Reidel, 1977), ch. 1.
4. On this issue see, Avi Sagi and Daniel Statman, *Religion and Morality*, trans. Batya Stein (Amsterdam and Atlanta, GA: Rodopi, 1995), especially ch. 2; Avi Sagi, *Judaism: Between Religion and Morality* (in Hebrew) (Tel Aviv: Hakibbutz Hameuchad, 1998).
5. For an extensive discussion of this question, see Sagi and Statman, *Religion and Morality*, ch. 1.
6. On R. Shapira's sermons, see Mendel Piekarz, *Ideological Trends of Hasidism in Poland during the Inter-War Period and the Holocaust* (in Hebrew) (Jerusalem: Bialik Institute, 1990).
7. Kalonymus Shapira, *Esh Kodesh* (Jerusalem: Va'ad Hasidei Piaseczno, 1960), 68. See also 172.
8. Ibid., 68–69. For further discussion, see Sagi, *Judaism: Between Religion and Morality*, 64–65.
9. Sagi and Statman, *Religion and Morality*, chs. 1 and 2.
10. This amendment was suggested by Nelson Pike, "Hume on Evil," *Philosophical Review* 72 (1963), 180–197.

[11] Sagi and Statman, *Religion and Morality*, 136–138.
[12] Ibid.
[13] See, for instance, George N. Schlesinger, "Suffering and Divine Benevolence" (in Hebrew), in *Modern Trends in Philosophy*, ed. Asa Kasher and Shalom Lappin (Tel Aviv: Yahdav, 1985), 53–55.
[14] Albert Camus, *The Rebel: An Essay on Man in Revolt*, trans. Anthony Bower (New York: Alfred A. Knopf, 1956), 101.
[15] Ibid.
[16] This is Eliezer Schweid's claim. See *Struggle Till Dawn* (in Hebrew) (Tel Aviv: Hakibbutz Hameuchad, 1991), 182–190.
[17] For a detailed analysis, see Avi Sagi, *Kierkegaard, Religion, and Existence: The Voyage of the Self*, trans. Batya Stein (Amsterdam-Atlanta, GA: Rodopi, 2000), 156–160.
[18] Emil L. Fackenheim, *God's Presence in History: Jewish Affirmations and Philosophical Reflections* (New York: Harper Torchbooks, 1972), 88.
[19] Ibid., 97.
[20] Emil L. Fackenheim, "Jewish Faith and the Holocaust: A Fragment," *Commentary* (August 1968), 32.

Chapter Seven

TIKKUN OLAM:
BETWEEN UTOPIAN IDEA AND
SOCIO-HISTORICAL PROCESS

Few ideas have boosted human thought and imagination as that of *tikkun olam* (repairing the world). Reformers have been leaving their mark since the dawn of human history, some crowned with a halo of sanctity and some condemned for their evil deeds. Prima facie, *tikkun olam* is a sublime notion expressing key features of human existence. The leading one is freedom. The amendment of reality necessarily assumes the ability to transcend factuality and be free to shape the world. *Tikkun olam* attests also to human creativity — we envisage how the world should be. Human beings are free creatures, capable of transcending their actual being and pursuing the possible, anticipated through imagination.

The fate of the *tikkun olam* idea, however, resembles that of many other sublime notions that are part of the general consensus — too little is invested in a critical effort that rigorously examines their nature. What do we intend when we speak of repairing the world? Is this a substantive idea, or do its inherent drawbacks deprive it of any justification? These are the central questions of this chapter.

CHAPTER SEVEN

My starting point is a distinction between two different and unrelated meanings of the concept of *tikkun olam*: (1) *Tikkun olam* as a utopian *idea*. (2) *Tikkun olam* as a concrete historical *process* unfolding in a concrete society. My central claim is that the first meaning of the concept is extremely problematic. We can still endorse the second meaning, however, because the concrete process of amending the world does not depend on the idea that directs it. The first step in the understanding of these claims and their implications, then, is to clarify the first meaning of *tikkun olam*.

Tikkun Olam as a Utopian Idea

According to this meaning of the term, *tikkun olam* is the realization of a specific idea that outlines the ideal vision. This perception assumes a contrast between real and ideal — the ideal negates actual reality and proposes to replace it with a utopian idea of the organization of the world. A critical discussion of all the aspects related to utopian thought exceeds the scope of this chapter,[1] and the following discussion will be confined to specific aspects necessary for clarifying the meaning of *tikkun olam*.

Martin Buber defines utopia as "something not actually present but only represented. The utopian picture is a picture of what 'should be.' What is at work here is the longing for that rightness."[2] Implicit in this definition is an essential characteristic of utopian thought, which Karl Mannheim analyzes in detail in his celebrated work *Ideology and Utopia*. Mannheim emphasizes that utopia works in human thought in two complementary and opposite directions. First, human thought transcends the reality in which the utopia is born, rejects it, and offers an alternative model of existence in its place. In Buber's terms, utopia places what "should be," which is opposed to what is. Second, utopian thought strives to return to reality in order to rebuild it. Mannheim rightfully emphasizes that transcendence alone is not utopia. Transcendence becomes a constitutive element of utopia only if joined by a passion to shape reality in light of the idea.[3]

What are the structural elements present in every utopia?[4] First, the idea of repairing the world rests on the notion of a perfect world. This perfection is related to the relationship between the components of the world on the one hand, and to the standing of each component on the other. The ideal world is an ordered world whose components are in perfect mutual harmony, while each one is also perfect in itself. In Yeshayahu Leibowitz's terms, the ideal world is the best of all possible worlds, which utopia counterposes to the real and imperfect one.

Second, since this world is ideal, it is harmonious — because it is more perfect than a non-harmonious world — and total — because it leaves no room for other options. Legitimizing another alternative as worthy means that the assumed perfection is not absolute because other and no less perfect options are also available.[5]

Finally, if the ideal world is perfect we must also conclude it is static and immutable, because change is an expression of imperfection and disharmony. This perfect world should therefore be characterized as one without progress or development.

Given this description of the ideal world, is it at all within human grasp? Some utopians have indeed assumed that utopia is synonymous with what, in principle, is unattainable. This is how Herbert Marcuse relates to the concept of utopia: "Utopia is a historical concept. It refers to projects for social change that are considered impossible."[6] Marcuse, therefore, holds that the present reality reflects the "end of utopia" because it has now become possible to realize options that had previously seemed unattainable. This approach to utopia, however, appears unsubstantiated. At most, it reflects, as Mannheim claims, the vantage point typical of those affirming the status quo.[7]

Various answers have been offered to the question of how this ideal world might be reached and, in this context, a distinction must be drawn between different versions of utopian and eschatological thought. Utopian thought assumes that progress toward the ideal world is a human endeavor unfolding within the confines of human time and history. By contrast, eschatological thought assumes that *tikkun olam* is God's endeavor and will occur at another place and another time, outside history.[8] Eschatological time seeks to establish a divine kingdom on earth, and thereby disregards the concreteness of human reality. According to Mannheim, this disregard is what excludes eschatological thought from the category of utopia.[9] Irrespective of whether Mannheim is correct, to the extent that the concern is to repair the world, the eschatological option must be excluded on the grounds that it does not seek to amend reality but to change it entirely. It speaks of a re-creation of reality involving cosmological implications.[10]

This schematic description enables us to summarize the idea of *tikkun olam* as postulating the idea of a perfect world, toward which we should strive from within empirical reality. Although ostensibly a noble and worthy cause, a more critical appraisal will show this to be a problematic idea.

Problems in the Utopian Idea of *Tikkun Olam*

The epistemological problem. This meaning of *tikkun olam*, as noted, seeks the realization of a perfect, harmonious, total, and static world. The specific content of this world is the concern of the different theories offering various ideal options. Precisely at this point, however, a significant epistemological problem emerges: a perfect world is not necessarily a rational idea. Karl Popper, who deals with a critique of utopia in several of his works, formulates this claim as follows: utopia sets goals to be achieved, but "it is impossible to determine ends scientifically. There is no scientific way of choosing between two ends...No decision about aims can be established by *purely* rational or scientific means."[11]

The utopian idea derives from a specific life context, from a particular culture that sets ideals and expectations. Finley postulates this as a guiding methodological principle in the study of utopias:

> Utopian ideas and fantasies, like all ideas and fantasies, grow out of the society to which they are a response. Neither the ancient world nor the modern world is an unchanging entity, and any analysis of Utopian thinking which neglects social changes in the course of the history of either antiquity or modern times is likely at some point to go badly wrong.[12]

The seemingly inevitable conclusion is that the utopian idea will be valid only for members of the specific culture who formulated it. Both structurally and in historical-realist terms, however, *tikkun olam* as a utopian idea transcends the specific context within which it was born. The ideal world of one culture and one society is presented as "the" ideal world for the other, for every other, even one wholeheartedly opposed to this particular version of *tikkun olam*. The utopian idea of *tikkun olam*, then, has metaphysical pretensions and claims universal validity. Its modes of justification transcend the social-historical context that sustains it and the criticism of local circumstances, so that its justification is unrelated to this background.

As for how this pretention is substantiated, the supporters of this ideal metaphysical world will probably claim it is validated by the truth of the utopia's constitutive idea. But how can this truth be determined outside the cultural-social-historical context within which this perfect world was born? An ideal world is always judged within a specific cultural narrative and we have no critical way of turning it into a meta-narrative. In other words, the notion of an ideal world is always within a *petitio principii* circularity and, therefore, merely conveys the beliefs of members of a particular society.

If this conclusion is correct, believers in an ideal world face a paradox: the notion of an ideal world rests on the assumption that the longed for world is perfect, harmonious, total, static, and universally valid. Epistemologically, however, the only claim that believers in an ideal world can substantiate is that this world is perfect for them and might therefore be imperfect for others.

The empirical-existential problem. The idea of *tikkun olam* takes a negative view of concrete reality, which it defines as flawed and lacking. But such a sweeping perception of the empirical world is surely a superficial and shallow view of human reality, which is by nature a far more complex amalgam of lights and shadows, ambiguously mixing good and evil.[13] It is to this evil, negative reality, that the notion of *tikkun olam* counterposes its idea of a utopian world.

Indeed, the meaning of the term "utopia" in Greek is "no place" (*ou topia*). Utopia transcends the familiar space and the known concrete world, but does so in order to enter a positive reality, as suggested by the link between the term utopia and the good place (*eu topia*).[14] In other words, the perfect reality does prevail somewhere in the world, but outside the familiar space. Thomas More's *Utopia*,[15] a paradigm of this literary genre, expressed this ambiguity when indicating that utopia is the name of a "new island,"[16] separated from land by a channel. The term, then, denotes a new and different place that is not part of reality. This issue is recurrently emphasized through several aspects of More's work: the precise name of the city is Amaurot, [from *amauroton* meaning "made dark or dim"][17]; the people residing in the city are the Achorians [from *a-* ("without") plus *choros* ("place, country": "the People without a Country,"[18] and the Polylerites, [from polus "much" plus "leros" ("nonsense"): "the People of Much Nonsense."[19] Utopia, then, is a place beyond all places, a reality that is not part of the world.[20] Yet, this is precisely the chink in the armor of the utopian idea: it traces a perfect, static, and unrealistic picture of the world.[21]

Moreover, the utopian idea assumes the existence of a uniform and simple ideal suited to all human beings.[22] As Berlin shows, this assumption is necessarily committed to the claim "that men have a certain fixed, inalterable nature, certain universal, common, immutable goals. Once these goals are realised, human nature is wholly fulfilled."[23]

But human creatures are by nature complex. The utopian idea disregards the unique character of individuals and of societies, failing to take into account that human beings are cultural creatures constituted by the historical and social contexts of their lives. The utopian idea is founded on a cultural "veil of ignorance" and is therefore unable to trace the contours of an ideal world that is real; the amendment it suggests is founded on the negation of human life's historical-cultural character.[24] Berlin, who endorses this criticism, concludes from it that the utopian idea of *tikkun olam* is "logically incoherent."[25] If the critique is correct, then, we must assume that the expression "the perfect society" is a family name for various real societies fitting this category. Each one is perfect, in that it realizes the ideals of the good, but it thereby denies the idea of a "single perfect society."[26]

The existentialist implication of *tikkun olam* as a utopian idea is no less problematic. Even if amending the world is not synonymous with the establishment of God's kingdom on earth, the idea does divert us from the present to the future. The present is negated for the sake of another future. The future-oriented utopian idea has nothing to say about the present, which it seeks to amend by transcending it altogether and thereby denying it as one of the foundations of human existence. Denying the present is also denying the past that has been brought into the present, that is, denying the temporal, historical character of human existence.

Erich Fromm calls this hope for the future passive hope, and describes its implications as follows:

> Time and the future become the central category of this kind of hope. Nothing is expected to happen in the *now* but only in the next moment, the next day, the next year, and in another world if it is too absurd to believe that hope can be realized in this world. Behind this belief is the idolatry of "Future," "History," and "Posterity."[27]

According to the utopian idea of *tikkun olam*, the purpose of the individual's life in the present is to engage in the constant nullification of his own existence for the sake of another existence. The real world in which the individual lives until the longed for future is realized is entirely meaningless. Is this not a return to Freud's death drive?

Finally, this idea assumes the possibility of absolute metamorphosis from one way of life to another. Although some individuals are indeed capable of such drastic conversion, the main course for human change and progress is far more moderate and constantly takes into account the surrounding reality that the utopian idea seeks to deny.[28]

The moral problems. Since people do not agree on the definition of the ideal, and since believers in the notion of an ideal world are sure that this is the only worthy and meaningful one, recourse to mechanisms of direct or indirect coercion and violence is inevitable.[29] As a result of social and cultural changes, the notion of what is ideal will also change. The utopian approach to the amendment of the world, however, ignores these changes, since it sets the idea as an a priori purpose. One way of avoiding this contradiction is to resort to violent power against the social-ideological changes opposed to the implementation of the utopian ideal.[30] Human history indeed shows that great ideas of *tikkun olam* have ended, more than once, in dreadful bloodshed; what began as a struggle against evil that offered ideas for a better world ended up in a worse world than the one it came to oppose.[31]

The uniformity and the simplicity of the idea of a perfect world is also harmful to human individuality. The harm is moral, because people's dignity is rooted in their individuality as expressed in human variance and differentiation.[32] An idea that is a priori valid, then, violates human dignity.

Prima facie, this criticism could be valid only if we assume a pluralistic world view supporting the existence of many alternative forms of the good, but this is not so. A moral monist claiming that every *moral question* has only one valid answer could still acknowledge that people have different cultural, social, and religious goals and values.

Finally, the utopian idea assumes that sacrificing humanity's present well being for the sake of its future is morally justified. In Kantian terms, however, this view breaches a fundamental moral duty by making human beings simply means for the advancement of future ends.

Supporters of *tikkun olam* as a utopian idea could claim that no reform is possible without it. We can change and reform reality precisely because of an idea of perfection that guides our critique of the current reality. According to Ernst Bloch, perfect utopia plays a dual role: it provides a criterion for judging the present and it supplies society with a dream to strive for.[33]

This pervasive idea, however, conceals a logical fallacy, since reform could also be driven by the idea of mitigating suffering, poverty, or distress. Implicit in the suggestion that we need utopia is the idea that suffering, misery, poverty, or any other social ill cannot be recognized without an ideal of perfection, but this is an unnecessary assumption. The recognition that suffering and distress are intolerable follows from a negative reality rather than from an idea of perfection.[34]

Many thinkers have indeed drawn a distinction between real social criticism and speculative thought nurtured by fanciful ideas. A particularly sharp articulation of the distinction between social critique and *tikkun olam* through the utopian idea appears in the Frankfurt school. Max Horkheimer offers the following formulation: "The dialectical [critical] theory does not formulate its critique solely through the idea...It does not judge according to what is over and beyond its era, but from it."[35] Horkheimer rejects philosophical speculation and, with it, also utopia. He claims that "utopia skips over time,"[36] and holds "it was a mistake to transcend the present and, because of a message about absolute perfection, fail to discern the possibilities latent in reality."[37] Marcuse summarizes this perception of a critical theory of society as follows:

> Up to now, it has been one of the principal tenets of the critical theory of society...to refrain from what might be reasonably called utopian speculation. Social theory is supposed to analyze existing societies in the light of their own functions and capabilities and to identify demonstrable tendencies (if any) which might lead beyond the existing state of affairs.[38]

Marcuse, who emphasizes the significance of negative critical thought about the present, holds this negative thought can become positive by discovering the options suppressed and denied in the present.[39]

Popper draws a similar distinction between utopia and social reform. Utopia imagines the ideal of the good society toward which it strives. The supreme concept of the utopian ideal is happiness and the perfect good. By contrast, social reform contends with a given reality of suffering and misery, and strives to amend it and reduce it as far as possible. Utopia focuses on what is not — on the future, whereas social reform focuses on the possible, that is, on the present.[40]

Criticism, change, or social progress, then, need not draw their contents from any absolute idea. We do not need to know what is the absolute good to identify an injustice and we do not need to know what is perfect happiness to identify human suffering. Quite the contrary, this criticism is particularly valuable because it returns to reality, examines the unfair and flawed aspects requiring correction, and points to the options latent within it.

CHAPTER SEVEN

Tikkun Olam as a Socio-Historical Process

A socio-cultural criticism more concerned with achieving reform in a particular society rather than with reforming the entire world is the sense covered by the second meaning of the concept, pointing to *tikkun olam* as a socio-historical process. This meaning of *tikkun olam* emerges against the backdrop of the first denotation, discussed above. Whereas *tikkun olam* as a utopian idea lies in the future, *tikkun olam* as a process is rooted in the present, in human reality. Whereas *tikkun olam* as an idea is a simple, uniform notion, *tikkun olam* as a process rests on the complexity of human reality. This process rests on a fragmented, local, and concrete perspective rather than on a total scheme.[41]

Tikkun olam as a utopian idea assumes a monistic world view, whereas *tikkun olam* as a process rooted in empirical reality is pluralistic, just like reality. This process, as noted, does not strive for an absolute change in complex human reality but seeks to disclose various possibilities latent in the social conditions of human existence. Hence, it is a family name for diverse phenomena, whose contents are not necessarily related. All societies and cultures engage or might engage in a struggle for reform whose contents are not dictated by a common idea.

The common denominator uniting all the manifestations of *tikkun olam* as a process is the sober understanding that empirical reality is the ultimate human reality, and cannot be transcended to shift into an absolutely good, united, and harmonious world. In this perception, human efforts are constant and infinite. Every social and cultural reality involves aspects that can be criticized, and new possibilities will invariably emerge. *Tikkun olam* as a process is, in Marcuse's terminology, "the end of utopia," constantly evolving out of existence rather than by virtue of an idea beyond history.

What epistemic instrument will serve to reveal reality's latent potentialities? According to Paul Ricoeur, utopia plays this critical role. In his view, "social imagination" or "cultural imagination" is in a key position, both as a deconstructive element that criticizes the extant social order and as a constructive element representing alternative options for the organization of social life.[42] Utopia or, more precisely, "the utopian mood" or the "utopian spirit,"[43] fill the important role of social imagination: "From this 'no place,' an exterior glance is cast on our reality, which suddenly looks strange, nothing more being taken for granted. The field of the possible is now opened beyond that of the actual, a field for alternative ways of living."[44]

Ricoeur assigns to utopia an entirely different role from the one it had played in classic utopian literature. According to Ricoeur, utopia denotes a reflective, critical process that precludes the unbridled sway of factuality.[45] Utopian thought presents alternative options of social order, of human relations, government, religion, and power, contrary to the classic utopias that pointed to a defined goal, a specific and mandatory conceptual content that all human beings must realize to attain a good existence. Ricoeur compares the role of utopia to the role of the "free variation" in Husserl's perception.[46] Just as for Husserl the free variation is what enabled reflection to attain liberation from the random factual datum by viewing it merely as one possibility among others, so also utopia.

This perception of utopia as a critical instrument is immune to the problems burdening classic utopias, and its orientation is concrete and empirical. At the same time, the key questions are: Do we need utopia, even as a mood or as critical thought, in order to be released from the coercing power of factuality? Is utopia identical to social imagination? Does utopia function like Husserl's free variation? My attempt to answer these questions will be guided by a renewed analysis of the relationship between Husserl's free variation and utopia. Epistemically, the free variation operates regarding a specific predicate of the object, such as color or shape. Through the free variation, we learn not to identify a given object with a specific color, since the variation enables us to think of another color as its predicate. Continued operation of the variation leads us not only to discover the available options but also, and mainly, to discover the "essence" (the *idos*), from which the free variation offers no release. This reflective process is thus a dual course: it discovers the possible as well as the essential. By contrast, utopia discovers the "possible" through the absolute denial and estrangement of factuality rather than as a variation of the same object. The process analogous to free variation is the discovery, through imagination, of the possibilities latent in a given social order rather than the absolute estrangement from it. Absolute estrangement points to distance and hence to utopia's irrelevance to concrete life.

This critique will be enriched by the adoption of Kierkegaard's distinction between imagination and fantasy.[47] Imagination is a reflective process that enables us to transcend factuality to the potential option latent within it. Although imagination is not entirely free from the given factuality, it does enable us not to see its concrete manifestation as the sole option. Fantasy, however, unlike imagination, is a process through which concrete existence detaches itself entirely from its real character. According to this distinction, utopian thought is a turn to fantasy, resting on complete liberation from empirical reality. Its constructive role in a process of social reform, which can occur by allowing imagination to reveal latent options, is thus hard to detect. Reform, then, cannot draw on utopia, even in the version Ricoeur describes.

What will justify the social reform process? What will lead people to act to amend the world? Believers in the need for a utopian idea as a condition of *tikkun olam* assume, as noted, that without an absolute, perfect idea we have no justification for concrete action in the world and no way of motivating individuals to engage in it. This assumption, however, is mistaken on both counts. Concerning the justification, the suffering and distress that are the lot of so many impose an obligation of action on individual and societies that is far stronger than that derived from the utopian idea. The utopian idea of *tikkun olam* relates to humanity in general but ignores concrete individuals living in dire circumstances. It also justifies, as noted, acts involving the sacrifice of individuals in the present for the sake of others' happiness in the future, thus affirming and demanding immoral, harmful deeds. By contrast, focusing on the difficult circumstances of individuals in the present discovers the suffering other, and this pain suffices to compel us into action. It is the other that imposes a moral obligation on us.[48] The real suffering of individuals or societies is an urgent moral task, and is indeed what creates the realm of the ethical: "Whoever explains *poverty* as the suffering of mankind, creates ethics."[49]

Human suffering is not only a decisive justification for concrete action but involves an element that motivates action. The need to find motivation for action in a metaphysical idea rather than in actual reality means that we seek "to make a Philosopher of man before making a man of him."[50] But the main factor motivating human action is compassion, care, and a sense of responsibility for the surrounding reality.[51]

Fromm describes this situation of human solidarity as resurrection:

> Resurrection in its new [non-religious] meaning...is not the creation of *another reality* after the reality of *this* life, but the transformation of *this* reality in the direction of greater aliveness.

> Man and society are resurrected every moment in the act of hope and of faith in the here and now; every act of love, of awareness, of compassion is resurrection...Every moment we give an answer. This answer lies not in what we say or think, but in what we are, how we act, where we are moving.[52]

This return to a human reality perspective also implies the development of an ongoing critical discourse. Believers in an absolute idea, in a truth that guides their lives can, at best, persuade the other or, if not, use violence in order to guide non-believers to the truth. But those who need to reform reality from within and have no recourse to absolute instruments require a continuous dialogue and the human commonality that will enable it. Buber resorted to strong terms to describe this reality:

> The real living together of man with man can only thrive where people have the real things of their common life in common; where they can experience, discuss and administer them together; where real fellowships and real work Guilds exist...We must be quite unromantic, and, living wholly in the present, out of the recalcitrant material of our own day in history, fashion a true community.[53]

This is a humble perception of *tikkun olam*, involving no Promethean idea of absolute rebellion for the sake of another world and hence none of the hubris typical of such a rebellion. But does not this humbleness turn *tikkun olam* into a random, local event? How can we fight for reform in the other's world when such amendments are called for? The struggle against evidence of evil in the other's world rests on the principle of human solidarity, on the ability to develop a true dialogue of compassion with other human beings. The limits of his reform, however, are determined by our concrete shared humanity: amending the other's world so that it may fit mine entails harm, paternalism, and contempt. Repair must be limited by what is common to all human beings — suffering and deprivation on the one hand, and aid to develop the other's immanent options on the other.

Tikkun olam as a process is now widening beyond the borders of a given community and culture, just as human solidarity is widening from a limited to an increasingly wider notion of "we."[54] But even if this broader definition were to include everyone in the entire world, the utopian *idea* of *tikkun olam* could never replace the *process* of *tikkun olam*.

Tikkun Olam and Jewish Tradition

Ostensibly, *tikkun olam* as a utopian idea definitely fits Jewish tradition, from its early days and until the Zionist era. Many scholars have indeed pointed to Jewish prophecy as one of the foundations of utopian discourse.[55] The term *tikkun olam* that appears in Jewish sources implies a whole and harmonious reality. Thus, for instance, the *Aleinu* prayer reads: "to repair the world in the kingdom of the Almighty." Maimonides defines in similar terms the test of the one destined to become the messianic king: "He will repair the entire world to serve God together."[56] *Tikkun olam* as a utopian idea acquires new strength in the Zionist era, when the utopian literary genre first appears in Jewish tradition.[57]

A view of *tikkun olam* as a real socio-historical process, however, is also clearly evident in Jewish tradition, as a constitutive element of the halakhic ethos. The system of commandments is, above all, a vote of confidence in empirical reality as it is — if concrete reality were negative, what would be the value of observing the commandments within it? Paulinian Christianity negated the commandments precisely because it negated current reality and material life, setting up as a goal the heavenly kingdom that is not in this world. It viewed the Torah as legitimizing carnal life and as luring us to it. The Torah therefore could not be the perfect expression of faith, which is an internal, spiritual matter.[58] By contrast, the basic halakhic ethos is one of molding and repairing the present world. The halakhic endeavor is inner-worldly and is not meant to attain a different, ideal reality.

The halakhic ethos does not ascribe decisive weight to messianism and to redemption beyond this world, as Maimonides clarifies when he utterly rejects any concern with the details of redemption and messianism:

> Said the Rabbis: The sole difference between the present and the Messianic days is delivery from servitude to foreign powers (B. San 91b). ...But no one is in a position to know the details of this and similar things until they have come to pass. They are not explicitly stated by the Prophets. Nor have the Rabbis any tradition with regard to these matters. They are guided solely by what the scriptural texts seem to imply. Hence there is a divergence of opinion on the subject. But be that as it may, neither the exact sequence of those events nor the details thereof constitute religious dogmas. No one should ever occupy himself with the legendary themes or spend much time on midrashic statements bearing on this and like subjects. He should not deem them of prime importance, since they lead neither to the fear of God nor to the love of Him.[59]

Maimonides, then, views the messianic idea as a marginal question that is not included in the principles of faith because it has no religious implications: it leads neither to love nor to fear.[60]

Gershom Scholem insightfully notes that halakhic tradition is the core of the "conservative forces" that strive to preserve existence as is and shape it within a halakhic context.[61] Scholem rightfully points to the dialectical and conflicting attitude of halakhic tradition toward messianic utopias:

> On the one hand, Messianic utopianism presents itself as the completion and perfection of Halakhah. It is to perfect what cannot yet find expression in the Halakhah as the law of an unredeemed world. Thus, for example, only in Messianic times will all those parts of the law which are not realizable under the conditions of the exile become capable of fulfillment…The law as such can be fulfilled in its total plenitude only in a redeemed world. But there is doubtless another side to the matter as well. For apocalypticism and its inherent mythology tore open a window on a world which the Halakhah rather preferred to leave shrouded in the mists of uncertainty. The vision of Messianic renewal and freedom was by its nature inclined to produce the question of what it would do to the status of Torah and of the Halakhah which was dependent on it.[62]

Despite this basic tension, we cannot ignore that the primary vector of the halakhic ethos is not toward the redeemed world. Furthermore, a decisive part of the laws that cannot be observed in exile can be observed in the Land of Israel, even in an unredeemed reality. In order to observe these laws, no overall, sweeping reorganization of reality is required. Settlement in the Land of Israel or sovereignty will suffice to enable observance of most of the missing laws. The assertion of Samuel, the Babylonian *amora*, fits the halakhic ethos that adheres to concrete reality: "The only difference between this era and messianic days is [Israel's] subjection to the nations" (BT Berakhot 32b).

Scholem seeks to emphasize the messianic — utopian in his terms — dimension of Jewish tradition, and claims that Maimonides' stance, as cited above, does not truly reflect it: "crucial parts of these theses have no legitimate basis whatever in the biblical and talmudic sources and are rather indebted to the philosophical traditions of Greece."[63] But even if Maimonides' position concerning messianism does not derive deductively from a specific halakhic text, it does successfully convey the halakhic ethos affirming concrete reality while also stressing the obligation of its perpetual reform.

The meaning of the term *tikkun olam* that appears in halakhic literature expresses the practical, non-utopian ethos of halakhic tradition, contrary to its meaning in the *Aleinu* prayer. The *olam* in this halakhic concept denotes the actual social reality within which human beings function, and the *tikkun* relates to the amendment of distortions or injustices in this context; *tikkun olam* is not the repair of the entire cosmos. In halakhic literature, *tikkun olam* denotes a concrete action meant to correct a specific wrong, not a comprehensive reorganization of reality by placing another, perfect world as an alternative to it. The act of correction reaffirms the concrete, routine social order; the act of correcting a specific wrong relates to one or another aspect of life that is reaffirmed through the limited character of the act of amendment, not to the whole of life.[64]

In modern Jewish thought, the non-utopian trend is indeed distinctively evident in the work of thinkers who shifted from speculative theory to halakhic praxis and are at the focus of this book. When embracing the meaning of the halakhic ethos, these thinkers also embrace the assumption that concrete reality is the only one available to us, and the purpose of observing the commandment is to amend this reality.

The first of these thinkers is Leibowitz, who takes this view of reality as his starting assumption: "The first mark of the religion of Halakhah is its realism. It perceives man as he is in reality and confronts him with this reality — with the actual conditions of his existence rather than the 'vision' of another existence."[65] The "anti-illusory," "anti-visionary" character of Halakhah precludes, according to Leibowitz, "flight" to another, perfect reality.[66] This understanding determines the way Halakhah contends with reality. Halakhah deals with the complex of questions raised by reality through the halakhic norm, not through theodicy.[67]

Leibowitz, as noted, rejects both the theodicean and the eschatological attempts to cope with reality by finding its meaning beyond it. The faithful live in this world without hope of finding redemption in another, better one. The concept of redemption undergoes a metamorphosis: it no longer denotes an occurrence in the world but a change in our being. The redeemed are those who transcend the shackles of natural givenness and concretize their freedom through the halakhic act *per se*: "Religion conceived as Torah and commandments redeems man from the shackles of nature. This is not redemption in the Christian sense, whereby a person is redeemed by virtue of his consciousness of being redeemed, but actual redemption, release from the bonds of natural, meaningless causality."[68]

Freedom is embodied in the endless, Sisyphean task incumbent on human beings to fulfill their halakhic obligations within the natural world. Believers struggle with reality and transcend it by observing the commandments. This is therefore an immanent transcendence because it does not imply detachment from natural reality and, therefore, "the project it sets for man is permanent and endless. No religious attainment may be considered final; the project is never completed."[69]

A similar approach is also suggested by Eliezer Goldman, when he analyzes the typology that differentiates "illusory religion" from "non-illusory religion." Illusory religion "holds that religion provides a chance for the transformation of human reality, releasing it from its flaws and allowing genuine closeness to God."[70] By contrast, non-illusory religion acknowledges

> that human reality must be accepted as is and without illusions that we will be able to extricate ourselves from it. It is from and within this reality that God must be worshipped, "for that is the whole duty of man" [Ecclesiastes 12:13]. This worship offers man the only possible option for attachment to his Creator, without fostering any false beliefs in its ability to eliminate the basic conditions of a created reality and redeem us from its flaws.[71]

The rejection of utopianism and the adherence to concrete reality do not ensure the development of a *tikkun olam* ethos or the shaping of an "ethic of suffering." Leibowitz indeed held that the only meaning of the religious obligation is to worship God, and set up a sharp dichotomy between "demanding" and "endowing" religions.[72] Whereas the former places the worship of God at the center, the latter places human needs. From the perspective of the demanding religion, human redemption neither is nor can be embodied in a utopian world or an eschatological event. The purpose of religious life is to worship God, not to repair reality. Hence, human redemption is embodied in the heroic effort to fulfill the religious obligation in this world. In a way, redemption is a kind of release from the illusion that the role of religion is to respond to human demands. Simply, then, redemption is the transparency of religious life.[73] In sum, Leibowitz neither did nor could have linked the rejection of utopia to the process of *tikkun olam*, since religiosity is absolute transcendence from the world within the world.

In his balanced way, Goldman offers an approach more closely attuned to halakhic practice. In several articles that examine the relationship between religion, Halakhah, and morality,[74] Goldman points to the decisive role of meta-halakhic norms in Halakhah.[75] These norms express the values and the ideology of "halakhic man," directing his halakhic decisions. In this way, Goldman points to the connection between Halakhah as a religious system and the real world within which it functions, although he did not develop an explicit view of *tikkun olam* as a process or an "ethic of suffering."

Contrary to Leibowitz and Goldman, Soloveitchik and David Hartman point to the link between Halakhah and processes of social reform. Soloveitchik's distinction between topical and thematic Halakhah, discussed in detail in Chapter Five, and Hartman's theological structuring of a non-utopian view of halakhic tradition, are explicit responses to this challenge, which Hartman sums up as follows: "The covenant does not suggest any promise of resolution for the finite human condition. Rather, it teaches the community how to be responsible for its social and political existence even within the uncertain and possibly tragic conditions of history and even though many events are beyond human control."[76]

In sum, for Halakhah as the mainstream Jewish tradition, the constitutive assumption of its meaning structure is a critical, non-utopian perception of *tikkun olam* and a system of norms meant to attain it.

Notes

1. On this issue, see Shyli Karin-Frank, *Utopia Reconsidered* (in Hebrew) (Tel Aviv: Hakibbutz Hameuchad, 1986).
2. Martin Buber, *Paths in Utopia*, trans. R. F. C. Hull (New York: MacMillan, 1958), 7.
3. Karl Mannheim, *Ideology and Utopia* (London: Routledge and Kegan Paul, 1979), 173–176.
4. For an extensive discussion, see Karin-Frank, *Utopia Reconsidered*, 37–40. See also Isaiah Berlin, *The Crooked Timber of Humanity: Chapters in the History of Ideas* (London: John Murray, 1990), 20–23.
5. See also Frances Theresa Russell, *Touring Utopia* (New York: Dial Press, 1932), 45, and Karin-Frank, *Utopia Reconsidered*, 40.
6. Herbert Marcuse, "The End of Utopia," in *Five Lectures: Psychoanalysis, Politics and Utopia*, trans. Jeremy J. Shapiro and Shierry M. Weber (Boston: Beacon Press, 1970), 63. See also Ilan Gur-Zeev, *The Frankfurt School and the History of Pessimism* (in Hebrew) (Jerusalem: Magnes, 1996), 120.
7. Mannheim, *Ideology and Utopia*, 176–177.
8. See also Buber, *Paths in Utopia*, 8–10.
9. See Mannheim, *Ideology and Utopia*, 198–203.
10. See also Buber, *Paths in Utopia*, 8–10.

11. Karl Popper, *Conjectures and Refutations: The Growth of Scientific Knowledge* (New York: Harper and Row, 1968), 359 (emphasis in the original). Berlin makes a similar claim in *The Crooked Timber of Humanity*, 20–48.
12. M. I. Finley, "Utopianism Ancient and Modern," in *The Critical Spirit*, ed. Kurt H. Wolf and Barrington Moore (Boston: Beacon Press, 1967), 6. See also Barbara Goodwin, *Social Science and Utopia* (Sussex: Harvester Press, 1978), 5.
13. See Mannheim, *Ideology and Utopia*, 177–178.
14. On this link between the two meanings of the term utopia, see Finley, "Utopianism Ancient and Modern," 3. See also Leah Hadomi, *Between Hope and Doubt: The Story of Utopia* (in Hebrew) (Tel Aviv: Hakibbutz Hameuchad, 1989), 44.
15. Thomas More, *Utopia*, edited by George M. Logan Robert M. Adams, and Clarence H. Miller (Cambridge: Cambridge University Press, 1995).
16. Ibid., 3.
17. Ibid., 113, note 7.
18. Ibid., 87, note 63.
19. Ibid., 71, note 37.
20. See Yosef Dan, *Apocalypse Then and Now* (in Hebrew) (Tel Aviv: Hemed, 2000), ch. 8.
21. See also Goodwin, *Social Science and Utopia*, 5.
22. Robert Nozick, *Anarchy, State and Utopia* (Oxford: Blackwell, 1974), 212–213.
23. Berlin, *The Crooked Timber of Humanity*, 20.
24. David C. Hoy and Thomas McCarthy, *Critical Theory* (Oxford: Blackwell, 1994), 103.
25. Berlin, *The Crooked Timber of Humanity*, 40.
26. Ibid.
27. Erich Fromm, *The Revolution of Hope: Toward a Humanized Technology* (New York: Harper and Rowe, 1968), 7.
28. See also Hoy and McCarthy, *Critical Theory*, 135; Berlin, *The Crooked Timber of Humanity*, 15–16.
29. Karl Popper, *The Open Society and its Enemies*, vol. 1 (London: Routledge and Kegan Paul, 1974), 159–161; Nozick, *Anarchy, State and Utopia*, 326–327.
30. See Popper, *Conjectures and Refutations*, 360.

[31] This issue is discussed at length in Albert Camus, *The Rebel: An Essay on Man in Revolt*, trans. Anthony Bower (New York: Alfred A. Knopf, 1956). See also Jacob Talmon, *The Origins of Totalitarian Democracy* (Harmondsworth: England: Penguin Books, 1952).

[32] See also John Stuart Mill, *On Liberty* (Harmondsworth, England: Penguin Books, 1974), 127–128.

[33] See Ernst Bloch, *A Philosophy of the Future* (New York: Herder and Herder, 1970), 91. Berlin too points out that this consideration is at the basis of the utopian idea of *tikkun olam*. See *The Crooked Timber of Humanity*, 25–26.

[34] See Popper, *Conjectures and Refutations*, 361; Hoy and McCarthy, *Critical Theory*, 107.

[35] Max Horkheimer, *Gesammelte Schriften*, vol. 5 (Frankfurt am Main: Fisher Taschenbuch, 1987), 224.

[36] Ibid., vol. 9, 242.

[37] Ibid., 246.

[38] Herbert Marcuse, *An Essay on Liberation* (Boston: Beacon Press, 1969), 3.

[39] Herbert Marcuse, *Negations* (Harmondsworth, England: Penguin Books, 1968), ch. 3. Marcuse discusses this issue at length in *Eros and Civilization: A Philosophical Inquiry into Freud* (London: Routledge, 1998).

[40] Popper, *Conjectures and Refutations*, 361.

[41] See Goodwin, *Social Science and Utopia*, 7.

[42] Paul Ricoeur, *Lectures on Ideology and Utopia* (New York: Columbia University Press, 1986), 3.

[43] Paul Ricoeur, *From Text to Action*, trans. Kathleen Blamey and John B. Thompson (Evanston, IL.: Northwestern University Press, 1991), 319.

[44] Ibid., 320.

[45] Ibid., 323.

[46] Ricoeur, *Lectures on Ideology and Utopia*, 16.

[47] Søren Kierkegaard, *The Sickness unto Death*, trans. and ed. Howard V. Hong and Edna H. Hong (Princeton, NJ: Princeton University Press, 1987), 30–31.

[48] See Popper, *Conjectures and Refutations*, 361. The similarities between Popper and Emmanuel Levinas are hard to ignore, and a comparative analysis is indeed called for.

Notes

49   Hermann Cohen, *Religion of Reason out of the Sources of Judaism*, trans. Simon Kaplan (New York: Frederick Ungar, 1972), 135 (emphasis in original).

50   Jean-Jacques Rousseau, *The Discourses and Other Early Political Writings*, trans. Victor Gourevitch (Cambridge: Cambridge University Press, 1997), 127.

51   Camus deals with this basic insight in *The Plague*, trans. Stuart Gilbert (Harmondsworth, England: Penguin Books, 1960), 104–105, 175 and in *The Rebel*. See chs. 3 and 5 above and my book, *Albert Camus and the Philosophy of the Absurd*, trans. Batya Stein (Amsterdam-New York: Rodopi, 2002), 159–172.

52   Fromm, *The Revolution of Hope*, 17 (emphasis in the original).

53   Buber, *Paths of Utopia*, 15.

54   Richard Rorty, *Contingency, Irony, and Solidarity* (Cambridge: Cambridge University Press, 1989), 192.

55   Rachel Elboim-Dror, *Yestersday's Tomorrow* (in Hebrew), vol. 1 (Jerusalem: Yad Yitzhak Ben Zvi, 1993), 12, and references in note 7.

56   Maimonides, *The Code of Maimonides, The Book of Judges*, trans. Abraham M. Hershman (New Haven: Yale University Press, 1949) Laws of Kings, 11: 4.

57   Elboim-Dror, *Yesterday's Tomorrow*, particularly vol. 2.

58   Paul develops this thesis extensively in Epistle to the Romans, particularly chs. 3–8.

59   Maimonides, *The Code of Maimonides*, Laws of Kings, 12:2.

60   For an analysis of Maimonides' position see Dov Schwartz, *Messianism in Medieval Jewish Thought* (in Hebrew) (Ramat-Gan: Bar-Ilan University Press, 1997).

61   Gershom Scholem, "Toward an Understanding of the Messianic Idea in Judaism," in *The Messianic Idea in Judaism and Other Essays on Jewish Spirituality* (New York: Schocken Books, 1995), 3.

62   Ibid., 19–20.

63   Ibid., 28.

64   For this use of the term *tikkun olam*, see, for instance, M. Gittin 4:2–7, 9; 5:3; 9:4; M. Eduyot 1:13; BT Gittin 33a. This is a particularly interesting text because of the talmudic commentary on the term *tikkun olam*: "What is 'for the sake of *tikkun olam*'? R. Johanan says, to prevent bastards, Resh Lakish said, to prevent deserted wives." See

also BT Gittin 34b, 36a, 40b–41b; 45a-b, and more. For a profound analysis of this issue, see Menachem Lorberbaum, "Maimonides' Conception of *Tikkun Olam* and the Teleology of Halakhah" (in Hebrew), *Tarbiz* 64 (1995), 65–82. See also David Schatz, Chaim I. Waxman and Nathan J. Diament, *Tikkun Olam: Social Responsibility in Jewish Thought and Law* (Northvale, NJ: Jason Aronson, 1997).

[65] Yeshayahu Leibowitz, *Judaism, Human Values, and the Jewish State*, trans. Eliezer Goldman et. al. (Cambridge, MA: Harvard University Press, 1992), (henceforth *Judaism*), 12.

[66] Ibid., 13.

[67] Yeshayahu Leibowitz, *Judaism, the Jewish People, and the State of Israel* (in Hebrew) (Tel Aviv: Schocken, 1976), 397.

[68] Ibid., 60.

[69] *Judaism*, 15.

[70] Eliezer Goldman, *Expositions and Inquiries: Jewish Thought in Past and Present* (in Hebrew), ed. Avi Sagi and Daniel Statman (Jerusalem: Magnes Press, 1996), 361.

[71] Ibid.

[72] *Judaism*, 14.

[73] Ibid., 69–70. Compare ibid., 46.

[74] See Goldman, *Expositions and Inquiries*, 265–305.

[75] Ibid., 300. See also ibid., 13–15. Leibowitz later adopted the concept of "meta-halakhic norms" introduced by Goldman and used it in a variety of contexts. See, for instance, *Judaism*, 128–131.

[76] David Hartman, *A Living Covenant: The Innovative Spirit in Traditional Judaism* (New York: Free Press, 1985), 261.

BIBLIOGRAPHY

Abraham b. Yitzhak of Narbonne, *Sefer ha-Eshkol*, edited by Shalom and Hanokh Albeck. Jerusalem, 1984.

Abulafia, Yitzhak. *Penei Yitzhak*. Izmir, 1898.

Ahituv, Yosef. *On the Edge of Change: A Study of Contemporary Jewish Meanings* (in Hebrew). Jerusalem: Ministry of Education, 1995.

————. "'Stuff the Wicked Until He Dies': Refraining from Saving a Sinner" (in Hebrew). *Tehumin* 9 (1985): 156–170.

Altman, Alexander. *Tolerance and the Jewish Tradition*. London: The Robert Waley Cohen Memorial Lecture — Council of Christians and Jews, 1957.

Asheri (Rosh). *Responsa*. Jerusalem: Or Hamizrah, 1994.

Bar Sheshet Barfat, Yitzhak (Ribash). *Responsa*. Jerusalem: Machon Yerushalayim, 1993.

Bein, Alex. *The Jewish Question: Biography of a World Problem*. Translated by Harry Zohn. New York: Herzl Press, 1990.

Benn, Stanley I. "Freedom, Autonomy, and the Concept of a Person." *Proceedings of the Aristotelian Society* 76 (1975–1976): 109–130.

Ben-Yitzhak, Shlomo (Rashi). *Responsa*. Bnei Berak, 1980.

Ben-Zimra, David (Radbaz). *Responsa*. Bnei Berak, 1975.

Berger, Peter. *The Heretical Imperative: Contemporary Possibilities of Religious Affirmation*. New York: Anchor Books, 1979.

————. *The Sacred Canopy*. New York: Anchor Books, 1990.

Berger, Peter, Brigitte Berger, and Hansfried Kellner. *The Homeless Mind: Modernization and Consciousness*. New York: Vintage Books, 1974.

Berlin, Isaiah. *Four Essays on Liberty*. Oxford: Oxford University Press, 1969.

------------. *The Crooked Timber of Humanity: Chapters in the History of Ideas*. Edited by Henry Hardy. London: J. Murray, 1990.

Bloch, Ernst. *A Philosophy of the Future*. New York: Herder and Herder, 1970.

Bloom, Allan. *The Closing of the American Mind*. New York: Simon and Schuster, 1987.

Buber, Martin. *Paths in Utopia*. Translated by R. F. C. Hull. New York: MacMillan, 1958.

Bultmann, Rudolf. "Is Exegesis without Presuppositions Possible?" In *The Hermeneutics Reader*. Edited by Kurt Muller-Vollmer. New York: Continuum, 1989.

Camus, Albert. *The Rebel: An Essay on Man in Revolt*. Translated by Anthony Bower. New York: Alfred A. Knopf, 1956.

------------. *The Fall*. Translated by Justin O'Brien. London: Hamish Hamilton, 1957.

------------. *The Plague*. Translated by Stuart Gilbert. Harmondsworth, England: Penguin Books, 1960.

------------. *Resistance, Rebellion and Death*. Translated by Justin O'Brien. New York: Alfred A. Knopf, 1966.

------------. *Lyrical and Critical Essays*. Translated by Ellen Conroy Kennedy. New York: Vintage Books, 1970.

------------. *The Myth of Sisyphus*. Translated by Justin O'Brien. Harmondsworth, England: Penguin Books, 1975.

Cohen, Hermann. *Religion of Reason Out of the Sources of Judaism*. Translated by Simon Kaplan. New York: Frederick Ungar, 1972.

Cohen, Raphael. *Da'at Kedoshim*. Altona: Judah Brothers, 1797.

Cruickshank, John. *Albert Camus and the Literature of Revolt*. New York: Oxford University Press, 1960.

Dan, Yosef. *Apocalypse Then and Now* (in Hebrew). Tel Aviv: Hemed, 2000.

Dent, Nicholas. "Rousseau and Respect for Others." In *Justifying Toleration: Conceptual and Historical Perspectives*. Edited by Susan Mendus. Cambridge: Cambridge University Press, 1988.

Doubrovsky, Serge "The Ethics of Albert Camus." In *Critical Essays on Albert Camus*. Edited by Bettina L. Knapp. Boston, MA: G. K. Hall, 1988.

Efrati, Benjamin. *The Defense in Rav Kook's Philosophy* (in Hebrew). Jerusalem: Mosad Harav Kook, 1959.

Eisenstadt, Samuel N. *Tradition, Change, and Modernity*. Malabar, Fla.: Robert Krieger, 1983.

Elboim-Dror, Rachel. *Yestersday's Tomorrow* (in Hebrew), vol. 1. Jerusalem: Yad Yitzhak Ben Zvi, 1993.

Fackenheim, Emil L. "Jewish Faith and the Holocaust: A Fragment," *Commentary* (August 1968): 30–36.

————. *God's Presence in History: Jewish Affirmations and Philosophical Reflections*. New York: Harper Torchbooks, 1972.

Finley, M. I. "Utopianism Ancient and Modern." In *The Critical Spirit*. Edited by Kurt H. Wolf and Barrington Moore. Boston: Beacon Press, 1967.

Fisk, Milton. *Ethics and Society: A Marxist Interpretation of Value*. New York: New York University Press, 1980.

Fromm, Erich. *The Revolution of Hope: Toward a Humanized Technology*. New York: Harper and Rowe, 1968.

Gadamer, Hans Georg. *Truth and Method*. New York: Harper, 1962.

Goldman, Eliezer. "Divine Good and Human Good" (in Hebrew). *News of the Religious Kibbutz*, 107 (March 1955): 15–17.

————. "Revelation in Philosophical Discourse" (in Hebrew). *De'ot* 46 (1977): 62–65.

————. *Expositions and Inquiries: Jewish Thought in Past and Present*. Edited by Avi Sagi and Daniel Statman (in Hebrew). Jerusalem: Magnes Press, 1996.

Goodwin, Barbara. *Social Science and Utopia*. Sussex: Harvester Press, 1978.

Gur-Zeev, Ilan. *The Frankfurt School and the History of Pessimism* (in Hebrew). Jerusalem: Magnes Press, 1996.

Guttmann, Julius. *Religion and Science* (in Hebrew). Jerusalem: Magnes Press, 1955.

Hacohen, Meir Simha of Dwinsk. *Or Sameah*.

Hadomi, Leah. *Between Hope and Doubt: The Story of Utopia* (in Hebrew). Tel Aviv: Hakibbutz Hameuchad, 1989.

Heidegger, Martin. *Being and Time*. Translated by John Macquarrie and Edward Robinson. Oxford: Blackwell, 1962.

Halevi, Judah. *The Kuzari*. Translated by Hartwig Hirschfeld. New York: Schocken Books, 1964.

Hardy, G. G. "Happiness Beyond Absurd: The Existentialist Quest of Camus." *Philosophy Today* 23 (1979): 368–369.

Hare, Richard M. *The Language of Morals*. Oxford: Oxford University Press, 1952.

------------. *Freedom and Reason*. Oxford: Clarendon Press, 1982.

Hartman, David *A Living Covenant: The Innovative Spirit in Traditional Judaism*. New York: Free Press, 1985.

------------. *Crisis and Leadership: Epistles of Maimonides*. Philadelphia: Jewish Publication Society of America, 1985.

Henkin, Herzl. "Better For Them To Be Mistaken Than Wanton" (in Hebrew). *Tehumin* 2 (1981): 272–280.

Henry, Patrick. *Voltaire and Camus: The Limits of Reason and the Awareness of Absurdity*. Banbury, Oxfordshire: The Voltaire Foundation, 1975.

Hick, John. *God Has Many Names*. Philadelphia: Westminster Press, 1982.

------------. *Problems of Religious Pluralism*. New York: St. Martin's Press, 1985.

------------. *An Interpretation of Religion: Human Responses to the Transcendent*. New Haven: Yale University Press, 1989.

Hochberg, Herbert. "Albert Camus and the Ethic of Absurdity." *Ethics*, 75 (1965): 78–102.

Hoffman, David Zvi. *Responsa Melamed Leho'il*. Frankfurt: Hermon, 1926–1932.

Horkheimer, Max. *Gesammelte Schriften*, vol. 5. Frankfurt am Main: Fisher Taschenbuch, 1987.

Hoy, David C. and Thomas McCarthy. *Critical Theory*. Oxford: Blackwell, 1994.

Illenburg, Isachar Ber. *Sefer Beer Sheva*. Jerusalem, 1982.
Ish-Shalom, Benjamin. "Tolerance and its Theoretical Basis in the Teaching of Rabbi Kook" (in Hebrew). *Daat* 20 (1988): 151–168.
------------. *Rav Avraham Yitzhak Ha-Cohen Kook: Between Rationalism and Mysticism*. Translated by Ora Wiskind-Helper. Albany: SUNY Press, 1993.

James, William. *The Varieties of Religious Experience: A Study in Human Nature*. London and New York: Longmans, Green 1928.

Kant, Immanuel. *The Doctrine Of Virtue: Part II of The Metaphysics of Morals*. Translated by Mary J. Gregor. New York: Harper and Row, 1964.
Karin-Frank, Shyli. *Utopia Reconsidered* (in Hebrew). Tel Aviv: Hakibbutz Hameuchad, 1986.
Kasher, Asa. "Paradox, Question Mark" (in Hebrew). *Iyyun* 26 (1976): 236–241.
------------. "Theological Shadows" (in Hebrew). In *The Yeshayahu Leibowitz Book: An Anthology of His Thought and in His Honor*. Edited by Asa Kasher and Jacob Levinger. Tel-Aviv: Tel Aviv University Students' Union, 1977.
Katz, Jacob. *Exclusiveness and Tolerance: Studies in Jewish-Gentile Relations in Medieval and Modern Times*. Oxford: Oxford University Press, 1961.
------------. *Halakhah in Straits: Obstacles in Orthodoxy at its Inception* (in Hebrew). Jerusalem: Magnes Press, 1992.
Keightley, Alan. *Wittgenstein, Grammar and God*. London: Epworth Press, 1976.
Kekes, John. *The Morality of Pluralism*. Princeton, NJ: Princeton University Press, 1993.
Kierkegaard, Søren. *Either/Or*, vol. 1. Translated by Howard V. Hong and Edna Hong. Princeton, NJ: Princeton University Press, 1987.
------------. *The Sickness unto Death*. Translated and edited by Howard V. Hong and Edna H. Hong. Princeton, NJ: Princeton University Press, 1987.

Kierkegaard, Søren. *Concluding Unscientific Postscript to "Philosophical Fragments."* Translated and edited by Howard V. Hong and Edna H. Hong. Princeton, NJ: Princeton University Press, 1992.

King, Preston. *Toleration.* London: George Allen and Unwin, 1976.

Kook, Abraham Yitzhak. *Iggerot ha-Rayha* (in Hebrew). Jerusalem: Mosad Harav Kook, 1962.

------------. *Eder Ha-Yakar ve-Ikvei ha-Tson.* Jerusalem: Mosad Harav Kook, 1972.

Larmore, Charles E. *Patterns of Moral Complexity.* Cambridge: Cambridge University Press, 1987.

Leibowitz, Yeshayahu. *Judaism, the Jewish People, and the State of Israel* (in Hebrew). Tel Aviv: Schocken, 1976.

------------. *Conversations on the Ethics of the Fathers* (in Hebrew). Jerusalem: Schocken Books, 1979.

------------. *Faith, History, and Values* (in Hebrew). Jerusalem: Academon, 1982.

------------. *Talks on Maimonides' Eight Chapters* (in Hebrew). Jerusalem: Keter, 1986.

------------. *Between Science and Philosophy* (in Hebrew). Jerusalem: Academon, 1987.

------------. *Notes on the Weekly Torah Reading* (in Hebrew). Jerusalem: Academon, 1988.

------------. *The Faith of Maimonides.* Translated by John Glucker. Tel-Aviv: Mod, 1989.

------------. *Judaism, Human Values, and the Jewish State.* Translated by Eliezer Goldman et. al. Cambridge, MA: Harvard University Press, 1992.

------------. *People, Land, State* (in Hebrew). Jerusalem: Keter, 1992.

------------. *Conversations about Moshe Hayyim Luzzato's "The Path of the Upright"* (in Hebrew). Jerusalem: n. p., 1995.

------------. *Five Books of Faith* (in Hebrew). Jerusalem: Keter, 1995.

------------. *Seven Years of Talks on the Weekly Torah Reading* (in Hebrew). Jerusalem: n. p., 2000.

Levinger, Jacob. *Maimonides' Techniques of Codification: A Study in the Method of the Mishneh Torah* (in Hebrew). Jerusalem: Magnes Press, 1965.

Bibliography

------------. *From Routine to Renewal: Pointers in Contemporary Jewish Thought* (in Hebrew). Jerusalem: De'ot, 1973.

Locke, John. *A Letter Concerning Toleration*, edited by Mario Montuori. Hague: Martinus Nijhoff, 1963.

Lorberbaum, Menachem. "Maimonides' Conception of *Tikkun Olam* and the Teleology of Halakhah" (in Hebrew). *Tarbiz* 64 (1995): 65–82.

Lovejoy, Arthur O. *The Great Chain of Being: A Study in the History of an Idea*. Cambridge, MA: Harvard University Press, 1970.

Maimonides. *The Book of Divine Commandments (The Sefer ha-Mitzvoth of Maimonides)*. Translated by Charles B. Chavel. London: Soncino Press, 1940.

------------. *The Book of Divine Commandments with Nahmanides' Glosses*. Edited by Hayyim Dov Chavel (in Hebrew). Jerusalem: Mosad Ha-Rav Kook, 1981.

Mannheim, Karl. *Ideology and Utopia*. London: Routledge and Kegan Paul, 1979.

Marcuse, Herbert. *Negations*. Harmondsworth, England: Penguin Books, 1968.

------------. *An Essay on Liberation*. Boston: Beacon Press, 1969.

------------. "The End of Utopia." In *Five Lectures: Psychoanalysis, Politics and Utopia*. Translated by Jeremy J. Shapiro and Shierry M. Weber. Boston: Beacon Press, 1970.

------------. *Eros and Civilization: A Philosophical Inquiry into Freud*. London: Routledge, 1998.

McConnell, Terrance C. "Moral Dilemmas and Consistency in Ethics." *Canadian Journal of Philosophy* 8 (1978): 269–287.

Mendelssohn, Moses. *Jerusalem: On Religious Power and Judaism*. Translated by Allan Arkush. Hanover: University Press of New England-Brandeis University Press, 1983.

Mill, John Stuart. *On Liberty*. Hammonsdworth, England: Penguin, 1984.

More, Thomas. *Utopia*. Edited by George M. Logan, Robert M. Adams and Clarence H. Miller. Cambridge: Cambridge University Press, 1995.

Moses of Coucy. *Sefer Mitzvot Gadol*. Bnei Berak, 1988.

Nagel, Thomas. "The Absurd." In *The Meaning of Life*. Edited by E. D. Klemke. New York: Oxford University Press, 2000.

Nehorai, Michael Zvi. "Can a Religious Deed Be Coerced?" (in Hebrew). In *Between Authority and Autonomy in Jewish Tradition*. Edited by Avi Sagi and Zeev Safrai. Tel Aviv: Hakibbutz Hameuchad, 1997.

Newell, J. David. "Camus on the Will to Happiness." *Philosophy Today* 23 (1979): 380–385.

Newman, Jay. "The Idea of Religious Tolerance." *American Philosophical Quarterly* 15 (1978): 187–195.

Nicholson, Peter. "Toleration as a Moral Ideal." In *Aspects of Toleration*. Edited by John Horton and Susan Mendus. London: Methuen, 1985.

Nietzsche, Friedrich. *Thus Spoke Zarathustra: A Book for Everyone and Nobody*. Translated by Graham Parkes. Oxford: Oxford University Press, 2005.

Nozick, Robert. *Anarchy, State, and Utopia*. Oxford: Basil Blackwell, 1974.

Pascal, Blaise. *Pensées*. London: J. M. Dent & Sons, 1932.

Piekarz, Mendel. *Ideological Trends of Hasidism in Poland during the Inter-War Period and the Holocaust* (in Hebrew). Jerusalem: Bialik Institute, 1990.

Phillips, D. Z. *The Concept of Prayer*. London: Routledge and Kegan Paul, 1968.

------------. *Faith After Foundationalism*. London: Routledge, 1988.

Pike, Nelson. "Hume on Evil." *Philosophical Review* 72 (1963): 180–197.

Piron, Mordechai. "The Principles of Religion v. the Perceptions of Toleration" (in Hebrew). *Mahanayim* 5 (May 1993): 44–51.

Plato. *The Collected Dialogues of Plato*. Edited by Edith Hamilton and Huntington Cairns. New York: Bollingen Foundation, 1961.

Pojman, Louis P. *Religious Belief and the Will*. London: Routledge and Kegan Paul, 1968.

Popper, Karl. *Conjectures and Refutations: The Growth of Scientific Knowledge*. New York: Harper and Row, 1968.

------------. *The Open Society and its Enemies*, vol. 1. London: Routledge and Kegan Paul, 1974.

------------. "Toleration and Intellectual Responsibility." In *On Toleration*. Edited by Susan Mendus and David Edwards. Oxford: Clarendon Press, 1987.

Raphael, D. D. "The Intolerable." In *Justifying Toleration: Conceptual and Historical Perspectives*. Edited by Susan Mendus. Cambridge: Cambridge University Press, 1988.

Ravitzky, Aviezer. "Rabbi J. B. Soloveitchik on Human Knowledge: Between Maimonides and neo-Kantian Philosophy." *Modern Judaism* 6 (1986): 157–188.

Rawls, John. *A Theory of Justice*. Cambridge: Harvard University Press, 1971.

Raz, Joseph. "Autonomy, Toleration, and the Harm Principle." In *Justifying Toleration: Conceptual and Historical Perspectives*. Edited by Susan Mendus. Cambridge: Cambridge University Press, 1988.

Ricoeur, Paul. *Lectures on Ideology and Utopia*. New York: Columbia University Press, 1986.

------------. *From Text to Action*. Translated by Kathleen Blamey and John B. Thompson. Evanston, IL.: Northwestern University Press, 1991.

Rorty, Richard. *Contingency, Irony, and Solidarity*. Cambridge: Cambridge University Press, 1989.

Ross, Ya'akov Yehoshua. "Anthropocentrism and Theocentrism" (in Hebrew). In *The Yeshayahu Leibowitz Book: An Anthology of His Thought and in His Honor*. Edited by Asa Kasher and Jacob Levinger. Tel Aviv: Tel Aviv University Students' Union, 1977.

Rousseau, Jean-Jacques. *The Discourses and Other Early Political Writings*. Translated by Victor Gourevitch. Cambridge: Cambridge University Press, 1997.

Rubinstein, Richard. *After Auschwitz*. Indianapolis, Bobbs-Merrill, 1966.

Russell, Frances Theresa. *Touring Utopia*. New York: Dial Press, 1932.

Sagi, Avi. "The Suspension of the Ethical and the Religious Meaning of Ethics in Kierkegaard's Thought." *International Journal for the Philosophy of Religion* 32 (1992): 83–103.

------------. "Religious Language in the Modern World: An Interview with Eliezer Goldman" (in Hebrew). *Gilayion* (August 1995).

------------. *Judaism: Between Religion and Morality* (in Hebrew). Tel Aviv: Hakibbutz Hameuchad, 1998.

------------. *Kierkegaard, Religion, and Existence: The Voyage of the Self*. Translated by Batya Stein. Amsterdam-Atlanta, GA: Rodopi, 2000.

Sagi, Avi. *Albert Camus and the Philosophy of the Absurd*. Translated by Batya Stein. Amsterdam-New York: Rodopi, 2002.
------------. *The Open Canon: On the Meaning of Halakhic Discourse*. Translated by Batya Stein. London: Continuum, 2007.
------------. *Tradition vs. Traditionalism: Contemporary Perspectives in Jewish Thought*. Translated by Batya Stein. Amsterdam-New York: Rodopi, 2008.
Sagi, Avi, and Daniel Statman. *Religion and Morality*. Translated by Batya Stein. Amsterdam and Atlanta, GA: Rodopi, 1995.
Sandel, Michael. *Liberalism and the Limits of Justice*. Cambridge: Cambridge University Press, 1982.
Sartre, Jean Paul. *Nausea*. Translated by Lloyd Alexander. Norfolk, CT: New Directions, 1959.
------------. *Existentialism and Humanism*. Translated by Philip Mairet. New York: Haskell House, 1977.
Scarman, Lord. "Toleration and the Law. In *On Toleration*. Edited Susan Mendus and David Edwards. Oxford: Clarendon Press, 1987.
Schatz, David, Chaim I. Waxman and Nathan J. Diament. *Tikkun Olam: Social Responsibility in Jewish Thought and Law*. Northvale, NJ: Jason Aronson, 1997.
Schick, Moshe (Maharam Schick). *Responsa*. Jerusalem, 1984.
Schlesinger, George N. *Religion and Scientific Method*. Boston: Reidel, 1977.
------------. "Suffering and Divine Benevolence" (in Hebrew). In *Modern Trends in Philosophy*. Edited by Asa Kasher and Shalom Lappin. Tel Aviv: Yahdav, 1985.
Scholem, Gershom. "Toward an Understanding of the Messianic Idea in Judaism." In *The Messianic Idea in Judaism and Other Essays on Jewish Spirituality*. New York: Schocken Books, 1995.
Schwartz, Dov. *Messianism in Medieval Jewish Thought* (in Hebrew). Ramat-Gan: Bar-Ilan University Press, 1997.
Schweid, Eliezer. *Struggle Till Dawn* (in Hebrew). Tel Aviv: Hakibbutz Hameuchad, 1991.
Searle, John. *Speech Acts*. Cambridge: Cambridge University Press, 1994.
Shapira, Hayyim Elazar. *Responsa Minhat Eliezer*. New York, 1958.
Shapira, Kalonymus. *Esh Kodesh*. Jerusalem: Va'ad Hasidei Piaseczno, 1960.

Shkop, Simeon. *She 'arei Yosher*, vol. 2. New York: Hava'ad Le-Hotsa'at Sifre Ha-Gaon R. Shimon, 1980.

Sigged, Ran. "Leibowitz and Kierkegaard" (in Hebrew). In *The Yeshayahu Leibowitz Book: An Anthology of His Thought and in His Honor*. Edited by Asa Kasher and Jacob Levinger. Tel Aviv: Tel Aviv University Students' Union, 1977.

Sofer, Moshe (Hatam Sofer). *Responsa*. Jerusalem, 1970–1972.

Sokol, Moshe. "Is There a 'Halakhic' Response to the Problem of Evil?" *Harvard Theological Review*, 92 (1999): 311–323.

Soloveitchik, Joseph Dov. "Kol Dodi Dofek: It Is the Voice of My Beloved that Knocketh." In *Theological and Halakhic Reflections on the Holocaust*. Edited by Bernhard Rosenberg. New York: Ktav, 1992.

------------. "A Halakhic Approach to Suffering." In *Out of the Whirlwind: Essays on Mourning, Suffering, and the Human Condition*. Edited by David Shatz, Joel B. Wolowelsky and Reuven Ziegler. New York: Ktav, 2003.

Statman, Daniel. *Moral Dilemmas*. Amsterdam: Rodopi, 1995.

Talmon, Jacob *The Origins of Totalitarian Democracy*. Harmondsworth: England: Penguin Books, 1952.

Tate, Robert S. "The Concept of Equilibrium in the Early Essays of Albert Camus." *The South Atlantic Quarterly* 70 (1971): 377–385.

Unger, Roberto Mangabeira. *Knowledge and Politics*. New York: Free Press, 1984.

Urbach, E. E. *The Sages: Their Concepts and Beliefs*. Translated by Israel Abrahams. Jerusalem: Magnes Press, 1979.

Vasil, Dean. *The Ethical Pragmatism of Albert Camus: Two Studies in the History of Ideas*. New York: Peter Lang, 1985.

Waldron, Jeremy. "Locke: Toleration and the Rationality of Persecution." In *John Locke: A Letter Concerning Toleration in Focus*. New York: Routledge, 1991.

Warnock, Mary. "The Limits of Toleration." In *On Toleration*. Edited by Susan Mendus and David Edwards. Oxford: Clarendon Press, 1987.

Weale, Albert. "Toleration, Individual Differences, and Respect for Persons." In *Aspects of Toleration*. Edited by John Horton and Susan Mendus. London: Methuen, 1985.

Winch, Peter. "Understanding a Primitive Society." In *Rationality*. Edited by Bryan R. Wilson. Oxford: Basil Blackwell, 1985.

------------. *Trying to Make Sense*. Oxford: Basil Blackwell, 1987.

Wittgenstein, Ludwig. *Lectures and Conversations on Aesthetics, Psychology, and Religious Beliefs*. Oxford: Basil Blackwell, 1970.

------------. *On Certainty*. Edited by G. E. M. Anscombe and G. H. von Wright. Translated by Denis Paul and G. E. M. Anscombe. New York: Harper and Row, 1972.

------------. *Tractatus Logico-Philosophicus*. London: Routledge, 1974.

------------. *Culture and Value*. Translated by Peter Winch. Oxford: Basil Blackwell, 1980.

------------. *Remarks on the Philosophy of Psychology*. Edited by G. E. M. Anscombe and G. H. von Wright. Translated by G. E. M. Anscombe. Oxford: Basil Blackwell, 1980.

Yaron, Zvi. *The Philosophy of Rabbi Kook*. Translated by Avner Tomaschoff. Jerusalem: WZO, 1991.

Zohar, Zvi. *Tradition and Change* (in Hebrew). Jerusalem: Ben Zvi Institute, 1993.

INDEX

Abraham 153, 156–158
Absolute Being 156
Absurd 69–71, 74–75, 79–83, 85–91, 102, 104, 169, 171, 214
Akedah (Sacrifice of Isaac) 131, 156
Alienation 79–80, 102, 170
Altman, Alexander
Tolerance and the Jewish Tradition 4
Anthropology 58–59, 88, 129, 174, 176
Aquinas, Thomas 8, 17, 36
Atheism 87, 91, 115, 131–132
Atheistic Interpretation 157
Augustine 8, 17, 36
Autonomy
Human 16, 24, 38, 124, 135

Barth, Karl 157
Berger, Peter 12, 29, 42, 45
Berlin, Isaiah 54–55, 64, 65, 213, 230
Two Concepts of Freedom 47
The Crooked Timber of Humanity 231

Bible 131
Biblical 29, 116–117, 145, 152–153, 155, 158, 226
Bloom, Allan
The Closing of the American Mind 55
Buber, Martin 208, 222
Bultmann, Rudolf 154, 158

Calvin 17
Camus, Albert 69–71, 75–76, 79, 83, 87–91, 98, 99, 100, 102, 103, 104, 106, 197–198, 233
The Fall 72
Myth of Sisyphus 72, 80–82, 85–86, 88–89, 94–95
"Nuptials at Tipasa" 82
The Plague 74, 92, 94–95, 172
The Rebel 72–73, 82, 85, 93
"*The Wind at Djemila*" 82
Castellion, Sebastian 17, 19
Choice 18, 24, 29, 38, 48, 53–54, 65, 85, 97, 152, 195
Faith as 49
Freedom of 16

Christianity   8, 11, 17, 97, 116, 125, 130, 152, 189, 223–224
   Anglican   19
   Protestant   118
   Redemption   91, 96, 227
Coercion   7, 10, 18–22, 24–25, 34, 39, 215
Cohen, Hermann   162–163, 173
Commandments   3, 23, 27, 51, 53, 77, 84–85, 91–94, 116, 118, 120, 121, 123, 128, 131, 224
   Observance of   4, 20, 21, 29, 31, 39, 96, 115, 117, 118, 223, 226, 227
Community   7, 22, 166, 175, 192, 222–223, 229
   Covenantal   180
   Jewish   4, 31
   Moral   149
   Natural   93
   Religious   59
   Western   4, 31
Compartmentalization   147
Consciousness
   Human   76, 85, 111
   Modern   78
   Self   94
   Transcendental   71, 170
"Copernican Revolution"   46, 75, 128
Covenant   31, 177–180, 229
Creation   75, 79, 85, 111, 115, 131, 156, 164, 179
   Human   73, 149
Cruickshank, John   87–88
Culture   ix, 6, 49, 58–59, 62, 66, 124, 154, 195, 211, 218, 223
   Christian   11
   Jewish   4
   Orthodox   63
   Pluralistic   12, 60
   Secular-liberal   37
   Tolerant   12
   Traditional   29, 53

Divine Transcendence   111, 199

Epistemology   147–148
Evil   23, 73–75, 143, 147, 150, 152, 158–163, 166–180, 189–199, 201–202, 222
   Good and evil   16, 57, 97, 145, 190, 195, 212
Exile   225
Existentialism   174
Explication   32, 80, 83, 88–90, 150

Fackenheim, Emil   201
Fallibility   14
Faith   18, 46, 49, 74–80, 83–84, 86–87, 90–92, 97, 110, 112, 116–119, 127–128, 130, 136, 152, 156–158, 163, 172, 176, 188, 201, 224
   Illusory   144
   Non-Illusory   144, 148
   "Thirteen Principles"   27, 121, 153
Freedom   19, 24, 25, 47, 49, 74, 85–88, 96, 121, 159, 162, 177, 179, 180, 196, 207, 225, 227
   Absolute freedom   91
   "Freedom from"   84, 95
   "Freedom to"   84, 95
   Model of   190, 195
   Of Thought and Action   8, 10, 13, 23
   Of Choice   16
Fromm, Erich   214

INDEX

God 18, 27, 45–46, 74, 90–91, 93, 96, 98, 101, 127, 134–135, 149, 153, 156, 162, 165–166, 172, 174, 176–177, 198, 202, 210, 214, 223
- Aristotelian 178
- Command of 61–62, 69, 126, 133, 191, 193
- "Death of God" vii, 78, 152, 188, 196, 200
- Faith in 110, 128, 158, 201
- Fear of 78, 131, 224
- Goodness of 113, 143, 150–151, 173, 189–190, 192–194, 197
- Living God 3–4
- Obedience to 51, 61, 73
- Of Abraham 199
- Of Creation 164, 179
- Transcendent viii, 79, 92, 132, 139, 144, 146–147, 199
- Uniqueness of 152
- Word at Sinai 28
- Worship of 17, 60, 75, 84, 87, 97, 111, 114–115, 118, 128–129, 132–133, 136, 228

Goldman, Eliezer viii, 41, 66, 117, 139, 144–151, 153–155, 227–229

Halakhah viii, 3–4, 23–24, 29, 31, 60, 75, 117, 128–129, 136, 225
- Human Creation 73, 93
- Thematic 166–171, 180, 229
- Topical 166–167, 170–171, 173

Halakhic Man 229

Hare, Richard 15, 37, 181, 182

Hartman, David viii, 144, 164, 173–180, 229

Hartman, Nicholai
- *Der Philosophe Gedanke und seine Geschichte* 109

Heidegger, Martin 83, 90,162
- *Being and Time* 104

Hermeneutics 153–154

Hick, John 33, 42

Holiness 92–93, 199

Holocaust 152, 165, 187–190, 193, 195–197, 200, 202

Hope 70, 87, 91–92, 94, 97, 147, 214, 222

Horkheimer, Max 216

Human Knowledge 144–145

Husserl, Edmund 89, 219–220

Identity 4, 132, 174

Idolatry 92–93, 110, 115, 126–127, 149, 152

Immanence viii, 98

Individuality 15–16, 215

Interpretation 9, 39, 112, 114, 123–125, 134, 153–154, 157–158, 166, 172, 202
- of Judaism 55, 58, 62
- of Leibowitz 90, 104, 127
- of the Sinai revelation 119–120, 124–125
- Self- 25

Israel 225
- God of 201
- People of 121
- Religion of 73
- State of 152, 165

Job 157–158, 169
- Suffering of 79, 156, 166, 170

Judah Halevi 116–117

Judaism 20, 45–47, 49, 55, 58, 60, 73, 75, 96, 113, 127, 129, 132, 136, 146, 148, 155, 161, 166, 169–170, 175
- Empirical 47, 62, 125

249

Historic   47, 62, 125
Secular   62
Traditional   62

Kant, Immanuel   65, 73, 128, 216
   Critique of Pure Reason   135
   Critique of Practical Reason   135
   Kantian legacy   51
Kasher, Asa   41, 101, 125, 127
Kekes, John   36–38, 55–56, 65
Kierkegaard, Søren   74, 80, 90, 93, 97, 101, 102, 104, 105, 109, 112, 130, 135–136, 200–201, 220
Kluger, Solomon   19–20
Knowledge   103, 115, 126, 168, 194, 199
   Human   144–145
   Self-   136
Kook, Abraham Yitzchak   24–25, 40

Lebenswelt   vii, 134, 154
Leibowitz, Yeshayahu   viii, 41, 49–50, 55–56, 65–66, 71–76, 78, 80–84, 86–87, 90–93, 95, 98, 100–101, 103–105, 109–111, 113–114, 124–129, 131–136, 137, 139, 144, 146–147, 155, 157–158, 163, 209, 226–229
   Philosophy of   45–48, 52–53, 58, 60–61, 69, 77
Locke, John   18–19, 38
   Letters Concerning Toleration   6, 17, 36
Lovejoy, Arthur   182
   The Great Chain of Being   195

Maimonides   20–21, 29, 39, 110–111, 113, 122–123, 139, 153, 164, 175, 179, 223–224, 226
   The Book of the Commandments   121
   Guide of the Perplexed   124, 168
   "Thirteen Principles"   27, 121, 153
Malcolm, Norman   59
Mannheim, Karl   209–210
   Ideology and Utopia   208
Marcuse, Herbert   209, 217–218
McConnell, Terrance   52
Meir Simha HaCohen   20–21
Mendelssohn, Moses   19, 38, 39, 46
Messianism   223–226
Metaphysics   14, 30, 39, 41, 51–52, 69–70, 82, 109, 115, 130, 132–135, 161, 163–164, 170, 174–175, 177, 180, 198, 201–202, 211, 221
   of Evil   74, 160, 167, 169
   Language of   165–166
   Rebellion   85–86, 91, 93, 95, 197
   of Suffering   162, 167, 169, 171–172
   and Theology   viii–ix, 27, 33, 45–46, 75, 110, 112–113, 126–128, 151
   of Value   134
   World   48, 58, 60, 73, 134, 212
Midrash   224
Mill, John Stuart   14, 38
   On Liberty   15
Modern   vii–viii, 15, 30, 32, 63, 78, 226
   Challenge of   75, 170
   Culture   46
   Man   171
   Outlook   169
   Values   45
   World   33, 98, 105, 211

Moral 48, 50, 52, 55, 57–58, 104, 149–150, 152, 156, 162, 177, 182, 190–192, 198, 215–216, 228
   Acclaim 9
   Dilemma 103
   Discourse 181
   Judgment 54, 151, 194
   Obligation 135, 221
   Order 193
   Value 8
   Weakness 7
More, Thomas
   Utopia 213
Moses of Coucy 23
Murdoch, Iris 157
Myth 59, 94, 125, 154, 225

Nahmanides 121–123
Newman, Jay 5, 7
Nietzsche, Friedrich 84, 95, 109, 188
Nozick, Robert 15

Ontology 76–77, 80
Oral Law 73, 100
Orthodox 45, 53, 55, 58, 63
"Other" 4, 8–10, 13, 15–16, 25–26, 32–33, 56–57, 63, 156, 166, 198, 221–222

Pascal, Blaise 76, 112, 199
Paternalism 9, 24–25, 223
Phenomena 75, 78–80, 83, 88, 103–104, 168, 188, 198, 218
   Historical 5, 60, 62
   Religious vii, 60, 127
Phenomenology 77, 103
Phillips, D.Z. 59
Pluralism 14, 31, 34, 36–38, 45, 47, 49, 53, 55, 57
   Descriptive 12–13
   Jewish 58, 62
   Normative 13
   Religious 32, 42
   Strong 13, 15–16, 26–28, 54, 61
   Toleration 3–5, 11, 33, 35
   Weak 13, 15–16, 26–27, 54, 61
Popper, Karl 14–15, 110, 211, 217
Praxis viii, 3–4, 20, 62, 74–75, 95–96, 105, 128, 163–164, 173
   Religious 27, 93, 110, 134, 226
Prayer 127, 198, 223, 226
Protestantism 17, 20, 101, 118, 136
Providence 112, 114, 149, 197

Rabbi Aha bar Yaakov 121
Rabbi Avdimi bar Hama 121
Rabbi Johanan 120
Radbaz 22
Raz, Joseph 15–16, 35, 38
Redemption 18, 71–72, 92, 96, 112, 180, 198, 224, 227
   Biblical 145
   Human 91, 228
   Transcendent 70
Relativism 5, 6, 14, 19, 26, 38, 47, 50–51, 55, 70
   Epistemic 27
   Normative 27
   Value 16, 50
Religion 18, 24, 27, 33, 42, 47, 59, 69–70, 74, 77, 83, 85–86, 91, 93, 96, 99, 102, 105, 111–113, 136, 143, 145–147, 154–155, 162, 172, 176, 178, 193, 197–198, 200, 216, 219, 221, 224, 226–229
   Act 20, 39, 73, 78, 97
   Commitment vii–viii, 28, 45, 110, 117, 124

Community 4, 59
Culture 12
Decision 87–88, 93
Experience viii, 33, 42, 150, 162, 197, 199
Facts 116, 119, 129
Faith 130, 132, 152, 201
Identity 174
Jewish vii–viii, 3–5, 20, 25–26, 28–29, 31, 46, 61–62, 71, 73, 84, 114–115, 118–119, 128–130, 134
Language 115, 125–127, 129, 133, 188, 200
Life vii–viii, 71, 92–93, 120, 130–131, 144, 150, 155, 163, 173, 187, 198, 202, 228
Morality 50, 57–58
Obligation 20, 72–73, 75, 95, 129, 133–135, 228
Phenomenon vii, 60, 127
Practice 198–199, 202
Test 200–201
Tradition 151, 153, 170
Toleration 17, 19, 24
Value 28, 131–132
World vii, 32–33, 52, 58, 60, 63, 75, 101, 132, 148, 202
Repentance 155, 176
Revelation 73, 99, 110, 115–116, 118, 120
"Sinai Revelation" 28, 31, 46, 51, 73, 114–122, 124–125, 133
Ricoeur, Paul 219–220
Rubinstein, Richard 188

Sabbath 30–31
Sartre, Jean Paul 52, 81
Skepticism 5, 12, 14, 19

Scholem, Gershom 224–225
Science 59, 72, 77, 110–112, 148, 153–154, 211
Searle, John 27–28, 129
Secular 12, 37, 40, 42, 62, 99
Secularization 26, 30–31, 46
Self 85, 88, 94, 104, 135, 150–151, 159, 171
  Self-Affirmation 83–84, 86–87
  Self-Awareness 89
  Self-Fulfillment 167
  Self-Interpretation 25
  Self-Knowledge 136
  Self-Perception 8, 20, 78, 161
  Self-Realization 167
  Self-Restraint 7–10, 36
  Self-Subversive 26
  Self-Transcendence 86, 92
Shapira, Kalonymos 191
Shkop, Simeon 118
Sinai Covenant 31
Soloveitchik, Joseph viii, 144, 159–173, 176, 180, 183, 229
  "A Halakhic Approach to Suffering" 158, 169–173, 179
  "Kol Dodi Dofek" 158, 165–166, 169–173, 179
Spinoza, Baruch 46, 109
Subjectivity 33
Suffering 162–165, 168, 175–176, 178–179, 197–198, 216, 223
  Ethic of Suffering 171, 228–229
  Human 164, 167, 169, 217, 221
  Job's Suffering 79, 156, 166, 170
  Suffering and Evil 158–161, 163, 166–167, 169–174, 177, 189, 191–192, 195

Theology   vii, ix, 113-114, 125, 127, 173, 176, 180, 196
   Classic   151
   Covenantal   177-178, 180
   Natural   187-188, 197
Theodicy   75, 143, 147, 150, 152, 158, 160-161, 167, 169, 170, 173-179, 187, 227
   Classic Theodicy   144, 149, 155
   Rejection of   155-157, 172, 180
Tikkun Olam   207-208, 210-212, 214-216, 218, 221-223, 226, 229
Time   14, 40, 49, 66, 80, 82, 115, 118, 121, 161, 192, 214, 216
   Historical   110, 210
   Transience of   95
Tolerance   4-8, 10-15, 17, 24, 26
   Paradox of   9, 25
Torah   20, 23, 72, 84, 97, 115, 120-121, 173, 178, 224
   Commandments   77, 91, 227
Transcendence   71, 73, 80, 84, 94, 96, 102, 120, 172, 209, 227-228
   Divine   79, 92, 111, 139, 144, 146-147, 199
   Human   76-77, 87
   Self   86, 92

Universalism   168
Utopia   16, 93-94, 208-221, 223, 225-226, 228-229

Value System   28-29, 77
Voltaire, Francois   14-15

Winch, Peter   59
   The Idea of Social Science   58
Wittgenstein, Ludwig   ix, 59-60, 62, 110-111, 125, 128-132, 188
   Tractatus Logico Philosophicus   112, 127

World   ix, 3, 18, 25, 27-29, 45-46, 48, 51, 56-63, 69-73, 75, 77-83, 87-94, 96, 98, 110-112, 115, 120, 127, 129, 131, 134, 136, 144-149, 153-154, 156-158, 160-161, 163-168, 171-176, 178-180, 188, 191, 195, 197-199, 207-208, 218, 220, 221-229
   Biblical   29
   Conceptual
   Cultural   60
   Halakhic   60, 71, 73, 93
   Human   71, 96, 167
   Ideal   209-213, 215
   Jewish   58
   Liberal   36
   Modern   33, 98, 105, 211
   Outside   4
   Pluralistic   viii, 32, 53-54, 57, 62, 215
   Religious   vii, 32-33, 52, 58, 60, 63, 73, 75, 77, 101, 132, 148, 202
   Secular   37
   Traditional   33
   Transcendental   71, 102, 228

www.ingramcontent.com/pod-product-compliance
Lightning Source LLC
Chambersburg PA
CBHW050847230426
43667CB00012B/2177